The European Central Bank at Ten

Jakob de Haan · Helge Berger
Editors

The European Central Bank at Ten

Springer

Editors
Prof. Dr. Jakob de Haan
University of Groningen
and
De Nederlandsche Bank
Research Department
PO Box 98
1000 AB Amsterdam
The Netherlands
e-mail: j.de.haan@dnb.nl

Prof. Dr. Helge Berger
Free University Berlin
and
International Monetary Fund
European Department
700 19th Street NW
Washington, DC 20431
USA
e-mail: hberger@imf.org

ISBN 978-3-642-14236-9 e-ISBN 978-3-642-14237-6

DOI 10.1007/978-3-642-14237-6

Springer Heidelberg Dordrecht London New York

Library of Congress Control Number: 2010933116

Cover design: WMXDesign GmbH

Printed on acid-free paper

Springer is part of Springer Science+Business Media (www.springer.com)

Contents

About the Authors

Helge Berger is a Deputy Division Chief in the European Department of the International Monetary Fund. He is on leave as a Chair of Monetary Economics at the Free University Berlin, Germany.

Martin Čihák is a Deputy Division Chief in the Monetary and Capital Markets Department of the International Monetary Fund; he is also a member of the Czech National Bank's Research Advisory Committee.

Jakob de Haan is Head of Research of De Nederlandsche Bank and Professor of Political Economy at the University of Groningen, The Netherlands.

Thomas Harjes is a Senior Economist in the European Department of the International Monetary Fund.

David-Jan Jansen is at the Research Department of De Nederlandsche Bank.

Dirk Schoenmaker is Dean of the Duisenberg School of Finance, and Professor of Finance, Banking and Insurance at the VU University Amsterdam, The Netherlands.

Emil Stavrev is a Senior Economist at the European Department of the International Monetary Fund; previously, he was a Senior Economist at the Czech National Bank.

Peter Stella is the former Chief of the Central Banking Division in the International Monetary Fund's Monetary and Capital Markets Department.

Jérôme Vandenbussche is an economist in the International Monetary Fund's European Department.

List of Figures

List of Tables

Chapter 1
Introduction

Helge Berger and Jakob de Haan

1.1 Background

As we write these lines, the pressure on Europe's sovereign and financial markets continues and the European Central Bank (ECB) continues to play a central role in euro area's crisis response. Indeed, its role has grown as the crisis evolved, from monetary policymaker to provider of emergency liquidity and temporary stabilizer of sovereign bond markets. Many books will be written about what transpired since the collapse of Lehman and how the ECB played its part in the euro area policy concert—but this book is not one of them. Rather than trying to predict the outcome of the ongoing crisis, we ask how the ECB grew into its current role, taking stock of the ECB's achievements during its first 10 years.

There was no shortage of doubters when the euro was introduced as a new currency and the Economic and Monetary Union (EMU) came to live in 1999. As the argument went, the ECB lacked the governance structure, institutional experience, strategy, and instruments required for running the euro area's monetary

The views expressed in this book are those of the authors and should not be attributed to De Nederlandsche Bank or the IMF, its Executive Board, or its management.

H. Berger
European Department, International Monetary Fund, 700 19th Street NW, 20431, Washington, DC, USA
e-mail: hberger@imf.org

H. Berger
Free University Berlin, Berlin, Germany

J. de Haan (✉)
Research Department, De Nederlandsche Bank, PO Box 98,1000 AB Amsterdam, The Netherlands
e-mail: j.de.haan@dnb.nl

J. de Haan
University of Groningen, Groningen, The Netherlands

J. de Haan and H. Berger (eds.), *The European Central Bank at Ten*,
DOI: 10.1007/978-3-642-14237-6_1, © Springer-Verlag Berlin Heidelberg 2010

policy effectively. And EMU showed too little economic convergence to make it work smoothly under one central bank but multiple fiscal and structural policies. But while the jury is still out on the latter (and the ruling is likely to be critical), the verdict on the ECB's first 10 years is in—and to a large degree it has it has been a resounding success. In fact, the ECB can look back with a certain amount of satisfaction. It has honed its tool kit and flexibly expanded it to meet the requirements of a changing world, adjusted its decision-making mechanism to better cope with the growing euro area membership, and after 10 years has earned the respect of financial markets, policymakers, and its peers in the US, Japan, and the UK. The questions of how exactly the ECB got there and what still might be lacking are the subject of this book.

It is difficult to overstate the significance of the establishment of the euro area. The decision of countries in this number, size, and global economic weight to voluntarily share a currency and to pool their monetary sovereignty was a historic premiere—and for first time since the Roman Empire, a large portion of Europe now shares a common currency. The euro area saw the light of day on 1 January 1999, with the adoption of the common currency by 11 of the then 15 member states of the European Union (EU), but the project of EMU had been a long way coming. Table 1.1 summarizes the main steps towards the creation of the currency union. The Single European Act, signed in 1986, was a major step in the European economic integration process. The act aimed at completing the European Community's internal market by December 31, 1992 by removing all barriers to the free movement of capital, labor, goods and services among its member states. This was an important step toward monetary unification, not least because it involved the formal end of exchange controls (e.g., Jonung & Drea 2010). The actual creation of the euro largely followed the steps foreseen in the Delors Report—named after Jacques Delors, president of the European Commission at the time—which proposed a three-stage programme of Economic and Monetary Union to turn the European Community into a true single market. A single currency was a key component of this programme. The report led to the 1992 Maastricht Treaty, which transformed the European Community into the more tightly knit European Union. Establishing a single currency became one of the EU's objectives and the Maastricht Treaty specified the institutional framework for achieving it. EMU kept on growing after its inception, with Greece joining the euro area in 2001. Slovenia entered the euro area in 2007, while Cyprus and Malta introduced the euro in 2008 and Slovakia in 2009. At the meeting of the European Council that took place in Brussels on the 17th June 2010, unanimous approval was given to Estonia to enter the euro area in 2011.

Since the start of the currency union, monetary policy in the euro area has been delegated to the ECB and its Governing Council alone is responsible for taking monetary policy decisions. This Governing Council consists of the Executive Board of the ECB—made up of the president, the vice-president and four other members—and the governors of the national central banks (NCBs) of the countries in the euro area. While the ECB is responsible for policy decisions, NCBs play a role in implementing monetary policy, as well as a provider of emergency

Table 1.1 Major steps toward the euro since 1989

February 1986	Signing of the Single European Act, advancing economic and political integration within the European Community.
April 1989	The Delors Report calls for Economic and Monetary Union (EMU) leading to a single European currency through three stages.
June 1989	The Madrid Summit of the European Council agrees that Stage 1 of EMU will start July 1, 1990. Stage 1 includes completing the internal market and removing all obstacles to financial integration.
October 1990	The Rome Summit of the European Council agrees that Stage 2 of EMU will begin January 1, 1994.
December 1990	The Dublin Summit of the European Council marks the beginning of intergovernmental conferences on EMU and political union.
February 1992	Signing of the Maastricht Treaty to establish the European Union, the successor to the European Community.
June 1992	Danish voters narrowly reject the Maastricht Treaty.
September 1992	Currency crises force Britain and Italy to abandon the Exchange Rate Mechanism (ERM).
July 1993	Member states agree to widen the "narrow" band in the ERM from 2.25 to 15% around the central rates.
January 1994	Stage 2 of EMU starts. The European Monetary Institute comes into operation and begins the transition from co-ordination of national monetary policies to a common monetary policy. Economic convergence is strengthened through adherence to "convergence criteria" set out in the Maastricht Treaty.
May 1995	The European Commission adopts a Green Paper "On the Practical Arrangements for the Introduction of the Single Currency."(A green paper is a document intended to stimulate discussion and start a process of consultation).
December 1995	The Madrid Summit of the European Council reaffirms January 1, 1999 as the date for the irrevocable locking of exchange rates, thus for the introduction of the euro. The "euro" is officially adopted as the name for the new single currency.
May 1998	Special meeting of the European Council decides that 11 member states satisfy the conditions for adopting the single currency.
June 1998	The European Central Bank and the European System of Central Banks are set up.
January 1999	Stage 3 of EMU begins. The exchange rates of the 11 initial participating nations are irrevocably fixed and the euro begins to trade on financial markets.
January 2001	Greece adopts the euro.
January 2002	Euro notes and coins enter into circulation in all participating member states.
January 2007	Slovenia adopts the euro.
January 2008	Cyprus and Malta adopt the euro.
January 2009	Slovakia adopts the euro.
January 2011	Estonia to adopt the euro.

Source: Updated from Jonung and Drea (2010)

liquidity. The Maastricht Treaty made "price stability" the ECB's primary objective, but left it to the ECB to give precise meaning to the words. The objective, first specified as inflation less than 2%, was made more precise in 2003 following an internal evaluation of the ECB's monetary policy strategy. Today, the ECB aims for maintaining inflation "below but close to" 2% in the euro area in the medium term. Over time, the ECB not only developed its monetary policy strategy and instruments to accomplish this objective, its communication strategy also evolved, guiding markets through statements, press conferences, and speeches.

This book takes stock of the ECB's experience during its first 10 years and offers guidance for the way ahead. The purpose of the book is to provide the reader with a comprehensive overview of the issues discussed. This introductory chapter outlines the issues covered and summarizes the main findings of the contributions.

1.2 Inflation Differentials

The ECB has been quite successful in maintaining price stability in the euro area, but rates of inflation continue to differ between countries. Price stability has been broadly achieved, with average inflation having been close to or slightly above 2% since January 1999 (Mongelli & Wyplosz 2008). Still, inflation rates in the various countries in the euro area have not converged and inflation differentials have been large and persistent. After converging sharply in the 1990s, national inflation rates started to diverge again in 1999 under the common currency. Since then, the standard deviation of the annual inflation rates among euro area members has fluctuated around 1%.

While some inflation differentials are a normal feature of a large currency area, in the euro area their presence is combined with a set of unique institutional and economic characteristics. In particular, limited labour mobility, heterogeneous degrees of rigidities in labour and product markets, the absence of a centralized fiscal authority, and still largely decentralised responsibility for fiscal policy, maintaining financial stability, and other economic policies tend to amplify rather than moderate heterogeneity in inflation. As a consequence, differences in price developments across the countries of the euro area have attracted substantial attention from policymakers and academics alike.

Under a common currency, heterogeneity in inflation will have real consequences. Price setting is subject to a variety of common and idiosyncratic shocks. For instance, an unexpected localized demand surge can lead to higher price level growth, forcing a real "appreciation" for countries with above area-average inflation, while countries having below-average inflation rates gain in price competitiveness. Consequently, exports and imports volumes will adjust, unleashing compensating adjustments in demand. In that sense, inflation differentials are "the product of an equilibrating adjustment process ... and, as such, are not only unavoidable, but also desirable" within a currency union (European Central Bank 2005, p. 61). However, shocks can interact with imperfections and rigidities in product, labour and other factor markets and lead to lasting inflation differentials. Furthermore, inflation differentials could be caused by inappropriate domestic policies or other unwarranted domestic developments, such as wage increases that are out of line with productivity growth, or inappropriate fiscal policies. Under these circumstances, inflation differentials can become a cause of concern as they could lead to sustained losses in competitiveness that will, ultimately, affect national output and employment growth (European Central Bank 2005).

Against this background, in Chap. 2, Jakob de Haan reviews the literature on inflation differentials in the euro area, focusing on two questions in particular: what generates inflation differences, and how, and how quickly, will they subside? He argues that the various explanations of inflation differentials broadly fall into five categories, namely: (1) convergence, (2) business cycle differences, (3) asymmetric demand and supply shocks and asymmetric adjustment mechanisms to common shocks, (4) characteristics of domestic product, labour and other factor markets, and (5) wage and price rigidities. These explanations are not mutually exclusive. For instance, asymmetric shocks may not only lead to inflation differentials, but also reduce business cycle synchronization. Likewise, the impact of shocks on inflation differentials depends on wage and price rigidities. He concludes that despite the research done to date, there is no clear consensus in the literature to what extent inflation differentials in the euro area are problematic. In part this is due to the fact that most recent research uses DSGE models that are all perfectly able to yield outcomes consistent with stylized facts, but that are very different in their explanation of these inflation differentials. Nevertheless it would be dangerous to ignore the potential dangers stemming from inflation differentials for the welfare and longevity of the euro area. Intriguingly, de Haan also concludes that recent research suggests that area-wide monetary policy can make a contribution to regional inflation stabilization.

1.3 ECB Monetary Policy Strategy

Credibility featured high in the ECB's early consideration of its monetary policy strategy. Arguably, this is one of the reasons why the Bundesbank's highly successful monetary approach, which combined a prominent role for monetary aggregates with great pragmatism in executing policy, also featured prominently in the ECB's strategy. Other than the Bundesbank, however, the ECB's favored a "two pillar" strategy that explicitly paired the discussion of monetary factors with a broad-based non-monetary analysis of the risks to price stability in the short to medium run, including, for example, standard Phillips curve modeling. However, many academics consider the ECB's approach as too complicated in comparison to a straightforward inflation targeting strategy, which emphasizes transparency and coherence between medium-term forecasts and policy actions (Mongelli & Wyplosz 2008). For instance, Favero, Freixas, Persson, and Wyplosz (2000, p. 6) argued: "[a]t a time when more and more central banks replace money-growth targeting with (expected) inflation targeting, and make efforts at being transparent, the ECB's strategy is unavoidably seen as obscure, often even archaic."

When the ECB's monetary policy strategy was initially introduced in 1998, the "first pillar" (the currently used term is "monetary analysis") was meant to examine the medium- to long-run implications of monetary developments for inflation (European Central Bank 2004). As inflation in the long run is considered to be a mostly monetary phenomenon, the ECB Governing Council announced under the "first pillar" a quantitative reference value for the annual growth rate of a broad monetary aggregate (M3). The focus on M3 was justified by its perceived favorable empirical properties, especially a relatively stable money demand relationship. Furthermore, M3 was shown to exhibit leading indicator properties for future inflation (Issing, Gaspar, Angeloni, & Tristani, 2001). As the ECB stressed, the reference value for M3 growth, which was set at 4.5%, was however not considered as intermediate monetary target, "in order to avoid an automatic monetary policy reaction to fluctuations in M3 growth that may not be associated with inflationary pressures, but that may result, for example, from ... financial innovations" (Issing 1999, p. 20). Although the "first pillar" is sometimes presented as only referring to M3 growth (see, for instance, Favero et al. 2000), the ECB examined—and continues to examine—not only to what extent M3 growth deviates from the reference value, but also analyzes its underlying causes. Considerable attention is being paid, for example, to the growth rates of the components of M3 and the role of financial intermediation for the transmission of monetary policy.

In December 2002 the ECB Governing Council decided to evaluate this strategy in the light of the experience, taking into account the public debate and the outcomes of research undertaken by ECB and NCB staff. The results of this evaluation were published in May 2003. Although many observers had expected that the ECB would abandon the "monetary pillar," the Governing Council made it clear that the ECB would continue to include monetary analysis in its policy strategy, although it needed some "clarification." As the Governing Council explained, the monetary analysis was to mainly serve as a means of "cross-checking," from a medium to long-term perspective, the short to medium-term indications from the economic analysis. To underscore the longer-term nature of the reference value for monetary growth, the Governing Council decided to discontinue the practice of an annual review of the reference value for M3 growth.

In Chap. 3, Helge Berger, Thomas Harjes, and Emil Stavrev take an in-depth look at the role of money in the ECB's monetary policy strategy. The chapter revisits the case for money in modern monetary policy, surveying the ongoing theoretical and empirical debate. The key conclusion is that, from a macroeconomic perspective, an exclusive focus on non-monetary factors alone may leave the ECB with an incomplete picture of the economy. However, treating monetary factors as a separate matter—as suggested by the "cross checking" in the ECB's current approach—is a second-best solution. Instead, a general-equilibrium inspired analytical framework that merges the economic and monetary analysis of the ECB's policy strategy appears the most promising way forward. The role played by monetary aggregates in such unified framework may be rather limited. Still, an integrated framework would facilitate the presentation of policy decisions by providing a clearer narrative of the relative role of money in the interaction with other economic and financial sector variables, including asset prices, and their impact on consumer prices.

The recent financial and economic crises led to new challenges for the ECB, forcing the bank to employ non-standard policy measures. This raises various questions. How effective have been the conventional and non-standard monetary policy measures implemented by the ECB? Have these measures helped maintain price stability and reduce tensions in the interbank market? Given the significant problems in the financial system, how effective is monetary policy in forestalling strong disinflationary pressure, particularly when policy rates are very low? In Chap. 4, Martin Čihák, Thomas Harjes, and Emil Stavrev analyze the ECB's response to the global financial crisis. Their results suggest that even during the crisis, the core part of the ECB's monetary policy transmission—from policy rates to market rates—has continued to operate, but at a decreased efficiency. They also find some evidence that the ECB's non-standard measures, namely the lengthening of the maturity of liquidity-supply operations and the provision of funds at a fixed rate, reduced money market term spreads, facilitating the pass-through from policy to market rates. Furthermore, their results imply that the substantial increase in the ECB's balance sheet may have contributed to a reduction in government bond term spreads.

1.4 ECB Communication

Since monetary policy is increasingly becoming the art of managing expectations, communication has developed into a key instrument in the central bankers' toolbox. Greater disclosure and clarity over policy may lead to greater predictability of central bank actions, which, in turn, reduces uncertainty and unwanted volatility in financial markets. Indeed, there is a strongly held belief among central bankers today that a high degree of predictability is important. As Poole (2001, p. 9) put it: "The presumption must be that market participants make more efficient decisions … when markets can correctly predict central bank actions."

The extent to which central bank communication has been successful is very much an empirical issue. Therefore, it is no surprise that the empirical literature on central bank communication has seen major developments in recent years.[1] Many of these studies refer to the communication policy of the ECB. In Chap. 5, Jakob de Haan and David-Jan Jansen review the literature on the communication policy of the ECB. Although the first-decade's record is filled with outside complaints about ECB communication with financial markets (Cecchetti & Schoenholtz

[1] See Blinder, Ehrmann, Fratzscher, De Haan, and Jansen (2008) for an extensive survey.

2008), the assessment of the ECB's communication policies by de Haan and Jansen is quite favourable. They conclude that, overall, ECB communication has contributed to the effectiveness of its monetary policy. One aspect is that ECB communications affect the level and volatility of financial prices—indicating that private sector expectations react to ECB communication. In addition, there is evidence that, on balance, communication has improved the predictability of interest rate decisions. Another aspect is anchoring market expectations in the longer run. Here de Haan and Jansen find that the evidence on the ECB's communication effectiveness is somewhat less clear. Finally, they examine the often contrasting signals from individual communication by ECB officials to market participants, concluding that dispersed communication has made it harder for market participants to forecast interest rate decisions.

1.5 Governance of the ECB

Beyond a policy and communication strategy, effective monetary policy also requires a well-designed decision-making mechanism. This is easier said than done. According to many observers, in the case of the ECB the sheer number of decision makers present in the Governing Council could pose serious problems. Indeed, the "one member, one vote" principle laid down in the Maastricht Treaty could mean that eventually all 27 EU members will hold a seat—and a vote—in the Governing Council through their NCB governors, should all current members decide to share EMU. Adding the six centrally appointed members of the ECB's Directorate (including the ECB's President and Vice-President), this would create a body of 33, making it by far the largest monetary policy-making institution among OECD countries. To paraphrase Richard Baldwin, a group that size would be too large to decide where to go to dinner, and most certainly too large to make efficient and timely monetary policy decisions. In another evolutionary step transforming the ECB's initial setup, the Treaty of Nice therefore called for a revision of the Governing Council's decision-making procedures. In March 2003, the Governing Council introduced a rotation system, in which NCB governors would receive voting weights as a function of their economic significance, once the number of governors (or, equivalently, euro area countries) reached 15. In December 2008, the ECB decided to postpone the actual implementation of the reform until the number of governors reached 18.

In Chap. 6, Peter Stella and Jérôme Vandenbussche assess the effectiveness of the current ECB governance arrangements. Reflecting on the ongoing debate on the optimal design of a monetary policy committee (MPC), they suggest that the ECB's longer-term governance structure could be dual: monetary policy decisions could be taken by a "denationalized" MPC consisting of 7–9 ECB bureaucrats while the larger council of NCB governors would meet regularly to do the oversight. However, this alternative may be at least one generation away as the legitimacy of the ECB and other EU institutions needs to be strengthened and further political integration is needed as well. Thus, for the time being, a rotation system may indeed provide a pragmatic compromise between the first best and the feasible. Rotation systems have proved durable working to satisfaction in the United States where there has been a similar legacy of "independent regional central banks" morphing into a unified structure.

1.6 Financial Stability

Although the primary objective of the ECB is to maintain price stability, there are explicit references to financial regulation and supervision in the Treaty on European Union. For instance, the treaty asks the European System of Central Banks (ESCB)—which includes the ECB central banks as well as the other, non-euro area EU central banks—to promote the smooth operations of payment systems. According to Article 105 (5), the ESCB shall contribute to the smooth conduct of policies pursued by the competent authorities relating to the prudential supervision of credit institutions and the stability of the financial system. Similarly, Article 105 (6) of the Treaty states that the Council may confer upon the ECB specific tasks concerning policies relating to the prudential supervision of credit institutions and other financial institutions with the exception of insurance undertakings. However, the Treaty is explicit on the principle of decentralisation and allocation of regulatory and supervisory powers to national central banks. Only in very special circumstances, and with unanimity in the European Council, will the ECB be allowed to regulate or supervise financial institutions.

Based on the experience during the financial crisis, a group of experts under the chairmanship of De Larosière proposed to set up a European Systemic Risk Board (ESRB) consisting of the members of the ECB General Council, plus the Chairs of the three European Supervisory Authorities (CEBS, CEIOPS, and CESR) and a member of the European Commission. The ESRB will become responsible for supervision of macro systemic risk. The micro (prudential) supervisory role is designated to a new European System of Financial Supervisors (ESFS), consisting of a network of national financial supervisors working in tandem with the new European Supervisory Authorities. The ECB will not have a direct role in micro prudential supervision, and this ESFS will operate separately from the ECB.

In Chap. 7, Dirk Schoenmaker discusses the challenges that the ECB faces under the proposed scheme. First, the ECB will need a tool to manage financial stability. What can the ECB do when an asset price bubble is building up or credit growth is excessive? Second, the ECB is dependent on the European Supervisory Authorities and the national central banks and supervisors for information. Timely information is crucial to make an up-to-date assessment of the stability of the European financial system and to act pro-actively when needed.

Schoenmaker argues that a tight link between macro and micro prudential supervision is important for a full and timely flow of supervisory information. But there are two hurdles for a micro supervisory role for the ECB. The Maastricht

Treaty requires a unanimous vote of all EU Member States for transferring financial supervision to the ECB. Even if this hurdle would be taken, the Maastricht Treaty only allows the transfer of banking/securities supervision and not that of insurance supervision. Schoenmaker concludes that a sectoral supervisory approach makes it difficult to take the cross-sectoral nature of the financial landscape fully into account.

References

Blinder, A. S., Ehrmann, M., Fratzscher, M., De Haan, J., & Jansen, D. (2008). Central Bank communication and monetary policy: A survey of theory and evidence. *Journal of Economic Literature*, *46*(4), 910–945.

Cecchetti, S. C., & Schoenholtz, K. L. (2008). *How central bankers see it: The first decade of ECB policy and beyond*, NBER Working Paper No. 14489.

European Central Bank (2005). Monetary policy and inflation differentials in a heterogeneous currency area. *Monthly Bulletin*, 61–77.

European Central Bank (2004). *The monetary policy of the ECB* (2nd ed.). Frankfurt: ECB.

Favero, C. A., Freixas, X., Persson, T., & Wyplosz, C. (2000). *One money, many countries: Monitoring the European Central Bank* (Vol. 2), London: CEPR.

Issing, O. (1999). The monetary policy of the Eurosystem. *Finance & Development*, *36*(March), 18–21.

Issing, O., Gaspar, V., Angeloni, I., & Tristani, O. (2001). *Monetary policy in the Euro area. Strategy and decision-making at the European Central Bank*. Cambridge: Cambridge University Press.

Jonung, L., & Drea, E. (2010). It can't happen, it's a bad idea, it won't last: US Economists on the EMU and the Euro, 1989–2002. *Econ J Watch, 7*(1).

Mongelli, F. P., & Wyplosz, C. (2008). *The Euro at ten: Unfulfilled threats and unexpected challenges*. Paper presented at the Fifth ECB Central Banking Conference: The euro at ten: lessons and challenges.

Poole, W. (2001). Expectations. *Federal Reserve Bank of St. Louis Review, 83*(1), 1–10.

Chapter 2
Inflation Differentials in the Euro Area: A Survey

Jakob de Haan

2.1 Introduction

The objective of the European Central Bank (ECB) is price stability, which the ECB has defined as an inflation rate in the euro area in the medium run that is below but close to 2%. The ECB does not focus on inflation in individual countries in the euro area. However, several years after the launch of the euro, inflation differentials among euro area countries are still subject to much debate. After converging sharply in the 1990s, national inflation rates started to diverge again in 1999; since then, the standard deviation of the annual inflation rates among euro area members has fluctuated around 1%—a substantial figure (Angeloni & Ehrmann 2007).

Differences in inflation are not unusual in large currency areas. In fact, in the absence of the possibility of nominal exchange rate adjustment and the presence of low labour mobility, they play an important role as a macroeconomic adjustment mechanism in response to asymmetric shocks. Thus, inflation differentials in the European Economic and Monetary Union (EMU) can be seen as "the product of an equilibrating adjustment process… and, as such, are not only unavoidable, but also desirable" (European Central Bank 2005, p. 61). At the same time, they may be problematic because "political economy considerations arise because of the euro area's institutional features. Inflation is unpopular, especially if it cannot be mitigated by a weaker exchange rate. National public opinion and politicians may misinterpret its causes and blame the currency instead. National differences also

The views expressed in this chapter are those of the author and should not be attributed to De Nederlandsche Bank.

J. de Haan (✉)
Research Department, De Nederlandsche Bank, PO BOX 98,1000 AB Amsterdam, The Netherlands
e-mail: J.de.Haan@dnb.nl

J. de Haan
University of Groningen, Groningen, The Netherlands

J. de Haan and H. Berger (eds.), *The European Central Bank at Ten*,
DOI: 10.1007/978-3-642-14237-6_2, © Springer-Verlag Berlin Heidelberg 2010

make the interpretation of euro area indicators more challenging for the Governing Council of the European Central Bank (ECB), which is mandated to set monetary policy for the area as a whole" (Angeloni & Ehrmann 2007, p. 1).

Furthermore, even if an inflation objective of "close to 2%" seems high enough to forego deflation in the euro area as a whole, it is possible that deflation occurs in an individual country, depending on how large inflation differentials are in the monetary union. In case of significant inflation differentials within the euro area it is possible for some countries to experience deflation, even if the euro area as a whole does not. Deflation is widely perceived as being more harmful than inflation. Sibert (2003) argues that the redistribution due to unexpected deflation may be more costly than the redistribution resulting from unanticipated inflation. Defaults may occur and the resulting bankruptcies and restructurings destroy real wealth. The deterioration in debtors' balance sheets brought about by unexpected deflation may thus lower both consumption and investment demand. Persistent deflation may turn into a deflationary spiral of falling prices, output, profits, and employment. With sticky wages, price declines cause real wages to rise, profit margins to fall, and employment to be cut back. This may set off a deflationary cycle.

In addition, inflation differentials can be harmful when they are caused by economic distortions (Beck, Hubrich, & Marcellino 2009). For example, structural inefficiencies in factor markets could affect production costs and, hence, lead to diverging goods prices in the countries concerned. This can have negative implications for the competitiveness of the high-inflation countries, particularly if the inflation differentials are long lasting. Harmful inflation differentials can also arise from rigidities in nominal wages and prices. Non-synchronised adjustments to shocks will lead to differences in inflation rates, which can lead to relative price distortions and thus inefficient allocations of households' spending.

Finally, inflation differentials within the euro area may also have a destabilizing effect on monetary policymaking. Since short-term nominal interest rates are identical in the euro area, differences in inflation rates across member countries cause differences in real interest rates. As a consequence, member countries with relatively high inflation rates experience relatively low real interest rates, which will boost investment and consumption and thus aggregate demand, which, in turn, may lead to even higher inflation rates.[1]

This chapter discusses two issues. The first is what generates these inflation differences in the euro area? The second related issue is how (and how quickly) these inflation differences will subside and what the possible mechanisms behind such convergence could be. Finally, the chapter discusses possible policy options and implications of diverging inflation rates for the ECB and other policy makers.

---

[1] However, what matters for investment and consumption decisions are ex ante measures of real interest rates, i.e., the difference between market interest rates and expectations for inflation developments over the relevant horizon. The dispersion across countries of ex ante measures of real interest rates is significantly lower than that of ex post measures (European Central Bank 2005).

2.2 Inflation in Countries in the Euro Area, 1999–2008

Inflation differentials in the euro area since the beginning of 1999 have been quite marked. Table 2.1 shows the annual inflation rate in the countries in the euro area. Most notably, Ireland, Spain, Greece and Portugal have been frequently at the top of the inflation league table, although Ireland more recently saw inflation differentials drop substantially and even occasionally had lower inflation than the euro area as a whole. Also price increases in the Netherlands in 2001/2002 were notably higher than average inflation in the euro area. In contrast, inflation in Germany and Austria has always been below the euro area average.

Figure 2.1 shows the degree of inflation dispersion in the euro area, measured in terms of the standard deviation. The figure shows that the standard deviation of the annual inflation rate (measured using HICP, the Harmonised Index of Consumer Prices) in the euro area has fluctuated around 1%. Before the start of the Economic and Monetary Union (EMU), the inflation dispersion in the founding countries of EMU decreased over time, especially during the second half of the 1990s. The non-weighted standard deviation declined from around 4% points at the beginning of the 1990s to about 1% point at the start of the monetary union (Angeloni & Ehrmann 2007). As Fig. 2.1 shows, since then the standard deviation initially declined, but more recently inflation dispersion slightly increased. This probably reflects the 2007/2008 enlargements of the euro area, as the new members had all an inflation rate above the euro area average since they became member of the currency union (see Table 2.1). Also differences in the transmission of shocks in commodity prices may play a role here.

Table 2.1 Inflation differential vis-à-vis euro area (HICP based, % points) in countries in the euro area, 1999–2008

	1999	2000	2001	2002	2003	2004	2005	2006	2007	2008
Austria	−0.91	−0.86	−0.69	−1.05	−1.09	−0.20	−0.21	−0.68	−0.16	−0.52
Belgium	−0.30	−0.14	−0.54	−1.20	−0.88	−0.29	0.21	−0.03	−0.54	0.75
Cyprus										0.64
Finland	−0.12	0.13	−0.32	−0.74	−1.09	−2.01	−1.55	−1.10	−0.78	0.17
France	−0.87	−0.99	−1.20	−0.81	−0.22	0.19	−0.42	−0.46	−0.75	−0.58
Germany	−0.79	−1.42	−1.08	−1.40	−1.36	−0.36	−0.40	−0.59	−0.08	−0.99
Greece			0.67	1.17	1.05	0.88	1.16	0.94	0.63	0.49
Ireland	1.04	2.43	1.01	1.97	1.61	0.15	−0.14	0.33	0.51	−0.63
Italy	0.23	−0.24	−0.66	−0.14	0.42	0.12	−0.11	−0.15	−0.32	−0.24
Luxemburg	−0.41	0.96	−0.58	−0.69	0.15	1.08	1.44	0.59	0.29	0.35
Malta										0.94
Netherlands	0.60	−0.48	2.13	1.12	−0.15	−0.77	−0.82	−0.72	−0.78	−1.53
Slovenia									1.40	1.79
Spain	0.81	0.66	−0.15	0.84	0.71	0.90	1.06	1.19	0.48	0.39
Portugal	0.74	−0.02	1.43	0.93	0.87	0.36	−0.19	0.67	0.06	−1.09

Source: ECB

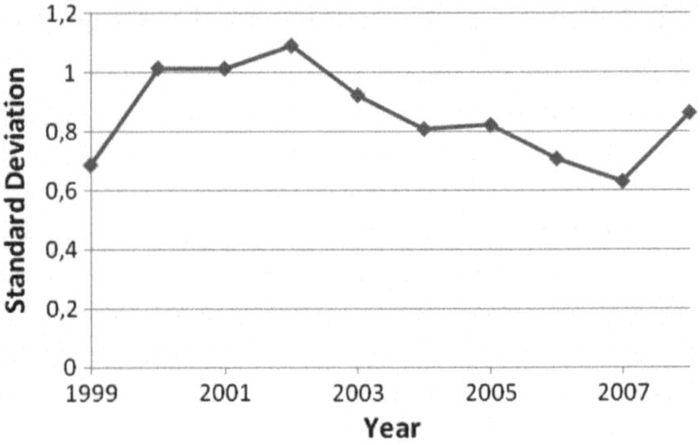

Fig. 2.1 Inflation dispersion in the euro area (standard deviation), 1999–2008. Source: own calculations using data shown in Table 2.1

Whereas most empirical studies on inflation differentials in the euro area focus on country-level data, Beck et al. (2009) use a novel monthly dataset of regional inflation rates from six countries in the euro area, namely Austria, Germany, Finland, Italy, Portugal and Spain, over the period 1996–2004. These authors argue that the use of regional inflation data may be helpful for three reasons. First, the understanding of the behaviour of regionally disaggregated inflation rate series helps to better understand aggregate inflation. Second, the use of regional data makes it possible to disentangle the importance of national from purely regional factors for inflation. Third, as there is more heterogeneity at the regional than at the national level, the identification of the sources of inflation heterogeneity may be easier.

Beck et al. (2009) employ a factor model to decompose regional inflation rates into a common area-wide, a country-specific and an idiosyncratic regional component. They find that at least half of the variation in regional inflation rates is explained by one area-wide factor (see Table 2.2). This common area-wide factor can be related to the common monetary policy in the euro area and to external developments, such as oil price changes and changes in the euro exchange rate. The national factor explains on average 32% of observed inflation variations,

Table 2.2 Variance in regional inflation differentials explained by euro area, national and regional factors

	All regions					
Proportion of variance explained	48.46					
	Austria		Germany		Spain	
	National	Regional	National	Regional	National	Regional
Proportion of variance explained	30.36	21.18	37.11	14.43	26.88	24.66
	Finland		Italy		Portugal	
	National	Regional	National	Regional	National	Regional
Proportion of variance explained	48.80	2.74	28.73	22.81	34.78	16.76

Source: Beck et al. (2009)

Table 2.3 Share of inflation differentials accounted for by area wide factors, 1993–2003

Overall	Services	Industrial	Energy	Proc. food	Unproc. food
0.66	0.58	0.67	0.52	0.65	0.42

Source: Altissimo et al. (2005)

although there are large differences across countries. The national factor is lowest in Spain (27%) and highest in Finland (49%). The remaining 18% of regional inflation differentials is due to regional elements. The authors also examine whether the estimated area wide and national factors have the same effects across all regions. They find that there is substantial heterogeneity in the effect of the euro area component within most nations, except in Spain and Portugal. There is also a lot of heterogeneity in the effect of the national component within nations.

Using factor analysis, Altissimo, Benigno, and Rodriguez Palenzuela (2005) have analysed to what extent five main subcomponents in the HICP, namely Services, Industrial Goods excluding Energy, Energy, Processed Food and Unprocessed Food, are driven by different reactions to area-wide factors or sectoral developments. The estimation period is 1993.01–2003.06. Table 2.3, which is reproduced from this study, shows the average across countries of the share of variance of the differentials accounted by common shocks, both for the HICP and for the subcomponents. The results show that the Energy and the Services sectors have the largest idiosyncratic components, while the Industrial Good excluding Energy and the Processed Food sectors have the lowest idiosyncratic components.

Figure 2.2 shows more recent figures on the contributions of the five main HICP segments to aggregate euro area inflation dispersion from 2005 to March 2009, measured as the covariance between inflation contributions of each sector and overall euro area inflation.[2]

The data show that euro area inflation differentials are mostly due to the energy component, whose contribution has considerably increased over time. Also the contribution of unprocessed food to inflation dispersion has increased during this period considered. On the other hand, the contribution from non-energy industrial goods has fallen since 2005, being particularly low in 2007 and 2009.

Following Rabanal (2009), the difference between inflation in country i and inflation in the rest of the euro area can be written as:

$$\Delta p_t - \Delta p_t^* = \Delta p_t^T - \Delta p_t^{T*} + (1-\gamma^*)(\Delta p_t^{T*} - \Delta p_t^{N*}) - (1-\gamma)(\Delta p_t^T - \Delta p_t^N) \tag{2.1}$$

where Δ is the year-on-year difference operator; p_t, p_t^T, p_t^N are the natural logarithms of the consumer price index, its tradable component, and its non-tradable component for country i; $p_t^*, p_t^{T*}, p_t^{N*}$ are the same variables for the rest of the euro area, while γ and γ^* are the share of tradable goods in the price index in country i

[2] The data refer to the current countries in the euro area. I am thankful to Lourdes Acedo-Montoya from the European Commission (DG ECFIN) for providing these data.

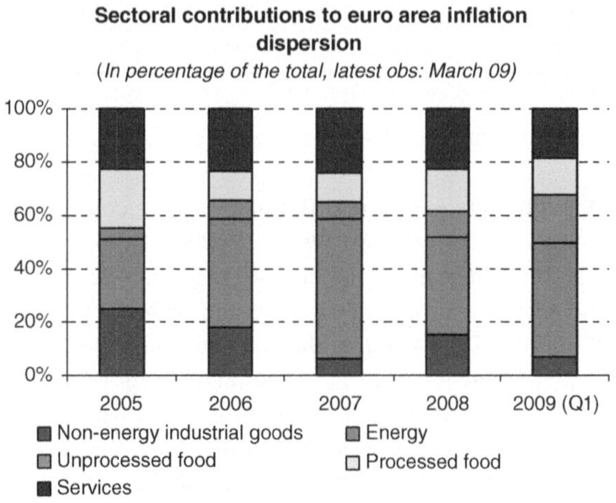

Fig. 2.2 Sectoral contributions to euro area inflation dispersion, 2005–2009. Source: European Commission

and in the rest of the euro area. As Eq. 2.1 shows, deviations from purchasing power parity can be explained by: (1) deviations from the law of one price for tradable goods and (2) movements of relative prices between tradable and non-tradable goods inside each country. As pointed out by Rabanal (2009), if the fraction of tradable goods in the consumer price index is the same across countries ($\gamma = \gamma^*$), and the law of one price holds for tradable goods ($\Delta p_t^{T*} = \Delta p_t^T$), then fluctuations in the inflation differential would be due to non-tradable inflation only. If the consumption basket differs across countries and there are deviations from the law of one price for tradable goods then fluctuations in the price of tradable goods will also matter.

Rabanal (2009) reports that the inflation differential between Spain and the rest of the euro area can largely be explained by the tradable component for most of the time since the start of the currency union. However, Altissimo et al. (2005) show that in a sectoral decomposition covering ten individual countries (all euro countries except for Greece and Luxemburg) between January 1990 to February 2004 most of the inflation differentials originate in the services category of the HICP, although in some periods also the energy category significantly contributed to overall dispersion. This suggests that the main source of dispersion in countries' inflation rates is in non-traded goods.

How does inflation dispersion in the euro area compare to inflation dispersion in the US? Beck et al. (2009) find a somewhat smaller degree of dispersion in regional inflation rates across US regions than across euro area regions. Moreover, regional US inflation rates exhibit slightly less persistence than euro area inflation rates. However, owner-occupied housing is included in the US CPI, but not in the European HICP. As argued by Remsperger (2003), this is important because there is hardly any other component where regionally divergent price developments have such a major impact as they do in housing. The interregional standard deviation of the changes in rents is greater than that of services, which, in turn, is larger than that of industrial goods (excluding energy). This suggests that an appropriate coverage of owner-occupied housing would result in the measured divergence of inflation rates in the euro area being larger.

2.3 Explaining Inflation Differentials

Several factors have been invoked to explain the size and the dynamics of inflation differentials in EMU that we capture in five categories, namely (1) convergence, (2) business cycle differences, (3) asymmetric demand and supply shocks and asymmetric adjustment mechanisms to common shocks, (4) characteristics of domestic product, labour and other factor markets, and (5) wage and price rigidities. These explanations are not mutually exclusive. For instance, asymmetric shocks may not only lead to inflation differentials, but also to differences in business cycle synchronisation. Likewise, the impact of shocks on inflation differentials depends on wage and price rigidities. For expository purposes, however, we will distinguish between these categories.

First, inflation rates of countries in the currency union could initially diverge because of a "catch-up" mechanism from different price levels (*convergence*). If price levels differed initially across countries forming a monetary union, price level convergence will generate temporary inflation differentials. Increased market integration and price transparency associated with the adoption of a common currency reduce the scope for deviations from the law of one price. Honohan and Lane (2003) conclude that a considerable part of the inflation differentials in the euro area in the early years of EMU can be explained by price level convergence. These authors estimated a multivariate panel where the spreads of national inflation rates from the area average depend on proxies for the catch-up effect and on three macroeconomic variables: nominal exchange rate changes; the fiscal balance, and the output gap. Their point estimate implies that a country with a price level one-third below the European average would experience an additional 1%-point of inflation.

One reason why countries may have different inflation rates that has attracted much academic attention is the so-called Balassa–Samuelson effect. This effect hinges on differences in labour productivity growth between the tradable and non-tradable sector. If this growth is higher in the tradable sector, wages will tend to increase in that sector without leading to higher unit labour costs. However, in case of high labour mobility between sectors wages will also tend to increase in the non-tradable sector, where—given the lower average labour productivity growth—prices will exhibit higher average increases. Therefore, countries with a large difference between labour productivity growth rates in the tradable and non-tradable sectors will also experience a higher inflation rate.[3] The Balassa–Samuelson effect is

[3] As pointed out by Rabanal (2009), the Balassa–Samuelson hypothesis could explain the higher inflation rate in the service sector (as a proxy for the non-tradable sector) than in the goods sector (as a proxy for the tradable sector).

often associated with the process of convergence in living standards across economies: countries that are in the process of catching-up normally display strong productivity growth in the tradable sector, while productivity developments in the non-tradable sector are normally more similar across countries (European Central Bank 2005).

However, there is evidence that the Balassa–Samuelson effect can provide only a partial explanation for euro area inflation differentials (see De Haan, Eijffinger, & Waller (2005) for a survey of older studies). As pointed out by the European Central Bank (2003), historically, catching-up has not always led to higher inflation or an appreciating nominal exchange rate, as the case of Ireland shows. Honohan and Lane (2003) argue that little if any of the Irish inflation deviation is due to the Balassa–Samuelson effect. According to these authors, Ireland's boom has been largely one of employment growth, and not exceptional productivity gains. Likewise, Rabanal (2009) concludes that the Balassa–Samuelson effect has not been an important source of inflation differentials between Spain and the rest of the euro area during the EMU period. Beck et al. (2009) argue that the Balassa–Samuelson effect implies a negative relationship between a region's initial income level and subsequent changes in the overall price level. They do not find much support for such a relationship.

Furthermore, some of the estimates of the Balassa–Samuelson effect are not in line with actual inflation after the start of the monetary union. For instance, Belgium and Finland are sometimes found to have high Balassa–Samuelson effects, but this is not confirmed by actual inflation differences. Conversely, in the beginning of the new century the Netherlands has had a higher inflation differential than predicted by the Balassa–Samuelson model (European Central Bank 2003a). Indeed, according to the European Central Bank (2005), differences in labour productivity trends across euro area countries contribute to inflation diversity, yet can only account for a relatively moderate share of inflation differentials.[4]

Second, *business cycle differences* among the countries in the euro area may contribute to inflation differentials. Countries with output above trend tend to have upward pressure on inflation, while countries with output below trend will experience downward pressure on inflation. Figure 2.3 plots the average inflation rate after the euro was adopted in each euro area country against its average output gap in the same period.[5] The figure suggests a positive relationship between the

[4] It may be argued that the Balassa–Samaulson effect may be more relevant for the new EU member states. However, according to Égert and Podpiera (2008), for the Czech Republic, Hungary, Poland, and Slovakia the relevant literature over the past 5 years failed to quantify a sizable Balassa–Samuelson effect, with the average effect from 20 recent studies accounting at best for one-third of the actual real exchange rate appreciation of more than 30% from 1995 to 2006. However, Mihaljek and Klau (2008) conclude that the Balassa–Samuelson effects are clearly present and explain around 24% of inflation differentials vis-à-vis the euro area (about 1.2% points on average) in their sample of 11 countries in central and eastern Europe covering the period from the mid-1990s to the first quarter of 2008.

[5] Inflation data come from the ECB, while the output gap data come from EconStats. The data for Ireland and the Netherlands run to 2006 only.

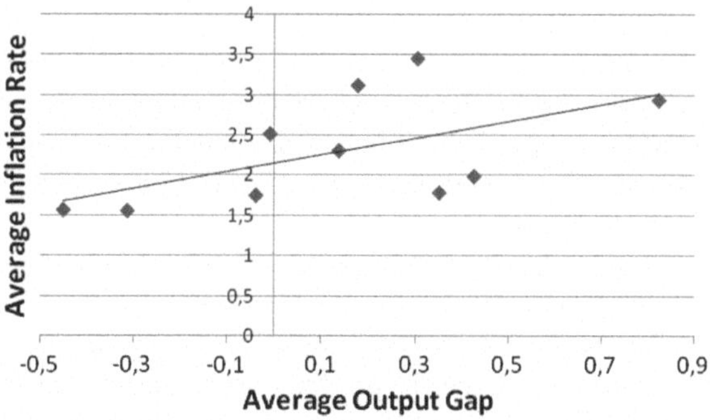

Fig. 2.3 Inflation and output gap, 1999–2008

average output gap and average inflation. Similarly, Honohan and Lane (2003) find that the effect of the output gap on inflation differentials is positive and statistically significant. In a more recent study, Andersson, Masuch, and Schiffbauer (2009) find that inflation differentials are primarily driven by different business cycle positions and to some extent by changes in product market regulations (to be discussed below). These author use panel estimations for annual inflation differentials for a sample covering the period 1999–2006 and 12 euro area countries (excluding Slovenia, Cyprus, Malta and Slovakia).

Business cycles may be out of sync for various reasons. Remsperger (2003) argues that one reason may have been the nominal convergence process in the run-up to EMU. The elimination of the residual foreign exchange risk since the beginning of 1999 and the dwindling of the risk premia brought about a largely uniform long-term interest rate level. In some countries, this is likely to have generated a substantial cyclical stimulus. The fall in real interest rates in those countries with above-average inflation sustained upward pressure on prices in exactly those countries that already had relatively high inflation. An important factor was the rapid rise in property prices encouraged by the convergence of interest rates (Remsperger 2003). Indeed, Honohan and Lane (2003) report a fairly strong negative cross-sectional correlation between real interest rate declines in the run-up to EMU and commercial property inflation in 1995–2001 (the correlation is -0.67).

The expansionary effects of real interest rate changes over time will probably be offset by the equilibrating effect of changes in national competitiveness triggered by an increase in inflation differentials (Angeloni and Ehrmann 2007). Owing to a real "appreciation", countries with higher-than-average inflation rates suffer a loss in price competitiveness, while countries with relatively low inflation rates gain in price competitiveness. The consequence is that export demand in countries with higher inflation rates tends to decline, which has a dampening impact on price developments in those countries. Conversely, demand tends to increase in countries with lower inflation rates. However, the coolant effect of real appreciation through a loss of competitiveness is likely only to operate at a more gradual pace. Still, as pointed out by Remsperger (2003), especially in the euro area, where the regional labour markets, owing to different languages and social security systems, are so far not very closely interlinked, short-term inflation differentials can help to stabilize output and the labour market through this "real exchange rate" effect.[6] Alternative adjustment mechanisms are high labour mobility, wage flexibility or a monetary union-wide fiscal transfer system. However, as pointed out by Beck et al. (2009), none of these mechanisms is very likely to play a role in EMU.[7]

Third, an important reason for continuing inflation differentials in the euro area consists in price reactions to constantly recurring *asymmetricsupply and demand shocks*.[8] Relative prices should fluctuate across countries—for example, in response to asymmetric productivity shocks—when the countries' consumption baskets are not identical; in a currency union, these fluctuations are necessarily reflected in inflation differentials (Duarte and Wolman 2008). Likewise, different national fiscal policy shocks can create or reinforce inflation differentials.

Also differences in the transmission mechanisms to common shocks could lead to inflation differentials. Different countries may be affected in different ways by the same shock due to differences in nominal rigidities (see below) or differences in their pattern of specialisation.[9] For another, they may react differently to common shocks because of differences in market structures.

One such common shock that may affect countries in the euro area differently and that has received quite some attention in the older literature is exchange rate shocks. The share of imported goods in private consumption and the strength of the pass-through effect determine the impact of exchange rate shocks on consumer prices. As discussed by De Haan et al. (2005), the pass-through of exchange rate changes into prices is not uniform across the countries in the euro area. Price developments may therefore differ in the medium term even with uniform shocks. One important factor influencing pass-through is the openness towards trading partners outside the euro area. In general, greater "extra-openness" should be reflected by a higher weight of extra-euro area goods in a country's overall goods basket and, therefore, a stronger pass-through effect from exchange rate changes

[6] This effect also occurs in relationship to countries outside the monetary union. Since the euro's (flexible) nominal exchange rate against the currencies of such countries is geared to economic developments of the euro area as a whole, euro-area countries with an above-average inflation rate see their competitive position vis-à-vis non-euro-area countries decline, while euro-area countries with a below-average inflation rate see their competitive position improve (Remsperger 2003).

[7] Financial integration may provide for insurance against asymmetric shocks. If residents of the member countries of a monetary union hold monetary union-wide diversified portfolios the costs of asymmetric shocks will be born by all residents (Beck et al. 2009). However, as De Haan, Oosterloo, and Schoenmaker (2009) show, despite substantial progress in financial integration in Europe, portfolios of many European financial institutions are still characterized by a high home bias.

[8] Asymmetric shocks and differences in the transmission of and the policy reaction to common shocks are, of course, among the driving forces of diverging business cycles.

[9] These factors can be related. According to the European Central Bank (2005), euro area energy and unprocessed food prices seem to change most frequently, while service prices appear to be modified less frequently.

on domestic prices. So, a member country that consumes imports from a non-member country will experience different inflationary pressures if the euro exchange rate depreciates as compared to a member country that conducts all its trade with other member countries (Hüfner & Schröder 2002). In addition to the direct impact of exchange rates on consumer prices, there may be a cyclical effect of exchange rate shocks via a change in the competitive position, which is also determined by an economy's degree of openness to countries outside the euro area. The econometric estimates of the inflation differentials of Honohan and Lane (2003) suggest a significant role for effective exchange rate changes. They estimate a multivariate panel where the spreads of national inflation rates from the area average depend on proxies for the catch-up effect and on three macroeconomic variables: nominal exchange rate changes; the fiscal balance, and the output gap. These authors conclude that a substantial part of the inflation divergence can be attributed to the euro exchange rate; euro area member countries are asymmetrically affected by changes in the euro exchange rate depending on their degree of external exposure. The point estimate of Honohan and Lane (2003) implies that a relative deprecation of 3.5% is associated with an additional 1% point of inflation. This is a quite a large effect. The Irish nominal effective exchange rate depreciated 11% during 1998–2000, while the French exchange rate weakened by only 4%. So, according to these estimates, differences in the effective exchange rates of Ireland and France led to an inflation differential of 2% points in this period. Angeloni and Ehrmann (2004) have shown that this conclusion is somewhat sensitive to the model specification, but Honohan and Lane (2004) have provided further evidence in support of their earlier thesis. However, the results of Angeloni and Ehrmann (2007), to be discussed in the following section, suggest a much smaller effect of the euro exchange rate on inflation differentials in the euro area. Also a recent study by Andersson et al. (2009) concludes that external factors such as differences in nominal effective exchange rates play only a minor role in explaining inflation differentials vis-à-vis the euro area.

The three sources of inflation differentials mentioned so far are probably not worrisome from a policy point of view (with a possible exception for fiscal policy differences), since they are either transitory (although potentially long lasting as will discussed in the next section) or reflect the result of convergence or equilibrating dynamics. Beck et al. (2009) identify two other factors that can lead to undesirable economic outcomes. These factors are: (1) *characteristics of domestic product, labour and other factor markets*, and (2) *nominal wage and price rigidities*. The importance of these factors is generally examined in conjunction with (symmetric or a-symmetric) economic shocks.

If wages diverge across countries due to structural inefficiencies in labour markets, also production costs and therefore goods prices may diverge. Labour market institutions may play a role here. For instance, according to Calmfors and Driffill (1988) differences in labour market institutions can give rise to different inflation rate outcomes because economies with either strong centralisation or strong decentralisation of wage bargaining are better equipped to face supply shocks than economies with an intermediate degree of centralisation. Likewise, the presence of

Table 2.4 Regression of mean inflation rates on mean economic structural variables

Variable	Area wide analysis		
	Estimate	Std. error	
U	−0.00679	0.005798	
DULC	−0.02321	0.036111	
DP_HOUS	0.227631	0.064476	
DENS_D	−0.01197	0.005862	
SERV	−0.00723	0.0034	
DY	0.002051	0.004318	
R-squared:	0.952	Obs.	66
Rbar-squared:	0.943		

Source: Beck et al. (2009)

rigidities affecting the price[10] and wage formation mechanism delays the necessary adjustment to shocks and gives rise to distortions in relative prices after such shocks, contributing to lasting inflation differentials. These differences can lead to relative price distortions and thus inefficient allocations of households' spending.

Beck et al. (2009) estimate a model explaining regional inflation differentials in which they take heterogeneity in product, labour and other factors markets into account. Table 2.4, which is copied from their paper, shows the results. The explanatory variables are the unemployment rate (*U*), the change in unit labour costs (*DULC*), change in rental costs (*DP_HOUS*), the number of suppliers (*DENS_D*), the percentage of services in gross value added (*SERV*), and growth of GDP per capita (*DY*). To capture the potential effects of labour market heterogeneity on inflation differentials, Beck et al. (2009) include average levels of unemployment (*U*) and average changes in unit labour costs (*DULC*) over 1995–2004. As proxy for the costs of non-traded input factors other than wages, they use the average year-on-year change in the COICOP (Classification of Individual Consumption by Purpose) index 'Housing, water, electricity, gas and other fuels' (*DP_HOUS*). As nominal rigidities are associated with imperfect competition in the goods and labour markets, which in turn can be approximated by the number of suppliers, Beck et al. employ a measure of market density in the manufacturing and in the wholesale sectors (*DENS_D*). As a proxy for differences in the production structure they use the relative sizes of the services sector (*SERV*), and to proxy business cycle movements, Beck et al. (2009) employ regional GDP per capita growth (*DY*). The latter variable is also their proxy for the Balassa–Samuelson effect that implies a negative relationship between income growth rates and inflation rates. As an alternative proxy they use average level of (log) per-capita income in 1995.

The results as shown in Table 2.4 suggest that labour market characteristics do not play an important role in explaining regional inflation differentials. The coefficients

[10] Evidence presented by Dhyne, Alvarez, Le Bihan, Veronese, Dias, Hoffmann, Jonker, Lünnemann, Rumler, and Vilmunen (2006) for the euro area suggests that prices are changed on average every 13 months.

of the unemployment rate and unit labour costs are insignificant. Also average per-capita income growth rate does not turn out to be significant. Likewise, using initial per-capita income instead of growth rates did not yield support for the Balassa–Samuelson effect. However, the results of Beck et al. (2009) lent support to the importance of the costs of non-wage input factors as the proxy for this variable (*DP_HOUS*) is highly significant. Also the extent of competitiveness of the economy seems to play an important role for inflation differentials as the coefficient of the proxy for this variable (*DENS_D*) is negative and significant at a 5% level. In other words, markets with more suppliers experience relatively lower inflation rates. The results of Beck et al. also suggest that the economic structure of a region significantly affects inflation differentials. The coefficient of the proxy for sectoral specialisation (*SERV*) is statistically significant. The authors conclude that the observed long-run differences in regional inflation rates do not reflect the response of integrated markets to economic shocks and are not the result of a convergence process in regional incomes but that they are caused by inefficiencies in factor markets and region-specific structural characteristics.

Using the OECD's index for product market regulations, Andersson et al. (2009) find that national differences in changes of product market regulations help explain inflation differentials in the euro area. In particular, an increase in product market regulations in a country relative to the euro area, *ceteris paribus*, leads to higher inflation relative to the euro area average.

Some other recent papers have examined inflation differentials in the euro area using general equilibrium multi-country models of the euro area. These studies will be discussed in the next section, which focuses on the persistence of inflation differentials.

2.4 Are Inflation Differentials Persistent?

Inflation differentials across European regions are not only quite large but also long lasting, not only across countries but also—to a lesser extent—within countries (see Table 2.5). The reported difference in the inflation rate between an average German

Table 2.5 Inflation in European regions, 1996–2004

	1996–2004		1996–1998		1999–2004	
	Mean	Std. dev.	Mean	Std. dev.	Mean	Std. dev.
All regions	2.18	0.63	1.89	0.61	2.26	0.70
Germany	1.35	0.15	1.21	0.21	1.31	0.20
Austria	1.62	0.1	1.19	0.17	1.73	0.11
Finland	1.41	0.09	1.07	0.05	1.60	0.13
Italy	2.26	0.22	2.13	0.33	2.22	0.22
Spain	2.87	0.22	2.45	0.25	3.06	0.24
Portugal	2.85	0.15	2.41	0.28	3.09	0.12

Source: Beck et al. (2009)

and an average Spanish region corresponds to a cumulative depreciation in the real exchange rate between an average German and an average Spanish region of around 15% over the sample period.

To examine whether there have been major changes in cross-regional inflation dynamics, Beck et al. (2009) split the sample into a 'pre-EMU' [1996(1)–1998(12)] and an 'EMU' [1999(1)–2004(10)] subsample. Two conclusions can be drawn. First, mean inflation rates are always lower in the 'pre-EMU' sub-period, probably reflecting the efforts of EU member states to meet the Maastricht convergence criteria. Second, inflation dispersion remains more or less stable across the two sub-periods. So, considerable inflation differentials across EMU regions continue to exist.

In the rest of this section we will discuss whether the various explanations for inflation differentials as discussed in the previous section, can also explain the persistence of inflation differentials.

As pointed out by Angeloni and Ehrmann (2007), nominal *convergence* could in principle account for both inflation differentials and their persistence. If imbalances in initial prices exist, it would probably take years before they are reabsorbed; until then, countries with lower initial price levels would systematically have above-average inflation rates. Furthermore, research for the US suggests that price level differences may be quite persistent in a monetary union. For instance, using consumer price data for nineteen US cities from 1918 to 1995, Cecchetti, Mark, and Sonora (2002) report that price level differences are large and persistent: annual inflation rates measured over ten-year periods can differ by as much as 1.55% points. Cecchetti et al. (2002) estimate the half-life of convergence to be 9 years, based on a panel of 15 cities from 1918 to 1995. Similarly, Parsley and Wei (1996) employ commodity level price data for 48 US cities from 1975 to 1992 and find persistent deviations from the law of one price for both traded and non-traded goods. The half-life of the price gap for tradable goods is roughly 4–5 quarters and 15 quarters for services.

Also *differences in business cycles* may be quite persistent, even in a monetary union. Two views have been put forward on this issue. In what we call the 'optimistic view', further economic and monetary integration will lead to less business cycle divergence. However, Krugman (1991) argues that in a further integrating Europe a similar concentration of industries may take place as in the US mainly because of economies of scale and scope. Due to this concentration process, sector-specific shocks may become region-specific shocks, thereby increasing the likelihood of asymmetric shocks and diverging business cycles. So, the 'pessimistic view' holds that business cycles in the euro may become more divergent in the future.

Various factors have been put forward that may affect business cycle synchronisation, ranging from trade relations (Frankel & Rose 1998), specialization (Imbs 2004), monetary integration (Fatás 1997), financial relations (Imbs 2006) and fiscal policy (Clark & van Wincoop 2001). However, "despite the theoretical and empirical analyses to date, it seems fair to say that there is no consensus on the important determinants of business cycle co-movement. The difficulty is that there are many potential candidate explanations." (Baxter and Kouparitsas 2005, p. 114). In their survey of the literature on business cycle synchronisation in Europe, De Haan, Inklaar, and Jong-A-Pin (2008, p. 266) conclude that "trade intensity is found to lead to more synchronisation. The trade relationships of the members of the European currency union are intense causing further synchronisation. However, the point estimates vary widely. Furthermore, the survey also showed that trade intensity only explains a fraction of business cycle correlations. The evidence for other factors affecting business cycle synchronisation is quite mixed. Although there are papers (like Inklaar, Jong-A-Pin, & De Haan 2008) suggesting that the well-known critique on EMU that a common monetary policy may not be equally good for all countries in the union ("one size does not fit all"), has lost force due to the economic and monetary integration process, others come to less optimistic conclusions."

According to Beck et al. (2009), the existence of *nominal wage and price rigidities* can also result in high persistence in inflation rates. In case of wage and price stickiness, the adjustment to exogenous shocks takes a long time, and persistent inflation differentials across member states can arise. Typically, nominal rigidities are associated with imperfect competition in the goods and labour markets.[11] In the final part of this section we will discuss some recent research based on dynamic stochastic general equilibrium (DSGE) models. This research focuses on the importance of shocks (including monetary and fiscal policy shocks) in view of differences in wage and price inertia, and characteristics of domestic product, labour, and other factor markets across countries.

Campolmi and Faia (2004) build a dynamic general equilibrium model with two regions that form a currency union and that are characterised by a variety of frictions: matching frictions and wage rigidity in the labour market, monopolistic competition in product markets and adjustment costs on pricing. The authors examine the impact on inflation differentials of common monetary policy and technology shocks after they have calibrated the model using euro area country data. They report that labour and/or product market institutions (proxied by differences in demand elasticities and unemployment benefits, respectively) are able to generate significant and persistent inflation differentials in case of common monetary policy shocks and symmetric technology shocks. Campolmi and Faia (2004) also find that the sensitivity of inflation in response to monetary and technology shocks is higher under either lower ratios of unemployment benefits to real wages or higher demand elasticity.

Altissimo et al. (2005) present a stylized model of a monetary union comprised of two regions to gauge the relative contributions in explaining inflation differentials of innovations in the shocks and structural differences in the regional economies. In each of the two regions two productive sectors are assumed, a traded and a non-traded goods sector. Each region is specialised in the production of a distinct, non-overlapping bundle of traded goods. The law of one price holds for

[11] In Sect. 2.5 we will discuss some recent research on labour market reform that aims to increase labour market flexibility.

each of the traded goods produced. Inflation differentials therefore arise in the model as a consequence of movements in the relative prices of non-traded goods. The authors conclude that inflation differentials are mainly driven by productivity shocks affecting the non-tradable sector. Symmetric sectoral productivity shocks (i.e., shocks that affect both sectors) in one country may generate sizeable inflation differentials. According to Altissimo et al. (2005), for plausible parameter values, a symmetric increase in productivity in one country has a negative and sizeable impact on the consumer price of the country relative to the rest of the area. They also find that government-purchase shock do not contribute significantly to inflation differentials.

The latter result is not in line with the findings of Duarte and Wolman (2008). These authors examine whether a regional government can affect the inflation differential relative to the union using a two-region model with both traded and non-traded goods, and with sticky prices. In each sector there are two types of firms, retailers and intermediate goods producers. There is an exogenous stream of government expenditures, and the regional fiscal authority has access to a labour income tax and can issue bonds to finance these expenditures. The model is driven by shocks to government expenditures and to productivity in the traded and non-traded goods sectors. Inflation differentials across regions arise from movements in the relative price of non-traded goods across countries and from price differentials for traded goods. Duarte and Wolman (2008) conclude that regional fiscal authorities do have the ability to affect their inflation differential. Specifically, by lowering the distortionary tax rate in response to a positive deviation of inflation from the union-wide average (and raising the tax rate in response to a negative deviation), a regional fiscal authority can decrease the volatility of its inflation differential in response to the shocks driving the model.

Andrés, Ortega, and Vallés (2008) use a two-country model with a common monetary policy. There are only traded goods. This is motivated by the authors arguing that inflation differentials in a monetary union are often assumed to stem mainly from the lack of competition in the non-traded sector but there is also evidence showing substantial differences among traded goods inflation rates. Each country produces differentiated goods traded in monopolistic competitive markets. Price discrimination across countries is possible due to differences in the degree of market competition. In the model, inflation reacts faster in countries with more competitive markets and with lower price adjustment costs. The model is calibrated so as to mimic the characteristics of the larger and less open euro area countries. The authors show that their model is able to generate substantial inflation differentials for reasonable parameter values. Small deviations in the degree of competition may be responsible for temporary inflation differentials up to 13 quarterly basis points when the economy is subject to a common monetary policy shock of an annual increase of 136 basis points. Small differences in the degree of nominal inertia also contribute to generating inflation differentials, but the relevance of this channel is less important. In case of regional (asymmetric) shocks, the elasticity of substitution between home produced and imported goods and the degree of openness also play a major role in producing sizeable inflation differentials.

Rabanal (2009) estimates a two-country, two-sector New Keynesian DSGE model of a currency union using Bayesian methods to explain inflation differentials between Spain and other euro area countries. His findings suggest that tradable sector productivity shocks explain about 65% of the variability of the inflation differential, while non-tradable sector technology shocks explain about 18% of the inflation differential. Demand shocks only explain 14% of inflation dispersion.

Finally, Angeloni and Ehrmann (2007) follow a different strategy than previous research that is based either on descriptive analyses, supported by correlation or regression results, or small calibrated models with microeconomic foundations. They argue that "Each of these lines of research alone is insufficient, we think. On the one hand descriptive analysis has probably reached a point of diminishing returns due to the scarcity of data. On the other, existing small micro-founded models, normally assuming two countries only, provide only partial answers." (p. 2). Instead these authors have estimated a model that includes 12 countries, each represented by an aggregate demand and an aggregate supply equation. Inflation differentials across countries, originating from nation-specific shocks, cumulate into changes in external competitiveness, which give rise to international trade spill over effects. Their sample is 1998:I–2003:II. In the model, inflation differentials also cause different national short-term real interest rates, which affect domestic aggregate demand in each country differently. The two mechanisms balance each other in a dynamic equilibrium whose characteristics depend on the model's parameter values. Angeloni and Ehrmann (2007) use the model to analyse inflation differentials, examining the contribution of the different sources of shocks to inflation differentials. Their results indicate that the main source of the differentials is given by national aggregate demand (or potential output) disturbances, followed by domestic cost-push disturbances. In contrast to the results of Honohan and Lane (2003, 2004), area-wide exchange rate shocks come third. According to Angeloni and Ehrmann, the euro exchange rate explains about one-third of the observed inflation differentials among euro area countries in 1998–2003. Angeloni and Ehrmann (2007) also conclude that inflation persistence potentially plays a central role in amplifying and perpetuating inflation differentials within the euro area.

2.5 Policy Implications

Ten years after, the launch of the euro, inflation differentials among countries in the euro area have not gone down. However, inflation differentials are a normal feature of any monetary union. Still, the evidence discussed in this chapter suggests that inflation differentials within EMU remain slightly larger and more persistent than those between regions of the United States. According to the European Central Bank (2005), "Inflation differentials across euro area countries may… reflect at least in part equilibrating changes in relative prices, which are an unavoidable and also desirable manifestation of the gradual but ultimately far reaching structural transformations to which monetary integration and the single market process give rise." The medium-term orientation of the ECB's policies facilitates the necessary adjustment of relative prices across regions and sectors in the presence of asymmetric shocks (European Central Bank 2005). However, as this chapter has made clear, not all inflation differentials are due to these equilibrating or convergence processes.

Unfortunately, despite the research done to date, there is no clear consensus in the literature to what extent inflation differentials in the euro area are problematic. In part this is due to the fact that most recent research—Beck et al. (2009) and Angeloni and Ehrmann (2007) being clear exceptions—uses DSGE models that are all perfectly able to yield outcomes consistent with stylised facts, but that are very different in their explanation of these inflation differentials. Still, there is quite some evidence that structural differences in product and labour markets play some role in explaining inflation differentials. Beck et al. (2009) argue that to reduce long lasting, potentially damaging inflation differentials structural reforms in factor and product markets are therefore needed to avoid inappropriate price movements. Also various other researchers come to this conclusion. However, most empirical research to date suggests that EMU has not spurred labour market reform (see Box 2.1).

What else can policy makers do to counteract inflation differentials? The ECB focuses on inflation in the euro area as a whole. In May 2003, the Governing Council of the ECB clarified its price stability objective, explaining that it aims to maintain inflation rates "below but close to 2%" over the medium term. According to the European Central Bank (2005), the aim of maintaining the inflation rate close to the upper bound of its definition of price stability signals the ECB's commitment to providing an adequate margin to guard against the risk of deflation in individual member countries. However, inflation differentials in the euro area cannot be affected by monetary policy directly, since there cannot be any regionally oriented monetary policy in a currency union.[12] Monetary policy in a currency union is uniform. However, Angeloni and Ehrmann (2007) also examine how this uniform monetary policy affects inflation dispersion and find an interesting result: minimising the deviations of area-wide inflation from its long-run level also helps keeping inflation differentials low. This result is in line with the findings of Beck et al. (2009). Their results suggest that the area-wide monetary policy can considerably contribute to regional inflation stabilization even though it cannot take regional developments into account when making its decisions.

[12] Fendel and Frenkel (2009) examine whether inflation differentials have influenced the behaviour of the ECB since the launch of the euro. They hypothesise that the ECB may have been less restrictive than euro area wide developments would dictate thereby preventing deflation in the low inflation countries. Their Taylor rule model outcomes suggest an influence of inflation differentials on monetary policy in the euro area. With higher inflation divergence, the ECB was more reluctant to fight an overall inflation gap.

Box 2.1 Has the euro led to more labour market flexibility?

It ids a popular belief that a currency union will create more *labour market flexibility*. The argument is that in EMU monetary policy is no longer available to individual countries to respond to asymmetric shocks, which increases the incentives to undertake structural reform (Bean 1998). Such reforms are likely to increase the flexibility of the labour market and, therefore, make adjustments to asymmetric shocks easier. In addition, structural reforms are also claimed to reduce the natural rate of unemployment

However, deregulating the labour market has high political costs. Labour market reform would include reductions in the level and duration of unemployment benefits, lower minimum wages, and possibly also reductions in employment protection. Politicians may be highly reluctant to pursue such policies because in the short run they may harm many voters. In addition, EMU might also reduce the incentives for governments to reform the labour market. Before the monetary union, a high inflation bias created an incentive for national policy makers to reform their labour market, because reform would reduce this bias. However, reform in any individual country in the monetary union is unlikely to affect the union-wide inflation bias and the country's incentive to reform is therefore smaller than before the start of the monetary union (Calmfors 2001). Furthermore, for most countries in the monetary union the delegation of monetary policy to the independent and conservative (i.e., inflation-averse) ECB has reduced the inflationary bias in comparison to the pre-monetary union situation. So, on theoretical grounds it is not clear whether the creation of the currency union will lead to more or less labour market reform

Most empirical research to date suggests that EMU has not spurred labour market reform (see Leiner-Killinger, López Pérez, Stiegert, and Vitale (2007) for an extensive survey). Duval and Elmeskov (2006) estimated a probit model over the period 1994–2004 to examine the impact of the EMU on major reforms in the labour market. Their dependent variable is a binary variable capturing major reforms that refer to: unemployment benefit systems, labour taxes, employment protection legislation, product market regulation, and retirement schemes. The key explanatory variable is a dummy variable that takes the value 1 if a country has a sovereign monetary policy and 0 otherwise. Duval and Elmeskov (2006) find that participation in a fixed exchange rate regime hardly influences labour market reforms. Alesina, Ardagna, and Galasso (2008) have also examined the impact of the euro on structural product and labour market reform. They find that the adoption of the euro has been associated with an acceleration of the pace of structural reforms in the product market. In line with the results of Duval and Elmeskov (2006), Alesina et al. (2008) conclude that the adoption of the euro does not seem to have accelerated labour market reforms. The measures they use capture the degree of employment protection related to the firing decisions and the level of insurance provided to the unemployed. Similar findings are reported by Bednarek-Sekunda, Jong-A-Pin, and De Haan (2010). They differentiate between reform enhancing the capacity of an economy to adjust to economic shocks and reform aiming to increase long-run output. Based on a panel model and using OECD data on labour market reforms for 27 OECD countries over the period 1994–2004, these authors find that both types of labour market reform are driven by different variables. Most importantly, their results suggest that the EMU has had no effect on reform enhancing the economy's capacity to adjust to shocks, while most of their evidence for reform increasing long-run output suggests that the EMU has not affected this type of reform either.

In contrast, Bertola and Boeri (2002) report that the adoption of the euro accelerated the pace of labour market reforms in those countries that joined the euro area. Although the euro area countries started out with a higher level of labour market inflexibility, as measured by employment protection legislation and benefits for the unemployed, euro area countries implemented more reforms between 1997 and 2002 than between 1986 and 1996 compared to non-euro area countries. However, the analysis of Bertola and Boeri (2002) is based on the number of reforms, which is a poor indicator of reform efforts (Leiner-Killinger et al. 2007).

Some authors have argued in favour of a monetary policy that takes inflation differentials into account. For instance, Benigno (2004) argues that it is optimal only to target inflation in the euro area as whole when the regions in the monetary union share the same degree of nominal rigidity. As nominal rigidities differ across the countries in the euro area, a feasible first-best solution consists of an inflation targeting policy in which higher weight is given to the inflation in the region with higher degree of nominal rigidity. The intuition for this can be described as follows. If an economy has two sectors of equal size, but with a different degree of rigidity, the two sectors have to adjust in a similar way upon the occurrence of an aggregate shock. However, the rigid sector bears a higher cost than the flexible sector in its adjustment to that macroeconomic shock. The implied welfare loss for the currency union could therefore be reduced by giving the more rigid sector a higher weight than that based on its overall size (European Central Bank 2005). However, as Benigno acknowledges, this conclusion is not robust to model changes.

The European Central Bank (2005) has various practical objections to this proposal. Not only would there be enormous problems related to the appropriate measurement of the degree of nominal rigidity in the various sectors or regions, it would also be very difficult to determine the level at which such nominal rigidity should be measured. Furthermore, it would be possible that by assigning greater importance to a particular country or sector-specific developments, monetary policy would in practice be accommodating behavioural or structural inefficiencies, ultimately creating perverse incentives and hampering the necessary progress towards more market-based adjustment mechanisms. Also the communication of monetary policy (discussed in more detail in Chap. 5) would face considerable challenges, since its conduct would become significantly more complex and difficult to explain to the public.

The results of Beck et al. (2009) suggest that national policies are still very important for regional inflation rate dynamics despite the fact that monetary policy is no longer conducted at the national level. They suggest that the strong influence of the national factor very likely results both from nationally conducted fiscal policy and nationally determined labour market institutions. However, the literature is somewhat divided about the role of national *fiscal policy*. Whereas Altissimo et al. (2005) conclude that government-purchase shock do not contribute significantly to inflation differentials, Duarte and Wolman (2008) find that regional fiscal authorities do have the ability to affect their inflation differential. Also studies using panel models for inflation differentials (like Honohan & Lane 2003 and Andersson et al. 2009) come to different conclusions. It seems safe to conclude that sound government finances are crucial in order for individual countries to be able to let automatic stabilisers work fully without running the risk of excessively high deficits. Governments should prevent discretionary policy measures from acting pro-cyclically over the business cycle, thereby exacerbating divergence across countries after asymmetric shocks (European Central Bank 2005).

References

Alesina, A., Ardagna, S., & Galasso, V. (2008). The Euro and structural reforms. NBER Working Paper No. 14479.

Altissimo, F., Benigno, P., & Rodriguez Palenzuela, D. (2005). Long-run determinants of inflation differentials in a monetary union. NBER Working Paper No. 11473.

Andersson, M., Masuch, K., & Schiffbauer, M. (2009). Determinants of inflation and price level differentials across the Euro area countries. ECB Working Paper No. 1129.

Andrés, J., Ortega, E., & Vallés, J. (2008). Competition and inflation differentials in EMU. *Journal of Economic Dynamics and Control, 32*(3), 848–874.

Angeloni, I., & Ehrmann, M. (2004). Euro area inflation differentials. ECB Working Paper No. 388.

Angeloni, I., & Ehrmann, M. (2007). Euro area inflation differentials. *The B.E. Journal of Macroeconomics*, Topics, *7*(1), article 24.

Baxter, M., & Kouparitsas, M. (2005). Determinants of business cycle comovement: A robust analysis. *Journal of Monetary Economics, 52*, 113–157.

Bean, C. (1998). The interaction of aggregate-demand policies and labour market reform. *Swedish Economic Policy Review, 5*(2), 353–382.

Beck, G.W., Hubrich, K., & Marcellino, M. (2009). Regional inflation dynamics within and across euro area countries and a comparison with the United States. *Economic Policy*, 141–184.

Bednarek-Sekunda, E., Jong-A-Pin, R., & de Haan, J. (2010). The European economic and monetary union and labour market reform. *European Union Politics, 11*, 3–27.

Benigno, P. (2004). Optimal monetary policy in a currency area. *Journal of International Economics, 63*, 293–320.

Bertola, G., & Boeri, T. (2002). EMU labour markets two years on: Microeconomic tensions and institutional evolution. In M. Buti & A. Sapir (Eds.), *EMU and economic policy in Europe* (pp. 249–280). Cheltenham: Edward Elgar.

Calmfors, L. (2001). Unemployment, labour-market reform and monetary union. *Journal of Labour Economics, 19*(2), 265–289.

Calmfors, L., & Driffill, J. (1988). Bargaining structure, corporatism, and macroeconomic performance. *Economic Policy, 6*, 13–61.

Campolmi, A., & Faia, E. (2004). Inflation differentials and different labour market institutions in the EMU. Mimeo: Pompeu Fabra.

Cecchetti, S. C., Mark, N., & Sonora, R. (2002). Price level convergence among United States cities: lessons for the European Central Bank. *International Economic Review, 43*, 1081–1099.

Clark, T. E., & van Wincoop, E. (2001). Borders and business cycles. *Journal of International Economics, 55*, 59–85.

De Haan, J., Eijffinger, S. C. W., & Waller, S. (2005). *The European Central Bank Credibility, transparency, and centralization*. Cambridge: MIT Press.

De Haan, J., Inklaar, R., & Jong-A-Pin, R. M. (2008). Will business cycles in the euro area converge? A critical survey of empirical research. *Journal of Economic Surveys, 22*(2), 243–273.

De Haan, J., Oosterloo, S., & Schoenmaker, D. (2009). *European financial markets and institutions*. Cambridge: Cambridge University Press.

Dhyne, E., Alvarez, L. J., Le Bihan, H., Veronese, G., Dias, D., Hoffmann, J., et al. (2006). Price changes in the euro area and the United States: some facts from individual consumer price data. *Journal of Economic Perspectives, 20*(2), 171–192.

Duarte, M., & Wolman, A. L. (2008). Fiscal policy and regional inflation in a currency union. *Journal of International Economics, 74*, 384–401.

Duval, R., & Elmeskov, J. (2006). The effects of EMU on structural reforms in labour and product markets. ECB Working Paper No. 596.

Égert, B., & Podpiera, J. (2008). Beyond Balassa-Samuelson in Visegrad-4 countries. VOX EU, 2 April 2008.
European Central Bank (2003). *Inflation differentials in the euro area: Potentialcauses and policy implications,* Frankfurt: European Central Bank. Available at: http://www.ecb.int/pub/pdf/other/inflationdifferentialreporten.pdf.
European Central Bank (2005). Monetary policy and inflation differentials in a heterogeneous currency area. *Monthly Bulletin,* 61–77.
Fatás, A. (1997). EMU: countries or regions? Lessons from the EMS experience. *European Economic Review, 41*(3–5), 743–751.
Fendel, R., & Frenkel, M. (2009). Inflation differentials in the euro area: did the ECB care? *Applied Economics, 41*, 1293–1302.
Frankel, J. A., & Rose, A. K. (1998). The endogeneity of the optimum currency area criteria. *Economic Journal, 108*, 1009–1025.
Honohan, P., & Lane, P. (2003). Divergent inflation rates in EMU. *Economic Policy, 18*(37), 358–394.
Honohan, P., & Lane, P. (2004). Exchange rates and inflation under EMU: An update. *Economic Policy Web Essay.* Available at: http://www.economicpolicy.org/responses.asp.
Hüfner, F.P., & Schröder, M. (2002). Exchange rate pass-through to consumer prices: A European perspective. ZEW Discussion Paper No. 02-20.
Imbs, J. (2004). Trade, finance, specialization and synchronization. *Review of Economics and Statistics, 86*, 723–734.
Imbs, J. (2006). The real effects of financial integration. *Journal of International Economics, 68*(2), 296–324.
Inklaar, R., Jong-A-Pin, R. M., & De Haan, J. (2008). Trade and business cycle synchronization in OECD countries: A re-examination. *European Economic Review, 52*(4), 646–666.
Krugman, P. R. (1991). *Geography and trade.* Cambridge Mass: MIT Press.
Leiner-Killinger, N., López Pérez, V., Stiegert, R., & Vitale, G. (2007). Structural reforms in EMU and the role of monetary policy A survey of the literature. ECB Occasional Paper No. 66.
Mihaljek, D., & Klau, M. (2008). Catching-up and inflation in transition economies: the Balassa-Samuelson effect revisited. BIS Working Papers No. 270.
Parsley, D., & Wei, S.-J. (1996). Convergence to the law of one price without trade barriers or currency fluctuations. *Quarterly Journal of Economics, 111*, 1211–1236.
Rabanal, P. (2009). Inflation differentials between Spain and the EMU: A DSGE perspective. *Journal of Money, Credit, and Banking, 41*(6), 1142–1166.
Remsperger, H. (2003). Inflation differentials in EMU. Causes and implications. Presentation at the CEPR/ESI Seventh Annual Conference on "The Euro Area as an Economic Entity" in Eltville on 13 September 2003.
Sibert, A. (2003). The New Monetary Policy Strategy of the ECB. Briefing paper for the Committee on Economic and Monetary Affairs of the European Parliament, May 2003.

Chapter 3
The ECB's Monetary Analysis Revisited

Helge Berger, Thomas Harjes and Emil Stavrev

3.1 Introduction

Money plays an important role in the European Central Bank's (ECB's) monetary policy strategy. According to the ECB, monetary analysis (formerly known as the "monetary pillar") helps to guide the policy-making process of the Governing Council by providing information on "medium to long-term trends in inflation, given the close relationship between money and prices over extended horizons" (ECB, 2003a, p. 79). It also serves as a communication device by stressing the ECB commitment to price stability. While a certain proximity to the monetary targeting framework of the German Bundesbank was intentional when the ECB announced its strategy, the ECB later made it clear that monetary analysis is neither its sole nor its most important guide to policy decisions. Today, the prime function of monetary analysis is to serve "as a means of cross-checking, from a medium to long-term perspective, the short to medium-term indications coming from economic analysis" (ECB, 2003a, p. 87), which is a broad-based analysis of price developments in the short to medium run based on non-monetary indicators. Still, the continued explicit

---

The views expressed herein are those of the authors and should not be attributed to the IMF, its Executive Board, or its management.

H. Berger (✉), T. Harjes and E. Stavrev
European Department, International Monetary Fund, 700 19th Street NW, Washington, DC, 20431, USA
e-mail: hberger@imf.org

T. Harjes
e-mail: tharjes@imf.org

E. Stavrev
e-mail: estavrev@imf.org

H. Berger
Free University, Berlin, Germany

J. de Haan and H. Berger (eds.), *The European Central Bank at Ten*,
DOI: 10.1007/978-3-642-14237-6_3, © Springer-Verlag Berlin Heidelberg 2010

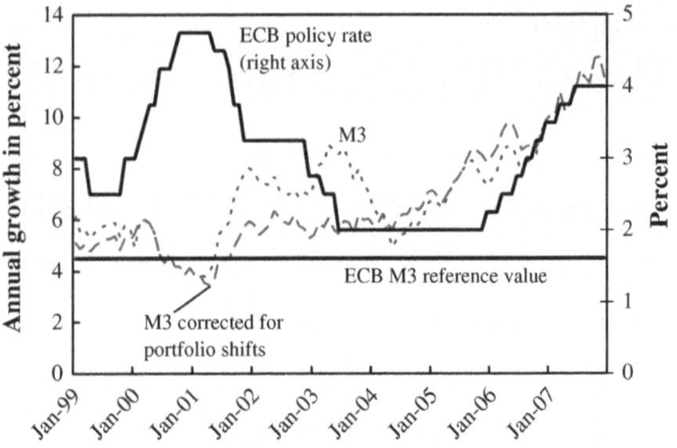

Fig. 3.1 M3 growth and policy rate in the euro area, 1999–2008. Source: ECB

reliance on money to guide monetary policy is a distinguishing feature of the ECB's framework compared to that of other central banks.

In practice, the implementation of the money-based element of the ECB's policy strategy has been challenging. In particular, the repeated surges of nominal M3 growth beyond the ECB's reference value (see Fig. 3.1) have made it increasingly difficult for outside observers to understand the transmission of monetary analysis into policy action, however indirect and conditional. Despite an impressive effort by the ECB to identify and explain to the wider public the various special factors (such as international portfolio shifts) potentially clouding the informational content of the monetary indicator, financial markets appear to no longer put appreciable weight on ECB communication relating to the monetary analysis. Instead, they appear to focus almost exclusively on communication related to the economic analysis.

At the same time, academic economists are debating intensively the ECB's monetary analysis. ECB watchers have criticized what they perceive as a breakdown in communication in the implementation of the "monetary pillar". More fundamentally, recent theoretical research casts doubt on the notion that monetary policy, almost by definition, needs to be based on a theoretical framework giving prominent role to monetary factors. Indeed, the standard New Keynesian dynamic general equilibrium (GE) model focuses almost exclusively on the interest rate channel of monetary policy, reducing the role of money to a unit of account. As a consequence, the underlying theoretical rationale of the "two pillar" approach has been questioned. Empirically, too, the case of a causal or even an informational role of money for inflation has been challenged. And while others disagree with these theoretical and empirical results, it is probably fair to say that there remains much debate about the role of money in monetary policy.

This discussion is highly relevant from the ECB's perspective, and policy makers appear to follow it closely. The ECB's evaluation of the role of money in its monetary strategy in 2003 already reflected some of the arguments discussed above, and the ECB has taken an even more active role in this debate since. For instance, in

November 2006 the ECB hosted a conference on "The Role of Money—Money and Monetary Policy in the Twenty-First Century", and the proceedings suggest a lively debate among both central bankers and academics.[1] That the topic is one where both areas often converge is also highlighted by a recent stream of working papers involving euro-area central bank staff members discussing, among other things, the stability of euro-area money demand and the implications for ECB policy.[2]

Against this background, this chapter revisits the case for the ECB's "monetary pillar". Starting from a brief description of the evolution of the ECB's monetary pillar (Sect. 3.2), the chapter surveys the ongoing theoretical and empirical debate on the role of money for inflation as well as arguments in support of a prominent role for money in monetary policy in partial as well in general equilibrium settings (Sects. 3.3, 3.4). In addition to the underlying macroeconomics, the chapter also reviews the more disaggregated aspect of the ECB's monetary analysis, taking a closer look at the ECB's experience with explaining the shorter-run movements of monetary aggregates in light of financial market integration and innovation (Sect. 3.5). Finally, some theoretical and institutional arguments for a steady hand in developing the ECB's monetary strategy further are discussed (Sect. 3.6). Section 3.7 concludes.

3.2 A Brief Guide to the Monetary Analysis in the ECB's Strategy and its Evolution since 1998

Money is a key ingredient in the ECB's monetary strategy, which guides its policy-making process and communication with the public (ECB, 1999, 2003b; see Fig. 3.2 for an overview).[3] Guidance for the policy process is provided by an analytical framework, encompassing (using the ECB's post-2003 terminology) monetary and economic analysis to ensure that the Governing Council has the information necessary to align monetary policy with the goal of price stability. The same framework also serves as a vehicle for communication, where it can help to establish confidence that the ECB is credibly committed to and able to achieve this

---

1 See Beyer and Reichlin (2008).

2 This exchange was reflected in a speech by Banque de France Governor Christian Noyer (2007), who suggested excluding from the ECB's money growth figures growth stemming from money holding by private equity or investment funds. ECB Vice-President Lucas Papademos, also in a public appearance, was later reported to refute the idea, however, pointing to the role of the broader aggregate as an inflation indicator (Reuters, 2007). Bloomberg (2007) reported around the same time that ECB President Claude Trichet and German Bundesbank Governor Axel Weber in public supported an important role for money in ECB monetary policy (see also Dow Jones, 2007).

3 According to the ECB (1999, p. 43), in addition to the guiding goal of price stability, the monetary strategy "imposes a clear structure on the policy-making process" and is a "vehicle for communicating with the public". See also ECB (2004a). In what follows, we focus only on the two latter elements.

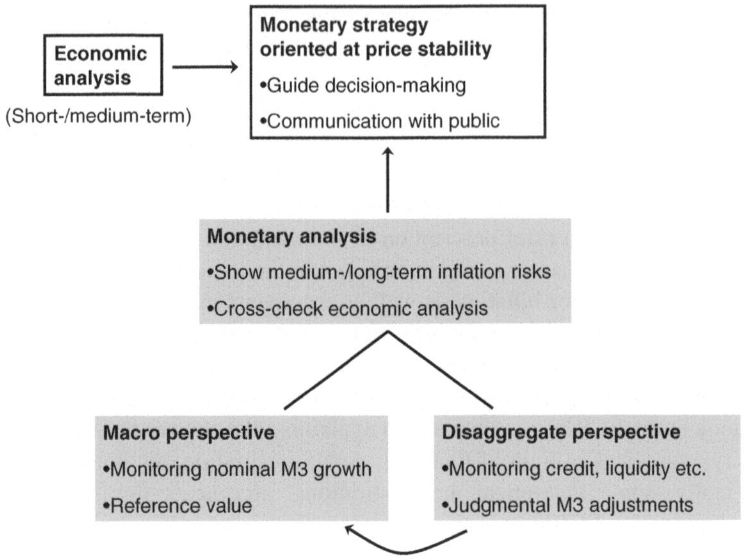

Fig. 3.2 A stylized view of the role of money in the ECB's monetary strategy. Sources: ECB (1999, 2003a, 2004a) and IMF staff

goal. While the economic analysis is focused on the short- and medium-run inflation outlook based on a broad range of non-monetary factors, monetary analysis aims at the medium- to long-run implications of monetary developments for inflation. Note that the medium-run time horizon where monetary and economic analysis overlap—probably best defined as between 1 year and 4–5 years, including the business cycle frequency—is perhaps to most relevant from a policy perspective. It is well known that monetary policy operates with lags and is commonly thought to influence inflation most after 6–8 quarters.[4]

Monetary analysis encompasses what, for the present purposes, can be called a macro-economic and a disaggregated (or more micro-oriented) perspective. The macroeconomic part of the analysis is implemented predominantly through a comparison of annual nominal M3 growth with a reference value, which is to reflect medium- to long-term monetary developments in line with the ECB's goal of price stability. However, early on the ECB (1998) was careful to state that interest rates would not be adjusted mechanically in response to deviations of actual growth from the reference value, and that it had not bound itself to an intermediate monetary target—as had one of its predecessors, the German Bundesbank. The reference value was to be used to discover and understand inflationary pressure building over the medium run: "in the first instance, a deviation of monetary growth from the reference value will prompt further analysis to identify and interpret the economic

[4] The notion of monetary analysis as a "cross check" of economic analysis also implies that both approaches apply to the same policy-relevant time horizon (see e.g., Jaeger, 2003).

disturbance that caused the deviation" (ECB, 1999, p. 49). And only if this analysis indicated a relevant threat to price stability, the ECB would act.[5]

In addition, monetary analysis takes a disaggregated perspective, focusing on other indicators of liquidity developments than M3. For instance, the ECB carefully looks not only at aggregate figures, but also scrutinizes other monetary aggregates, private credit growth, as well as their counterparts in the aggregate balance sheet of monetary and financial institutions. As the ECB (1999, p. 79) wrote, the general idea of looking beyond M3 was to provide useful "background information" for the assessment of aggregate developments—for example, to help separate transitory from price-relevant movements in monetary conditions.

These salient features of the ECB's monetary analysis have remained in place throughout its short history, but difficulties in implementation occurred early on, building pressure for changes in the framework. As Faruqee (2005) and De Haan, Eijffinger and Waller (2005) describe in some detail, starting as early as 2000, observed nominal M3 growth rates relative to the reference value were increasingly difficult to square with the interest rate decisions taken by the Governing Council. The ECB stressed in its communications that it had never intended to interpret the M3 reference value mechanistically and pointed to some of the specific disaggregate circumstances, such as portfolio shifts, that suggested that not all movements in M3 were likely to be price-relevant. But, for many, hearing these arguments "caused the impression that the ECB was looking for some kind of argument to ensure that developments under the first pillar were in line with the decision taken" (De Haan et al., 2005, p. 53).

As a consequence, ECB watchers took an increasingly critical view of the "monetary pillar" during this period. For instance, Cukierman (2001) stressed that a focus on inflation alone may provide for a more effective communication with the public. Bernanke, Laubach, Mishkin and Posen (1999) also argued that inflation targeting is a communication device well suited to establish and uphold a price-stability oriented reputation with economic agents even in the absence of an explicit monetary component.[6] And Alesina, Blanchard, Galí, Giavazzi and Uhlig (2001a, b, p. 4) speaking about a "breakdown in communication," agreed that the ECB should abandon the two-pillar approach in favor of a simple inflation targeting strategy. While they conceded that there may be good theoretical and

[5] The ECB is constantly working on improving its monetary analysis. For example, Papademos (2006, p. 4) points out that the ECB is carrying out research aimed at "...incorporating a richer financial sector into dynamic stochastic general equilibrium models, in order to study the role of financial variables in the conduct of monetary policy". He goes on to note that (p. 5) "...the monetary analysis of the ECB has evolved over time and is fairly comprehensive, going beyond the standard assessment based on the quantity theory of money and the stability of money demand". Beyond the improvements of the macroeconomic part of the monetary analysis, Papademos (2006, p. 6) also emphasis "the usefulness of monitoring and assessing monetary and credit developments...for the safeguarding of financial stability".

[6] More recently, Fatás, Mihov and Rose (2007) showed that empirically any (and not just monetary) nominal target that is systematically achieved by the central bank is associated with low inflation.

empirical reasons why monetary aggregates may provide information about future euro-area inflation, they found it hard to "justify why it should be assigned any special role beyond that of a potentially useful leading indicator of inflation—and, hence, an additional element in the ECB's current second pillar." That the ECB at times seemed to ignore M3 developments altogether when setting interest rates was recommendable, "but it should do it for the right reasons." Arguing a similar case, Bini-Smaghi and Gros (2000, p.159) stated that "no clear explanation has been given about the operational role that such a monetary reference value should play in the ECB's strategy. It is obviously not an intermediate target, not even in the way that Bundesbank has intended it to serve in the past, that is, as a main explanatory factor for policy decisions".

During this period, the ECB and its staff maintained that the M3 reference value at the core of monetary analysis was valuable. For instance, Issing, Gaspar, Angeloni and Tristani (2001) repeated the strong empirical relationship between long-run money growth and inflation and their theoretical underpinnings, making it a crucial part of monetary analysis and, thus, any monetary policy strategy. Other arguments raised in support of the ECB's monetary strategy included the historical precedence of the Bundesbank's monetary policy regime and the necessity of some form of continuity in this regard (De Haan et al., 2005). Finally, Issing (2001, p.23) stressed that, in the ECB's experience at least, monetary analysis had fared better than sometimes assumed: "the signals given by 'headline' growth rates of key monetary aggregates...have proven more reliable guides for monetary policy decisions than many external observers anticipated when the strategy was announced". But Issing also repeated that "the Governing Council has always clarified that it will not react in a mechanistic way to monetary developments and that a careful reading and analysis is always needed".

Nevertheless, acknowledging that the "two pillars" had posed "challenges for communication" (ECB, 2003a, p. 86), in May 2003 the ECB decided to refine its monetary strategy—and, in particular, monetary analysis.[7] As the ECB (2003a, p. 79) explained, while careful evaluation had "confirmed the main elements of the strategy originally announced in 1998," there was reason to "clarify to the public some aspects of the strategy." A first aspect was a more precise definition of the ECB's definition of price stability, which is now meant to imply inflation of below but "close to" 2%. The other pertained to the Governing Council's wish "to clarify communication on the cross-checking of information" on future price developments coming from the two elements of its monetary strategy.

As to monetary analysis, the 2003 changes stressed the medium- to long-term nature of the M3 reference value, put greater emphasis on the disaggregate perspective, and generally seemed to downgrade the relative importance of monetary analysis compared to its economic counterpart. Already the use of the word "cross-checking" signaled that the Governing Council intended to put its

[7] See also European Central Bank (2003a, p. 79) and Issing, Angeloni, Gaspar, Klöckers, Masuch, Nicoletti-Altimari, Rostagno, and Smets (2003).

monetary and economic analysis on a more equal footing. In fact, by announcing a new structure of the introductory statement read by the ECB president to the media after Governing Council meetings, the Council seemed intent to reverse the previous order of the two aspects of its monetary strategy. Since 2003 the statement starts with the economic analysis identifying risks to price stability and only then turns to the monetary analysis, which now "mainly serves as a means of cross-checking, from a medium to long-term perspective, the short to medium-term indications coming from economic analysis" (ECB, 2003a). However, with the ECB's (2003b, 2004a) overall orientation at price stability over the medium-term, both remain relevant.

An important change underscoring the medium- to long-term nature of the reference value for monetary growth implemented in 2003 is that the Governing Council no longer reviews the reference value on an annual basis (ECB, 2003a). The ECB (2003b, p. 91) explained that this change was in line with the "medium-term nature" of the assumptions underlying the computation of the reference value since 1999. Presumably, the assumed stability of the money demand parameters and trends in velocity and potential output were then also responsible for the fact that the reference value had remained unchanged since 1999. However, the Council also signaled that it will update the reference value when necessary and remains committed to track monetary developments to identify medium- to long-term trends in inflation.

In addition, the ECB (2003a, p. 89) stressed the micro perspective of the monetary analysis. Citing a heightened need to distinguish "temporary phenomena" from more permanent changes in money demand, which it viewed "as a condition for setting a reference value for M3 growth", the ECB (2003a, p. 91) announced an even more systematic monitoring of liquidity conditions beyond M3. The ECB pointed to M3 developments driven by increased asset price volatility and the resulting portfolio shifts into more liquid assets as an example for sizable yet probably temporary factors to be monitored in the future.

It seems clear, however, that the ECB's evaluation of its monetary analysis is ongoing along a number dimensions. For instance, judging by the steady flow of high-quality research conferences on relevant subjects and the publications of ECB and euro area central bank staff, there is a high interest in the theoretical underpinnings of the macroeconomic perspective. This interest includes empirical evidence on the validity of theories supporting the reference value approach. But there are also strong efforts to draw theoretical and empirical conclusions from contemporaneous dynamic general equilibrium models. In Sects. 3.3 and 3.4, we will discuss the ongoing theoretical and empirical debate along these lines.

3.3 Survey of the Theoretical Debate

There is an ongoing theoretical discussion on the role of money in monetary policy. In the wake of the monetarist revolution, it seemed natural that central banks charged with keeping inflation at bay should be predominantly concerned with controlling money growth—or, more generally, with monetary analysis in terms of the ECB monetary strategy. However, modern macroeconomics in the New Keynesian tradition makes a strong case for focusing on interest rate setting alone (e.g., Clarida, Galí, & Gertler, 1999; Woodford, 2003). As Woodford (2007, p. 14) argues, "there is nothing structurally incoherent about a [monetary] model that involves no role whatsoever for measures of the money supply". Based on this strand of the literature, the ECB should be focusing on its economic analysis alone. McCallum (2001), on the other hand, warns that the sheer fact that a model can be written without any direct reference to monetary aggregates does not mean that money should be ignored as a structural or informative factor for inflation, and there may be a number of reasons to suspect that the Woodford-type model may be over-simplified in this respect. The implication of McCallum's view, of course, would be that monetary policy may have a rationale to continue to pay attention to money.

In what follows, we survey the main aspects of this discussion, covering both general and partial equilibrium models. The survey reinforces some of the advantages of a general equilibrium approach, which provides, among other things, a more complete picture of the economy, allows the formulation of model-consistent forward-looking expectations, and shows greater robustness to the Lucas critique than partial approaches. Even more importantly, the development of generalized versions of the "cashless" New Keynesian standard model allows a unified treatment of essential monetary and non-monetary determinants of inflation in a consistent framework. This suggests that merging the two analytical pillars of the ECB's monetary strategy is a distinct and quite attractive possibility. In addition to freeing the arguments for a strong role of money in monetary policy from the confinement of partial equilibrium models, a unified analytical framework also helps focusing the debate on the relative weight of the economic and monetary factors. The survey also shows, however, that there is little hope to settle this issue on theoretical ground alone.

3.3.1 The Cashless Benchmark: The Standard New Keynesian General Equilibrium Model

In the cashless New Keynesian model (NKM), money plays little or no role for inflation and is introduced, if at all, more or less as an afterthought (see Galí & Gertler, 2007). Central banks influence the economy only through the interest rate and its impact on consumption and investment decisions. And while interest rate control presupposes control of the money supply at the technical level, the central bank will supply money elastically at the set rate. As a consequence, aggregate output as well as the resulting time path of inflation is independent of the money supply. One way to characterize the cashless NKM in light of the ECB's monetary strategy would be to say that it focuses exclusively on important elements of its economic analysis.

To illustrate, consider a standard dynamic stochastic general equilibrium (DSGE) model as described, for instance, in Woodford (2003). The aggregate supply equation typically features a Calvo-style staggered price mechanism, where profit maximizing firms take into account the current output gap and expected future price developments when setting prices. Others may index prices to past inflation, a theoretical feature that helps the model to better capture some of the persistence found in real-world inflation data. In a log-linearized form around the steady state, the aggregate supply equation (or Phillips curve) then takes the form

$$\hat{\pi}_t = \theta_\pi \hat{\pi}_{t-1} + \theta_{E\pi} E\hat{\pi}_{t+1} + \theta_x x_t + \varepsilon_{\pi,t}, \tag{3.1}$$

where $\hat{\pi}_t$ is the rate inflation, $x_t = y_t - y_t^n$ is the output gap, defined as the difference of output y_t from its flexible-price (or natural) potential y_t^n, and $\varepsilon_{\pi,t}$ is a cost-push shock.[8] The coefficients $0 < \theta_{E\pi} < 1$, θ_π, $\theta_x > 0$ summarize deep structural parameters of the underlying micro-founded model and are, in principle, independent of the monetary policy regime. Finally, E is the expectations operator, and it is assumed that expectations are formed in a way that is consistent with the full model and the period t information set.

Aggregate demand is derived from household optimization based on a period utility function that, in the standard NKM, either excludes real money balances or includes them as a fully separable argument—a case we will discuss shortly. In both cases the Euler equation yields

$$x_t = \varphi_{Ex} E x_{t+1} - \varphi_i \left(\hat{i}_t - E\hat{\pi}_{t+1}\right) + \varepsilon_{x,t}, \tag{3.2}$$

where $\hat{i}_t$ is the nominal interest rate set by central bank and $\varepsilon_{x,t}$ is an aggregate demand shock. The coefficients $\varphi > 0$ summarize parameters in the representative household's utility function. The presence of the interest rate in the aggregate demand equation gives rise to the so-called interest rate channel, the core mechanism through which monetary policy influences the economy and, ultimately, inflation in the NKM.

Similar to the introduction of partial indexation in the Phillips curve, this formulation of the Euler equation is often extended to allow for habit persistence in consumption. The resulting introduction of additional leads and lags of the output gap (not shown) is said to greatly enhance the model's fit with the data (see e.g., Fuhrer, 2000; Christiano, Eichenbaum, & Evans, 2005).

Lastly, the central bank determines the nominal interest rate. In an optimal policy framework, the bank bases it decisions on a welfare function derived from the household utility under commitment. Alternatively, we may assume that it commits to follow a simple rule that links the time path of the interest rates to current and expected inflation and output gap. For instance, monetary policy could be following a Taylor-type rule of the form

---

[8] Unless otherwise stated, all variables in Sects. 3.3.1 and 3.3.2 are defined as (log) deviations from the steady state marked by a "^".

$$\hat{i}_t = \kappa_{i_{t-1}}\hat{i}_{t-1} + (1 - \kappa_{i_{t-1}})\left(\kappa_{\pi_t}\hat{\pi}_t + \kappa_{x_t}x_t\right), \tag{3.3}$$

where the coefficients $\kappa > 0$ are chosen so that the model's equilibrium is well defined.[9]

If Eqs. 3.1, 3.2, and 3.3 completely describe the equilibrium time path of output and inflation based on non-monetary or economic factors, what then is the role of money in this model class? As Woodford (2003) demonstrates, there are various ways of introducing money into the model without changing its core mechanism. For instance, households could face cash-in-advance constraints or employ money to reduce transactions costs for certain goods. Under some assumptions, this can be modeled by including real monetary balances as a separate argument into the period utility function. Then household optimization will, in addition to Eq. 3.2, yield a standard money demand function

$$\hat{m}_t = \gamma_y\hat{y}_t - \gamma_i\hat{i}_t + \varepsilon_{m,t}, \tag{3.4}$$

with $\hat{m}_t$ and $\hat{y}_t$ representing the deviation of real monetary balances and output from their steady state levels, respectively, $\varepsilon_{m,t}$ a liquidity preference shock, and where the coefficients $\gamma > 0$ are based on parameters in the household's utility function.

But while the New Keynesian model can be amended to explain the demand for monetary balances, money performs no function of relevance from a policy perspective. Given Eqs. 3.1, 3.2, and 3.3, money has no structural or causal role to play in determining the equilibrium time path of inflation. In addition, money is also denied any informational function. As Woodford (2007) carefully points out, the time path of real balances described in Eq. 3.4 is merely a reflection of contemporaneous developments elsewhere in the economy distorted by a money demand shock.

It is important to note that the neutrality of money with regard to inflation extends to the long run—which reinforces the relevance of the result for the ECB's current monetary strategy. The ECB (2003a, p. 87) stresses that its monetary analysis is focused predominantly on the medium- to long-run and asserts that there is a close association between the "more drawn out and persistent trends" in inflation and the "medium- to long-run trend of money growth".[10] However, as Woodford (2008) illustrates in some detail, the NKM model with added money demand implies a long-run correlation between money and inflation (which are both endogenous variables in the model) despite the absence of a causal or structural relationship. In other words, while the New Keynesian DSGE model is tuned to short- to medium-term business cycle frequencies, its implications include

[9] Equilibrium determinacy is discussed, for instance, in Woodford (2003). Also see Sect. 3.3.2. Note that, except for the notation in deviations from the steady state, Eq. 3.3 is similar to a forward-looking Taylor rule with inertia, where the central bank reacts to deviations of inflation from its inflation target (assumed to be identical with the steady state) and the output gap from its steady state (assumed to compatible with the inflation target).

[10] Fischer, Lenza, Pill and Reichlin (2008) stress that the ECB's Quarterly Monetary Assessment is mostly (albeit not exclusively) targeted at medium- to long-term inflation forecasting. See also the background study by Masuch, Nicoletti, Altimari, Rostagno and Pill (2003).

the longer run (of course, a corollary of this is that any causal or informational role of money for inflation that could be established within the NKM framework—see Sect. 3.3.2 below—would not only be relevant in the long-run but also at shorter-run business cycle time horizons).

As a consequence, the policy recommendation stemming from the cashless NKM is that central banks would be well advised to ignore monetary developments altogether. Conditioning monetary policy on monetary developments—e.g., by including money in one form or another in the Taylor-type rule (Eq. 3.3)—will do little to improve the central bank's control over inflation. On the contrary, because money demand is subject to shocks, conditioning interest rates on monetary developments would add unwanted volatility to the economy. Taken literally, the implication for the ECB's monetary strategy would be to forgo monetary analysis and focus on economic analysis alone.

3.3.2 The Case for Money in the Generalized New Keynesian Model

The policy recommendations based on the NKM approach could hardly be more straightforward—but then the standard model may not be a good description of a monetary economy. In what follows, we will review some of the key arguments made for a more prominent role of money, including non-separability and financial frictions, which give money a causal or structural role in the economy. Another argument could be equilibrium indeterminacy. Finally, the NKM model can be amended in various ways to show that money could have an important informative function for monetary policy.

3.3.2.1 Non-Separability: Money and the Interest Rate Channel

Those arguing in favor of a more prominent role of money often stress the lack of generality of the NKM, and a fairly direct approach to generalization is to lift the separability assumption of the household utility function. As, among others, Nelson (2002) and Ireland (2004) have shown, introducing non-separability of money and consumption will introduce a causal link from monetary aggregates to the output gap and inflation.[11] From the perspective of the ECB's monetary

[11] As far as the aggregate implications are concerned, the non-separability argument is conceptually close the idea that real monetary balances have a direct demand effect in the tradition of Pigou and Patinkin. Ireland (2001) develops a real balance effect in a cash-in-advance DSGE framework under separable utility. However, the real balance effect has been met with skepticism, owing, in part, to the dominance of non-money holdings in private wealth and the fact that outside money (i.e. currency in circulation) is only a small fraction of monetary aggregates (see Nelson, 2003; Brand, Reimers and Seitz, 2003). The Bundesbank (2005) summarizes the evidence on the real balance model as weak at best for the US, the UK, and the euro area as a whole.

strategy, this effectively integrates elements of monetary and economic analysis in one unified analytical framework.

With the separability assumption lifted, money influences inflation through two channels. Real balances now enter as an argument into the dynamic demand equation because they influence the household's consumption decisions. For the same reason, money enters the stochastic discount factor of price-setting firms and, thus, the dynamic supply equation.[12] As Andrés, López-Salido, and Vallés (2006) show, instead of Eqs. 3.1 and 3.2 in the NKM we then have

$$\hat{\pi}_t = \tilde{\theta}_\pi \hat{\pi}_{t-1} + \tilde{\theta}_{E\pi} E\hat{\pi}_{t+1} + \tilde{\theta}_x x_t - \tilde{\theta}_m \hat{m}_t + \varepsilon_{\pi,t} \tag{3.5}$$

$$x_t = \tilde{\varphi}_{Ex} E x_{t+1} - \tilde{\varphi}_i \left(\hat{i}_t - E\hat{\pi}_{t+1} \right) + \tilde{\varphi}_m \hat{m}_t - \tilde{\varphi}_{Em} E\hat{m}_{t+1} + \varepsilon_{x,t}, \tag{3.6}$$

with $0 < \tilde{\theta}_{E\pi} < 1, \tilde{\theta}_\pi, \tilde{\theta}_x, \tilde{\theta}_m > 0$, and all $\tilde{\varphi} > 0$.[13] Household optimization will also yield a standard money demand function comparable in form to Eq. 3.4. Finally, to close the model, a plausible assumption is that the central bank takes into account that money now plays a causal role in the economy when setting interest rates. To that end, one can define a Taylor-type rule

$$\hat{i}_t = \kappa_{i_{t-1}} \hat{i}_{t-1} + (1 - \tilde{\kappa}_{i_{t-1}}) \left(\tilde{\kappa}_{\pi_t} \hat{\pi}_t + \tilde{\kappa}_{x_t} \hat{x}_t + \tilde{\kappa}_{M_t} \hat{M}_t \right), \tag{3.7}$$

where $\hat{M}_t$ represents the deviation of nominal balances from their steady state value, and where the $\tilde{\kappa} > 0$ guarantee a well-defined equilibrium (see Rudebusch & Svensson, 2002; Nelson, 2003; Andrés et al., 2006).

While a relatively straightforward way to ensure money a causal role as a determinant of inflation in a generalized NKM approach, non-separability is rarely considered a strong argument among theorists. McCallum (2001) argues that non-separability effects tend to be small under plausible specifications of the utility function. Woodford (2003) comes to similar conclusions in his discussion of the "cashless limiting economy". The basic idea is that, while money may influence marginal utility from consumption, it is usually required for only a small fraction of transactions. In the limit, the non-separability argument can therefore be neglected.

The small empirical literature on money separability also sends ambivalent signals. Kremer, Lombardo and Werner (2003) estimate a structural NKM model for German data using a Bayesian approach and find evidence for the non-separability of money and consumption. These results are at odds with the negative

---

[12] Note that—assuming a standard household utility function $u(.)$ with u_c, $u_m > 0$, u_{cc}, $u_{mm} < 0$, and $u_{cm} > 0$—the direct and indirect impact of contemporaneous money on inflation move into opposite directions, with the overall impact being a question of the underlying parameters and, thus, ultimately an empirical matter.

[13] A variant of the above model introduces, in addition, non-separability across period—that is, habit persistence in consumption. Andrés, López-Salido and Nelson (2007) show that this adds inertia to output and inflation, and money demand conveys forward-looking information on output similar to what we discuss in Sect. 3.4 around Eq. 3.8.

findings of Ireland (2004) for the US and Andrés et al. (2006) for the euro area, suggesting that there may be cross-country differences to take into account.[14] Jones and Stracca (2006) provide more mixed evidence employing a non-parametric approach. They find that additive separability cannot be rejected for their full sample period 1991–2005 in the euro area. On the other hand, this result seems to be driven by a small number of observations, which to the authors suggests that additive separability holds "most of the time" (Jones & Stracca, 2006, p. 6). They speculate that additive separability could be regime-dependent, prevailing mostly in credible low-inflation environments.

Overall, this suggests that non-separability provides a qualitatively interesting but quantitatively not compelling reason for integrating monetary factors into the cashless standard NKM. The question is whether additional arguments can be mustered to strengthen the case for money in the analytical framework.

3.3.2.2 Information: Money as an Indicator

Another argument brought forward to underline the relevance of money in monetary policy is that of informational frictions. The general idea is that money may complement the information set of policy makers seeking to control inflation no matter whether it has a structural or causal role to play in the economy or not. In what follows, we first discuss the general issue whether money can provide relevant real-time information for policy makers. In the next step, we return to general equilibrium modeling to take a closer look at the idea that money could reveal crucial forward-looking information. From the viewpoint of the ECB, the information content of money captured in the latter approach could be a further reason to integrate monetary and economic analysis in one analytical framework.

Nelson (2002), following earlier ideas by Meltzer (2001), points out that money may be a superior index of monetary policy effects than the interest rate. The basic argument is that money demand is a function of various asset yields (e.g., interest rates of all terms, yields of real assets such as housing, share yields, the exchange rate, etc.) as well as of unobservable yields to human capital. As a consequence, monetary aggregates will reflect (equilibrium) changes of these asset prices and, thus, provide important information to monetary policy beyond what can be captured by a specific short-term rate. In particular, if the various asset prices shaping money demand are also relevant for consumption and investment decisions, real money balances could also be a good indicator of the overall policy stance.[15]

---

[14] The results of Kremer et al. (2003) are more pronounced in some time samples than others. Also note that their solution technique deviates from Ireland (2004) and Andrés et al. (2006) in that it does not force a non-explosive solution in the Taylor-type rule.

[15] See also Brand et al. (2003). Masuch et al. (2003) discuss empirical evidence supporting the view that the money stock serves as a proxy for a spectrum of interest rates. As Nelson (2002) shows, the adjustment-cost approach discussed below can be interpreted as a simple formalization of this idea within a DSGE model.

Monetary aggregates may also have important real time informational content within a standard NKM framework with a traditional money demand function. For instance, it has been said that money can serve as a real time indicator of real GDP growth, which is observed with significant lags and subject to (often significant) data revisions (Bundesbank, 2005; Masuch et al., 2003). Output data is revised substantially for a period of up to 9 months after their first release, while monetary (like price) data are subject to only minor revisions within a short period after release. Thus, as Coenen, Levin and Wieland (2005) conclude, monetary aggregates could have a significant role in providing information about the current level of aggregate demand and therefore about the resulting pressures on inflation.[16] This also seems to play some role in practice (Calza, Gerdesmeier, & Levy, 2001). Fischer et al. (2008, p. 5) report that the ECB looks to short-run money demand dynamics to complement its economic analysis: for instance, "money demand equations might suggest that strong monetary growth was a result of strong real income growth and/or a low level of interest rates in the economy. Strong monetary dynamics would thus be seen as confirmation of signals coming from conjunctural indicators".

However, the real-time informational content of monetary aggregates is not undisputed. At a theoretical level, Galí (2008) argues that the information contained in monetary aggregates can be misleading. For example, consider a simple economy blessed with a productivity boom that was fully accommodated by output growth. In such a scenario, output growth would prompt an increase in money demand that could be taken to signal upward inflation pressure. However, with the output gap unchanged, inflation would likely remain constant.[17] He concludes that a stable money demand relationship does not imply that monetary indicators are useful in assessing inflation risks.

An additional problem is the (in)stability of money demand, which can introduce a Pool-type tradeoff between the relative variances of money demand shocks and output mismeasurements (Coenen et al., 2005; Dotsey & Hornstein, 2003). More specifically, while there may be reason to believe that, as a rule, real money demand reflects the true level of output because households have full information over individual private income, the underlying household preferences for liquidity may be subject to temporary changes. And even the Bundesbank (2005, p. 21) concedes that "the degree of inaccuracy in measuring GDP appears to be relatively small in relation to an indirect observation via money growth".

Finally, the informational advantages of monetary aggregates are disputed from a practical viewpoint as well. One argument is based on the observation that alternative measures of real activity other than GDP are readily and timely available (Galí, Gerlach, Rotemberg, Uhlig, & Woodford, 2004). What is more,

---

[16] Svensson (2003b, p. 1070), too, calls the idea of money as an indicator variable "the potentially most useful role for money in monetary policy analysis". See also Smets (2003).

[17] Stepping outside the DSGE approach, he looks at a simple economy with a Phillips curve and a standard money demand function. If the productivity increase was fully accommodated by output growth, inflation would remain constant but the money stock would (still) increase.

the computation of usable figures for monetary aggregates at higher frequencies requires a number of interventions, too. For instance, the ECB, just as the Bank of England or the Bundesbank, corrects the monthly level of monetary aggregates for seasonality, end-of-month effects, reclassifications (e.g., the enlargements of the euro area in 2001 and 2007), and revaluations (Fischer et al., 2008).[18]

Despite these issues, Beck and Wieland (2007a) argue that the real-time observability of money could help policy makers reduce uncertainty about the true time path of potential output. The basic idea is that—through a standard money demand function—the long-run component of money growth is correlated with the long-run component of output growth and, thus, or so the authors argue, the growth rate of potential output.[19] As a consequence, long-run money growth can be used to "cross check" inflation forecasts based on non-monetary factors and correct any permanent information gap or structural bias of the central bank with regard to the output gap argument in its policy rule.

More specifically, the authors suggest that the central bank adjusts its interest rate upward whenever the (appropriately filtered) long-run component of money growth in excess of observed long-run output growth (weighted by the output elasticity of money demand) exceeds a critical threshold anchored by the inflation target. If inflation remains below this threshold, the interest rate follows a conventional Taylor-type rule based on observed inflation and the output gap. In a simulation exercise using a (backward-looking) DSGE model calibrated to the euro-area economy they show that—assuming that the central bank indeed persistently misjudges the output gap—an interest rate rule based on the idea of cross-checking can produces sizable stability gains.

While intriguing, the cross-checking idea can be questioned along a number of dimensions. Obviously, cross-checking requires long-run monetary developments to be correctly identified, which requires a suitable amount of data. Moreover, it is not entirely clear why the central bank does not directly exploit excess long-run money growth to directly improve its estimate of the output gap. In addition, Galí et al. (2004, p. 27–29) remark that the ECB need not observe the development of monetary aggregates to receive information whether policy has gone off track—it can directly observe the price level instead. And while information on the price level may be slower in arriving than monetary data, it is very likely available early enough to allow accurate identification of medium- or long-term trends in time to alter them. Finally, the question arises whether the assumption of more or less permanent information impairment on the side of the central bank is the most straightforward way to introduce an important informational function for money.

[18] Fischer et al. (2008) also document at some length how the increasing importance of portfolio-related changes for the development of monetary aggregates from the year 2001 onward have reduced the usefulness of mechanical money demand functions for the ECB's Quarterly Monetary Assessment.

[19] Also see Orphanides (2003). The concept of potential output in current New Keynesian DSGE models is not necessarily identical with the long-run trend of output. See, for example, Clarida et al. (1999) and Woodford (2003) for a discussion.

For instance, the model of Andrés et al. (2007) discussed below makes a similar case for money based on the assumption that household money demand is forward-looking.

In addition to their potential real-time information qualities, monetary aggregates may also be a forward-looking indicator of economic activity—a quality that may be of particular value to policy makers. Nelson (2002, 2003) argues that monetary aggregates will anticipate interest rates and output—and, by extension, also inflation—if money demand was forward-looking.[20] This will be the case in the presence of adjustment costs for real balances because already small adjustment costs give cash-holding households an incentive to smooth their stock of real monetary balances over time.[21]

This idea can be incorporated in the standard NKM model discussed in Sect. 3.3.1, while otherwise keeping the framework (Eq. 3.1) and (Eq. 3.2) intact. Andrés et al. (2007) show that in this case real money demand becomes

$$\hat{m}_t = \bar{\gamma}_y \hat{y}_t - \bar{\gamma}_i \hat{i}_t + \bar{\gamma}_m \hat{m}_{t-1} + \bar{\gamma}_{Em} E\hat{m}_{t+1} + \varepsilon_{m,t}, \tag{3.8}$$

where all $\bar{\gamma} > 0$ and $\varepsilon_{m,t}$ is a money demand shock stemming from household preferences. Note that money demand is now influenced by lagged as well as expected real balances, the latter of which implies that it will reflect the entire expected future time path of interest rates and output.[22] Nelson (2003) then argues that in the presence of informational frictions—for instance, if current private sector shocks are unknown to the central bank (see Aoki, 2006)—incorporating money into the policy function along the lines of Eq. 3.7 will be optimal.[23] While this will also hold in the absence of adjustment costs, the weight given to monetary aggregates in the policy rule is particularly large when money demand is forward-looking.

Andrés et al. (2007) produce evidence that a model along the lines of Eqs. 3.1, 3.2, 3.7, and 3.8 provides a reasonably good fit of the euro-area and US economies.

---

20 Given potential output, the link to inflation would be provided by a dynamic AS-equation such as Eq. 3.1. The fact that monetary policy involves complex transmission processes, including port-folio rebalancing, has also recently been stressed by Goodfriend (2000).

21 Note that a simple cash-in-advance constraint of the form $M_{t-1}/P_{t-1} > Y_t$ (with P indicating the price level and M the nominal level of the money stock) would, in principle, also create forward-looking behavior of households or investors. The standard assumption is $M_t/P_t > Y_t$, which is mimicked by money-in-utility frameworks where the contemporaneous money stock enters the utility function.

22 Habit persistence in consumption would further enrich the dynamics of Eq. 3.8. As Nelson (2002) notes, one interpretation of the equation is that it illustrates the dependence of money demand on long-run asset prices (i.e. interest rates) in the spirit of Meltzer's (2001) argument discussed earlier. See Coenen et al. (2005) for a related discussion.

23 In general, this will also hold for a policy rule conditioning the interest rate on expected inflation. Assume, for instance, the central bank does not observe the output gap. Based on Eq. 3.5, neither current inflation nor expected inflation will be perfectly correlated with the output gap. Thus money is always likely to add to the central bank's information set because, just like the output gap itself, it depends on the future time path of interest rates (see also Nelson, 2002).

Like the non-separability result, this seems to suggest that the standard NKM model may indeed be somewhat less general—and the role of money somewhat more prominent—than often thought.[24] Of course, some of the arguments mentioned earlier with regard to real time information still apply. For instance, the information content of money would be diminished in the presence of strong money demand shocks.

In summary, it would seem that the information angle has the potential to add to the non-separability argument in support for a prominent role of money in monetary policy in principle. However, the discussion of the extent of its quantitative relevance has only just begun.

3.3.2.3 Financial Frictions: Money and the Credit Channel

The absence of an explicitly modeled monetary transition mechanism including money—in particular one that involves banks and credit supply—is another of the principal criticisms of the cashless NKM approach. Prominent examples for DSGE models including such mechanisms can be found in the credit channel literature (Bernanke & Gertler, 1995).[25] The basic idea is that banks and financial markets fulfill a crucial function in investment financing in the presence of information asymmetries. This function can give rise to an additional transition channel that complements the interest rate mechanism at the heart of the NKM approach. Similar to the interest rate channel, the credit channel's influence on inflation is an indirect one working through the demand side and, ultimately, the output gap.

The credit channel is often broken down into two separate mechanisms: the traditional bank-lending channel and the balance-sheet channel. The bank-lending channel emphasizes that monetary policy influences the real economy though bank loan supply, which depends to a large degree on the banks' ability to draw demand deposits. Money matters in this regard because the availability of demand deposits is influenced by the supply of central bank liquidity or money (Bernanke & Blinder, 1988). The link exists, for instance, if there are binding reserve requirements for banks or because the supply of central bank liquidity influences the ability of banks to attract nominal demand deposits. Banks may be interested in attracting nominal deposits since they allow them to share profit risk associated with real shocks with depositors (Diamond & Rajan, 2001, 2006).

The other relevant mechanism is the so-called financial accelerator or balance-sheet channel, describing the way credit markets can amplify the effects of monetary policy. Behind this is the fact that the external finance premium paid by

---

[24] In a broadly related result, Leeper and Roush (2003) find that adding a monetary argument to the interest rates equation improves the fit of empirical impulse responses to monetary shocks for US data (see, e.g., Leeper, Sims and Zah, 1996 and Christiano, Eichenbaum and Evans, 1998 for earlier work). Smets (2003) interprets this as supporting the informational content of money.

[25] Also see, for instance, recent contributions from Christiano and Rostagno (2001), Christiano et al. (2005), and Goodfriend and McCallum (2007).

borrowers is a negative function of the value of the collateral (i.e., their balance sheet) required by banks, which, in turn, depends on the interest rate set by the central bank. For instance, a policy interest rate hike that worsens the balance sheet positions of firms will cause external borrowing costs to increase, which can limit firms' ability to invest over and beyond the immediate impact of the initial policy measure (Bernanke, Gertler, & Gilchrist, 1996). Note that, to the extent that banks use external sources of finance instead of demand deposits to extend credit, they may themselves be subject to balance-sheet effects. In this case borrowers are likely to see any change in the banks' external finance premium reflected in their credit costs, which will also reduce their ability to invest.

The credit channel clearly indicates a role for money in the transmission process of monetary policy—but the extent to which this is the case is under some dispute. As to the balance sheet or financial accelerator channel, Greiber and Setzer (2007, p. 5) argue that money may play some role as an indicator variable, since "[i]n a rather mechanical sense the creation of a new loan is likely to go along with the creation of new deposits". However, Galí et al. (2004) stress that the balance sheets of households and firms or solvency indicators of the banking system should be more important state variables than the growth of monetary aggregates.

And even for the bank-lending channel, where money has a more central function by construction, its relevance has been questioned. One issue is the reduction in the importance of bank lending in more advanced financial markets. As Bernanke (2007) points out, the development of financial markets tends to go along with an increase in market-based financing, which reduces the relevance of the bank-lending channel and, by extension, of central bank liquidity. But even in the presence of strong bank-based financing, more developed financial markets will tend to reduce the importance of money because banks get access to other sources of liquidity and depend less on demand deposits.[26] This does not necessarily mean that financial development makes the credit channel obsolete. As already mentioned, there may be non-traditional credit channel effects operating through bank balance sheets.[27] Overall, however, it would seem that the traditional money-based credit channel is destined to gradually loose significance even in relatively bank-based financial systems such as the euro area.

And indeed, summarizing the exhaustive research effort of the Eurosystem's monetary transmission network for the euro area, Angeloni, Kashyap, Mojon and Terlizzese (2002, p.44) write that "the overall role of banks in the transmission mechanism is somewhat different, and perhaps smaller, than what might have been

---

[26] The same holds for the reduction in the stringency of reserve requirements. For the US case, Loutskina and Strahan (2008) show empirically how financial innovation, in particular securitization, has reduced the impact of lending conditions set by monetary policy on credit supply.

[27] See Bernanke (2007). Making a related point, Van den Heuvel (2007) models bank lending in the presence of capital adequacy regulations but without reserve requirements. The results imply lending will depend, among other things, on banks' financial structure and interest rates.

expected based on prior work". The interest rate channel seems to explain most of the reaction of the euro-area economies to monetary policy. And, even though there is some evidence that credit supply changes with monetary policy, these effects vary largely with the liquidity position of banks and are not uniform across euro-area member countries (e.g., Ehrmann, Gambacorta, Martinez-Pages, Sevestre & Worms, 2003).[28]

This suggests that the credit channel argument adds some support to non-separability and information in justifying a significant position for monetary factors in monetary policy overall. However, this support is very limited.

3.3.2.4 Equilibrium Selection: Money and the Price Level

Finally, at a more technical level, another argument in favor of a prominent role for money in monetary policy could be equilibrium indeterminacy in DSGE models. In a classical contribution, Sargent and Wallace (1975) argued that an interest rate rule may leave the economy's price level indeterminate if the interest rate policy rule reacts to the history of exogenous disturbances only. McCallum (1981) later pointed out that money could provide a solution. He stressed that the central bank could anchor the economy and avoid any unwanted volatility caused by multiple equilibria by conditioning the interest rate, in addition, to monetary developments.

There is, however, some debate whether this result extends to modern DSGE models. Woodford (2003) argues against money as a unique anchor, pointing out that, in principle, any commitment to a real or nominal endogenous state variable can anchor the economy's price level locally around the steady state.[29] For instance, an interest rate rule of the type (Eq. 3.3), while not including a monetary argument, will still determine the price level if the central bank's reaction to the output gap and the rate of inflation are correctly chosen, that is, if a version of the so-called Taylor principle holds.[30] However, Christiano, Motto and Rostagno (2008) illustrate that small changes in the NKM approach, such as introducing a real cost (or supply-side) channel of interest rates, can re-introduce indeterminacy.[31] In this case, money may play an important role in the sense of an escape

---

[28] On the financial accelerator, Greiber and Setzer (2007) and Bundesbank (2005) report that expansionary monetary conditions have positive feedback effects on housing prices, which Greiber and Setzer (2007, p. 2) take to imply that "a stronger case can be made for ... the indicator properties of money." See, however, the discussion above.

[29] McCallum (2001), von Hagen (2004), and Masuch et al. (2003), among others, make similar points.

[30] As Woodford (2003) shows, the determinacy conditions may involve both lower- and upper-bounds for the reaction to state variables if the Taylor-type rule is forward-looking and the $\kappa \geq 0$.

[31] See also Christiano and Rostagno (2001), Benhabib, Schmitt-Grohe and Uribe (2001a), and Carlstrom and Fuerst (2002). As Christiano et al. (2008) explain, balance-sheet effects along the lines previously discussed could also be part of the supply-side impact of interest rates.

clause: if economic variables fluctuate in response to non-fundamental (or expectation) shocks, abandoning the Taylor-type rule in favor of a policy strategy stabilizing the money stock can be beneficial.

But there remain doubts whether indeterminacy indeed robustly supports a money-based monetary strategy. As Christiano et al. (2008) readily concede, for instance, stabilizing any other economic variable under the escape clause would serve the same purpose as stabilizing the money supply. The argument has to be made that the central bank can indeed control the relevant monetary aggregate better than any other variable in the economy.[32] Moreover, as Uhlig (2008) argues, the type of boom-and-bust cycles the money-based escape clause strategy could prevent may not be empirically relevant. Finally, from a theoretical perspective, other principles of equilibrium selection on the basis of learning dynamics (Lucas, 1986) may also shape the relevance of the issue. For example, McCallum (2003) qualifies multiple equilibria as theoretical curiosities with little relevance for actual economies, and that can be overcome by the adaptive learnability of the bubble-free solution.[33]

3.3.3 The Case for Money in Partial Equilibrium Models

Leaving the realm of DSGE models, there is an interesting partial-equilibrium literature focusing on the contribution of money as a direct determinant of inflation. While severely criticized for their less-than-complete description of the underlying economic forces, partial equilibrium models are not without theoretical background (inspired by the quantity theory of money) and often appear well-anchored in empirical research (stressing the long-run correlation of money and inflation). In addition, they seem to be popular among practitioners of central banking. From the mainly theoretical perspective entertained in the present

[32] Galí et al. (2004, p.31) stress that rules that bind the central bank's nominal policy rate to endogenous variables, including real variables, can be interpreted as a commitment to as money supply target—albeit one that excludes money: "A commitment to a money-supply target implies a commitment to raise nominal interest rates at a certain rate in response to increases in the general level of prices above that characteristic for the optimal equilibrium, and similarly to raise interest rates in response to increases in real activity; otherwise, the central bank would be accommodating the increased money demand that would result from increases in either prices or real activity".

[33] Similar conclusions seem to hold for the related debate on multiple global equilibria. As, for instance, Benhabib et al. (2001a, b) demonstrate, local determinacy may go hand-in-hand with global indeterminacy—for instance, in the case of a self-fulfilling deflationary trap where the nominal interest rate drops to its zero lower bound. However, Woodford (2003) argues that some plausible learning processes can ensure that the forces anchoring the locally stable equilibrium also anchor the global equilibrium if shocks to expectations are not too large. Moreover, the problem of globally indeterminate equilibria is not confined to Taylor-type rules and can also occur under monetary strategies based on money targeting.

section, however, the main question is whether partial equilibrium models add to list of arguments discussed in Sect. 3.3.2. With that in mind, we will describe the two core models in this domain.

3.3.3.1 The P* Model: Money and the Price Level

A well-known approach motivated by the quantity theory of money is the so-called P-star (or P*) model, favored by some economists and central bank practitioners.[34] Starting point of the P* model is the assumption that deviations of the (log of the) actual price level, p, from the equilibrium price level, p^*, the so-called price gap, can be used to predict future price adjustments and, thus, inflation.[35] Based on Svensson (2000), this can be illustrated using a simple version of the Phillips curve such as

$$\pi_t = \alpha_\pi \pi_{t-1} + \alpha_{E\pi} E\pi_{t+1} + \alpha_{P*}\left(p^*_{t-1} - p_{t-1}\right) + \varepsilon_{\pi,t}, \tag{3.9}$$

where all $\alpha > 0$.[36] Note that the P* model does not restrict the expectations term, which, in principle, could take any form.

Following Gerlach and Svensson (2003), the price gap can be related to the monetary gap or excess liquidity, defined as the difference between the real money stock and its equilibrium level, $m^*_t \equiv m_t - p^*_t$. That is,

$$p^*_t - p_t = m_t - m^*_t. \tag{3.10}$$

Reynard (2007), alluding to the quantity theory of money, defines p^* as the equilibrium price level supported by the current nominal quantity of money in circulation, M_t, given potential output and the equilibrium velocity, v^*_t (all in logs),

$$p^*_t \equiv c + M_t + v^*_t - y^*_t, \tag{3.11}$$

where c is a constant. In line with Orphanides and Porter (2000), v^*_t can be modeled as $v^*_t = \eta i^*_t$, where i^*_t is the level of the equilibrium short-term interest rate proxying the opportunity costs of money holdings and $\eta > 0$ is the semi-elasticity of money demand with regard to i^*_t. This implies that the P* inflation process involving money is a function of the excess of real balances over equilibrium money demand:

$$\pi_t = \tilde{c} + \alpha_\pi \pi_{t-1} + \alpha_{E\pi} E\pi_{t+1} + \alpha_{P*}\left(m_{t-1} + \eta i^*_{t-1} - y^*_{t-1}\right) + \varepsilon_{t,\pi}, \tag{3.12}$$

with $\tilde{c} = \alpha_{P*} c > 0$.

[34] See, among others, Hallman, Porter and Small (1991), Tödter and Reimers (1997), Neumann (1997), Orphanides and Porter (2000), and Masuch, Pill and Willeke (2001).

[35] Unless otherwise stated, all variables in Sect. 3.3 are defined as (log) levels.

[36] Equation 3.9 nests a number of P* approaches. Hallman et al. (1991), for instance, assume $\alpha = 1$, which seems to be in line with Reynard's (2007) empirical observation that the price gap influences inflation with considerable lags and some persistence.

Versions of the P* model are reported to do well in some empirical applications (e.g., Masuch et al., 2001), but the approach also has no lack of critics. On the empirical level, Reynard (2007) and Nelson (2007) have pointed to the difficulties of identifying equilibrium changes in velocity in a plausible manner. And Gerlach and Svensson (2003, p. 1653) rather bluntly state that "the microfoundations of the P* model are not clear (to us, at least)...," a sentiment echoed by Andrés et al. (2007). But perhaps the most interesting observation is that, at least to some extent, Eq. 3.11 resembles the Phillips curve under the generalized New Keynesian DSGE model allowing for non-separability in Sect. 3.3.2. Both Eqs. 3.11 and 3.5 add a monetary factor to an otherwise traditional Phillips curve, even though this factor takes the form of the deviation of the money stock from its steady state level and Eq. 3.10 focuses on excess demand.

However, if the principal idea of money directly influencing inflation can be plausibly expressed in either a partial or a general equilibrium approach, the latter holds a number of advantages. Clearly, a DSGE model gives a more complete and ultimately more informative picture of money's potential role in the economy. While the P* model postulates that the impact of money can be captured by the Phillips curve alone, the Phillips curve in the DSGE model describes only one of two channels through which money impacts inflation.[37] Moreover, its microfoundations make the DSGE model less prone to parameter instability in structural empirical applications—a particularly attractive feature for policy makers who are interested in predicting the impact of policy changes (see e.g., Lubik & Surico, 2006; Woodford, 2008).

Among other things, these observations suggest that the P* model adds little to the arguments in favor of a more prominent role of money listed in Sect. 3.3.2.

3.3.3.2 The Two-Pillar Phillips Curve: Money and Long-Run Inflation

Another prominent partial-equilibrium approach is the two-pillar Phillips curve, developed most recently in a series of papers by Gerlach (2004) and Assenmacher-Wesche and Gerlach (2006a, b).[38] This strand of the literature focuses on the "trend", "core", or "low-frequency" movements (i.e., movements that continue long enough un-reversed to qualify as a long-term depending on a particular definition) of money. Similar to the price gap discussed above, these long-run movements in money growth are added as a "second pillar"—a term explicitly linking this approach to the ECB's self-description of its monetary analysis—to a conventional Phillips curve approach.

[37] As discussed, the other channel works through the demand (or Euler) equation (Eq. 3.6), and both interact in the general equilibrium. In addition, the parameters in Eq. 3.5 are structural in nature.

[38] See Benati (2005), Gerlach and Svensson (2003), Jaeger (2003), Neumann and Greiber (2004), Christiano and Fitzgerald (2003), Backhus and Kehoe (1992), or Lucas (1980) for other (also mostly empirical) work in the same direction.

Somewhat more formally Assenmacher-Wesche and Gerlach (2006a, b) describe the two-pillar approach as:

$$\pi_t = \beta_\pi \pi_{t-1} + \beta_x x_t + \beta_m(\Delta m_t^L + \tau \Delta i_t^L - \Delta y_t^L) + \varepsilon_{\pi,t}, \tag{3.13}$$

with all β, $\tau > 0$, and where Δm_t^L,Δy_t^L, and Δi_t^L represent the growth rate of the long-term component of real money balances, real GDP growth, and the nominal interest rate change, respectively. The expression in parenthesis on the right-hand-side of Eq. 3.13 marks the growth rate of the long-term component of the supply of real balances corrected for long-term changes in money demand based on a standard demand function. There is obviously some resemblance between Eqs. 3.13 and 3.12, but the precise formulation of the role of money is quite different.[39]

While most of the recent literature is agnostic about the theoretical underpinnings of the two-pillar Phillips curve, others have made attempts to reason for it from a theoretical perspective. One possibility is to start from a standard forward-looking Phillips curve and simply to assume that money growth determines inflation expectations as in Gerlach (2004).[40] Another would be to follow Neumann and Greiber (2004), who argue that if the behavior of actual inflation was linked to longer-run (or core) inflation, and core inflation was driven by the longer-run component of money growth by way of the quantity theory and a standard money demand function (Eq. 3.13) might be a valid causal model of inflation.

The concept enjoys some support among monetary policy practitioners (Assenmacher-Wesche, Gerlach, & Sekine, 2007) and is reported as describing euro-area inflation well (e.g., Assenmacher-Wesche & Gerlach, 2006a, b)—but the approach is not without drawbacks. As Nelson (2007) writes, in this model class identification of a link between money growth and inflation requires multi-decade averages of data. And, in a related comment, the OECD (2007) points out that this type of results is not always robust to changes in the sample period. For instance, excluding the 1970s period, a time of large common swings of money and inflation before what is now called the great moderation, tends to weaken the link between money and inflation.

However, the most severe criticism of the model has come from the theoretical side. As already highlighted in Sect. 3.3.1, the standard NKM approach with added money demand can be shown to produce long-run empirical implications that are observationally equivalent with the empirical facts captured by the two-pillar Phillips curve while rejecting causality of money for inflation across both in

39 The difference to the P* model is less pronounced in Gerlach and Svensson's (2003) specification of the two-pillar Phillips curve which is based on the real money gap instead of long-run excess money growth.

40 See Bordes and Clerc (2007) for a similar discussion of the underpinnings of Eq. 3.13. Interestingly, according to Gerlach (2004), the ECB (2001b) in an early description of its policy framework explicitly allowed for the possibility of a direct impact of money on inflation expectations—a statement that was removed from later editions of the book (ECB, 2004a, b).

short- and long-run (Woodford, 2008).[41] Therefore Nelson (2003) concludes that models such as of the two-pillar Phillips curve variety provide no valid test for evaluating a possible causal role of money for inflation. And Woodford (2007) points out that, once a structural general equilibrium model such as the NKM is available to account for the relation between money and inflation across all time horizons, there is little need for a partial modeling effort to capture the longer-run inflation dynamics separately. By extension, this argument also holds for generalized versions of the New Keynesian DSGE model that—other than the standard model favored by Woodford (2007, 2008)—allow money a causal role in the determination of money.

This discussion suggests that, not unlike the P* approach, the two-pillar curve does not add significantly to the arguments for a more prominent role of money in Sect. 3.3.2.

3.3.4 Summary

The theoretical debate suggests that there are a number of advantages to the general equilibrium approach. One obvious point is that the DSGE framework allows a fuller view of the role of money in the economy than any partial equilibrium model, including by capturing equilibrium feedbacks and by allowing for model-consistent forward-looking expectations. DSGE models are also less prone to the Lucas critique.

What is even more important, however, is that taking advantage of DSGE modeling does not mean ignoring the potential role of money in the economy. On the contrary, as Papademos (2006, p. 6) rightly points out, DSGE models have "…the potential to incorporate in a substantive way the role and effects of money and credit in the monetary transmission mechanism". While supporters of a strong role of money in monetary policy might have been tempted to look at partial equilibrium models for support in the past, the advent of generalized versions of the "cashless" New Keynesian baseline model makes this less of a necessity. These models allow for a causal as well as an informative role for money in the economy and, thus, seem to capture well most arguments made within the confinements of the partial equilibrium approach. This holds for the short as well as the long run, where it has been convincingly argued that the implications of the DSGE models are well in line with the empirical predictions of the quantity theory. Also, much like many pragmatically minded partial equilibrium models, modern DSGE approaches have been amended to better describe the data, for instance

[41] Compare Nelson (2007) and Beck and Wieland (2007b), who discuss the two-pillar Phillips curve but ultimately reject it as a-theoretical. Ireland (2004), too, states that a thorough analysis of the role of real balances in the macro economy may require more than adding money to the Phillips curve.

through the introduction of habit persistence arguments or partial indexation to complement the purely forward-looking models.

In the light of these findings, a merger of the two pillars of the ECB's monetary strategy is recommendable. The ongoing discussion of the relevance of money in the macro economy suggests that an exclusive focus on non-monetary (or "economic", in ECB parlance) factors alone may leave euro-area policy makers with an incomplete picture of the economy. And treating monetary factors as a separate matter, using potentially inferior partial-equilibrium tools to cross-check the implications of the "economic pillar", is obviously a second-best solution to this problem. Indeed, the natural approach seems to be a merger of the two analytical "pillars" of the ECB's monetary strategy within a general-equilibrium inspired analytical framework incorporating both monetary and non-monetary determinants of inflation. Of course, just as the current "monetary pillar" is not explicitly linked to a particular partial equilibrium model, the merged framework will not be reduced to a particular model, rather than to the general idea or narrative.

Even a focus on general equilibrium models does not necessarily guarantee a clear-cut answer to the question about the weight to be attached to monetary analysis in such a unified analytical setup. In fact, it seems difficult (if not impossible), to come to a final view on theoretical grounds alone (see Table 3.1). One the one hand, not all general-equilibrium arguments in favor of a prominent role of money are considered quantitatively important in the literature. This holds, for instance, for the non-separability and credit channel effects within

Table 3.1 Arguments in favour of a more prominent role for money: overview

Argument	Mechanism	Monetary variable to watch
General equilibrium:		
Causal	Non-separable utility function: money influences consumption decisions and price setting	Real money, deviation from steady state
Causal	Financial frictions: bank lending influenced by money supply, impacts investment decisions	Real money, deviation from steady state
Determinacy	Multiple equilibria: policy strategy focused on money prevents volatility from equilibrium indeterminacy	Real money, deviation from steady state
Information	Adjustment costs: smoothing of balances conditions money on future output and interest rate path	Real money, deviation from steady state
Information	Long-run correlations/cross-checking: long-run money growth indicates potential output growth	Real long-run money growth, excess over observed long-run output growth
Partial equilibrium:		
Causal	P* model: price level ultimately determined by money stock	Real money, excess over equilibrium demand
Causal	Long-run correlations/two-pillar Phillips curve: inflation reacts (also) to long-run money growth	Real long-run money growth, excess over long-run demand growth

the New Keynesian approach. And while there is something to be said for the idea that monetary indicators can provide helpful forward-looking information for policy makers, the discussion of its economic relevance has just begun. On the other hand, money may matter through the sum of all these factors, leaving the option for a relevant role of money overall.

Against this background, there is an increased interest in assessing the validity of these arguments empirically. Section 3.4 will take a closer look at the existing literature and present some new results.

3.4 The Importance of Money for Inflation Forecasts

There are several reasons why an empirical perspective might be informative with regard to the role of money in monetary policy. First, the theoretical debate is hardly conclusive. In fact, while there are indications that money has at least some causal influence on inflation or might, in addition, provide information about its future time path, the economic relevance of these channels remains mostly an empirical question. Second, there could also be a purely empirical argument in favor of a prominent role for money in monetary policy. A forward-looking policy maker may take the pragmatic position that money deserves attention if it proves helpful in forecasting inflation, no matter the precise channels through which this occurs. Thus, both on theoretical and empirical grounds, a monetary strategy placing special weight on money would seem particularly convincing, if money proved exceptionally helpful in forecasting inflation.

However, the picture emerging from the empirical literature so far is fairly mixed. On the one hand, a number of studies conclude that money provides relevant information about euro-area inflation; on the other, results for the US and cross-country studies often point in the opposite direction. What is more, there is a discussion on the economic relevance of monetary in comparison to other factors. In light of this, in what follows we will briefly review the existing literature, including recent IMF research on this topic.

3.4.1 A Brief Survey of the Empirical Literature

A number of studies suggest that the indicator properties of money for inflation may be limited—either because money-based models do not perform well in a cross-country framework or because money is severely outperformed by other indicators. For example, Roffia and Zaghini (2007) show that, over a 3-year horizon, in a panel of 15 industrialized countries starting in early 1970s, episodes of strong money growth are related to higher inflation only in about half of the 71 cases. De Grauwe and Polan (2005), looking at a large panel of about 160 countries since the 1970s find that the relationship between money and longer-run inflation is weak at best for low-inflation regions comparable to today's euro area. Gerlach and Svensson (2003, p. 1669) find that the growth rate of nominal M3 adds little to the forecasting accuracy of an output-gap based model of euro-area inflation, which to them suggests "considerable doubt on its usefulness for policy purposes." Similarly, Stavrev (2006) finds that inflation forecasts for the euro area based on some quantity-theory inspired inflation models are outperformed by non-monetary approaches. And, finally, the OECD (2007) reports results from an euro-area inflation forecasting "horse race" between alternative time-series models suggesting that money played a prominent role only up to 2000. After 2000, for instance, real time measures of the output gap out-performed money as a predictor of inflation (OECD, 2007).

In contrast, another strand in the literature suggests that partial equilibrium models can help forecasting euro-area inflation. Among others, the Bundesbank (2005) reports that P* models akin to the ones discussed in Sect. 3.3.3 are linked to euro-area inflation trends. Fischer et al. (2008) report that the ECB has internally used P* models to forecast inflation. Gerlach (2004) and Assenmacher-Wesche and Gerlach (2006a, b) show a significant contribution of longer-run movements in money growth (appropriately filtered) in two-pillar Phillips-curve type dynamic inflation equations along the lines of Eq. 3.13 in Sect. 3.3.3. And, according to Gerlach and Svensson (2003), a real money gap representation of the P* model along the lines of Eq. 3.12 adds to the predictive power of a conventional Phillips curve approach.

Other studies imply that trend M3 growth is a predictor of inflation over medium-term horizons. For example, following Nicoletti-Altimari (2001), Hofmann (2008) finds that trend growth of M3 is, as a rule, useful for inflation forecasts at medium-term horizons, although its forecasting performance has declined recently. Scharnagl and Schumacher (2007) use a Bayesian estimation framework to identify single monetary and real variables as well as groups of such variables that significantly predict euro-area inflation. The results suggest that a measure of trend M3 growth is the only monetary variable with relevant and time-invariant predictive power on its own, and that monetary variables as a group work well in forecasting models that also feature some real variables.

Finally, Berger and Österholm (2008a) show that, while M2 as well as M3 growth can help improve forecasting models of euro-area inflation in a mean-adjusted Bayesian VAR framework, the size of this improvement tends to be very small. Using a model based on data from 1970 to 2006 and forecasting horizons of up to 12 quarters, they find surprisingly strong evidence that adding money to both univariate and trivariate models (including, in addition to inflation, real GDP growth and interest rates) improves forecasting accuracy. The results are very robust with regard to alternative treatments of priors and sample periods. However, the predictive marginal power of money growth for inflation is substantially lower in more recent sample periods compared to the 1970s and 1980s. Interestingly, the result seems not to be an artifact of the particularities of the euro area: a related paper reports similar findings for M2 growth in the US (Berger & Österholm, 2008b).

3.4.2 A Systematic Analysis of the Information Content of Money

A number of things may explain these widely differing results, with important implications for any systematic approach to evaluating the information content of money in forecasting inflation. One factor is *sample selection*. D'Agostino, Giannone and Surico (2006) make the point that the predictability of macroeconomic variables in general may have been lowered as macroeconomic volatility declined during the great moderation. In a related result, De Grauwe and Polan (2005) report that the relationship between money and longer-run inflation is the strongest in high-inflation countries. This suggests focusing any comparative analysis of competing models of inflation on a unified sample period, preferably a recent one to maximize the relevance of results for policy makers.

Another factor will be differences in the *empirical approach*. The literature has employed a wide variety of inflation models, both empirical and structural, ranging from simple time-series models to sophisticated general dynamic factor model (GDFM) approaches and more structural, theory-guided setups.[42] While all these models incorporate money one way or the other and can, in principle, be compared with non-monetary approaches, their comparison would be more straightforward in a nested framework. In particular, the marginal contribution of money to inflation forecasting accuracy should be evaluated for a particular model class, comparing the forecasting performance of a model that encompasses monetary variables with a related one that does not. Such an exercise is akin to a Granger causality test in a multivariate environment (Ashley, Granger, & Schmalensee, 1980; Berger & Österholm, 2008a).

Finally, it would be helpful to employ structural models in addition to the idea of Granger causality testing. As among others Woodford (2008) and Galí et al. (2004) warn, empirical correlation does not necessarily imply *theoreticalcausality*. In particular, the identification of an empirical link between money and inflation may not be sufficient to give money a special role in the determination of inflation. After all, both variables may be simultaneously determined by an omitted driving variable, as the New Keynesian DSGE model would suggest (see Sect. 3.3.1).

Following these arguments, Berger and Stavrev (2008) provide a systematic analysis of the information content of money for inflation in the euro area. They compare the simulated out-of-sample forecasting performance of models with and without money for the period 2000–2007 for a number of typical model classes in the literature using Bayesian estimation techniques where appropriate.[43]

---

[42] Yet another strand of research, as e.g. in Stavrev (2006) and Hofmann (2008), combines a variety of approaches for inflation forecasting. While perhaps helpful as a forecasting tool, this approach provides little guidance for the question at hand.

[43] All models are initially estimated over the same training period, 1993Q1–1999Q4, and their inflation forecasting performance is assessed for the period 2000Q1–2007Q2. See Berger and Stavrev (2008).

The model classes include, on the empirical side, pure time series and GDFM approaches and, on the structural side, both partial and dynamic general equilibrium models that are conceptually equivalent to the ones discussed in Sect. 3.3. The within-class comparison is based on the out-of-sample root mean square errors (RMSEs) at forecasting horizons of 1, 4, 8, and 12 quarters ahead. A lower RMSE implies better forecasting accuracy at a particular horizon. Figure 3.3 summarizes key results from their paper.

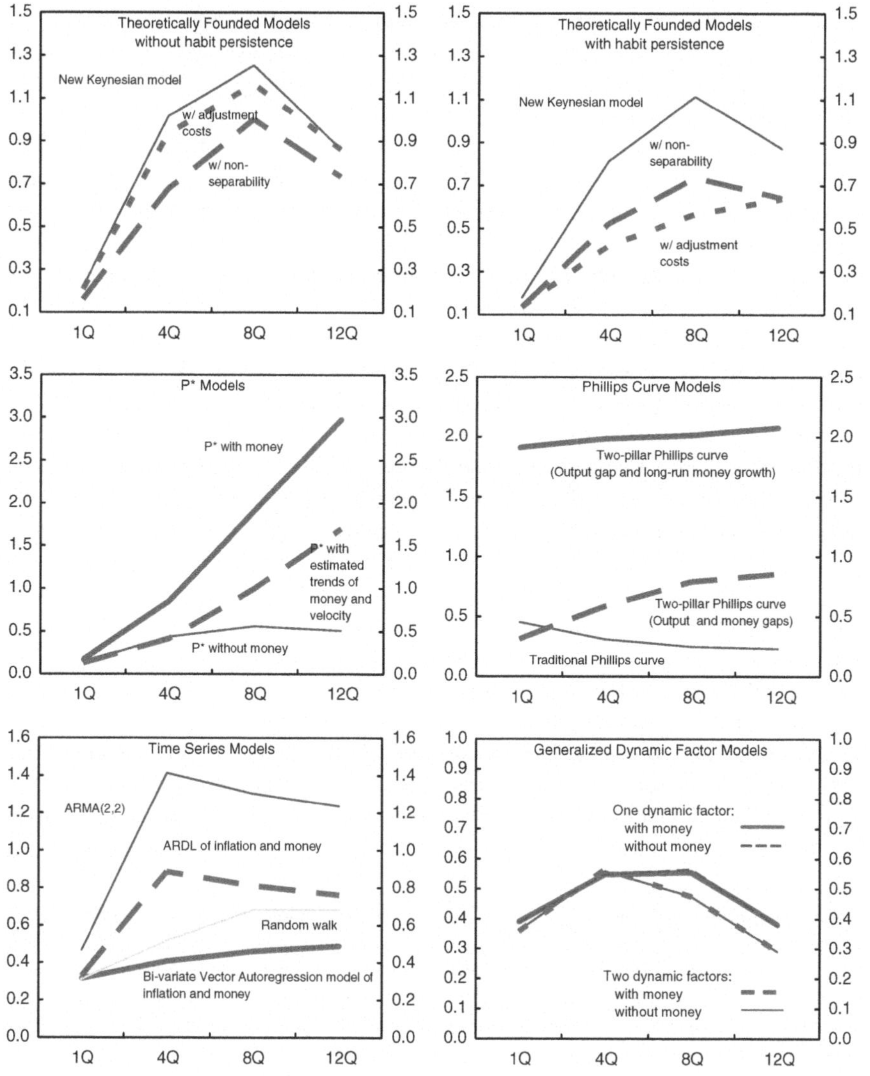

Fig. 3.3 Forecast performance of various inflation models. (RMSE of dynamic forecasts, in percentage points of year-on-year inflation). Source: Berger and Stavrev (2008)

An important first finding is that among the structural New Keynesian DSGE models, the money-enhanced generalized approaches perform well compared to the cashless NKM baseline (Fig. 3.3, first row).[44] The size of the improvement in forecasting accuracy from adding money is a matter of perspective. For instance, at a forecasting horizon of eight quarters, introducing non-separability reduces the RMSE compared to the cashless baseline without habit persistence by about 0.25 percentage points of inflation, while the improvement from adding adjustment costs is only about 0.1 (left figure). At about 0.4 and 0.5, the improvements from adding money to the baseline NKM with habit persistence at the same horizon (right figure) are higher and seem to have a more relevant empirical dimension. On the other hand, viewed across all forecasting horizons, the average improvement in RMSE is no higher than 0.3 percentage points for either group of models in the NKM class.[45]

In addition, they find that money does improve inflation-forecasting performance of some time-series models (Fig. 3.3, third row, left panel). An autoregressive distributed lag (ARDL) single equation approach containing money, while not beating the simple random walk model, delivers better inflation forecasts than the ARMA approach. The best time-series model in terms of RMSEs across all horizons is a bivariate BVAR model. At about 0.5–1.0 percentage points on average, the reduction in RMSE gained by the bivariate VAR model against the ARMA model is considerable, but the improvement against the random walk model is modest at best. These results are consistent with other studies in the literature that have used time-series models (e.g., Berger & Österholm, 2008a; Fischer et al., 2008). On the other hand, Berger and Stavrev (2008) also report that incorporating monetary indicators in the GDFM models does little to improve inflation forecasting performance once a broader set of economic indicators is taken into account (Fig. 3.3, third row, right panel). The two-factor GDFM model with money does better in forecasting inflation than the two-factor model without money, but the reduction in RMSEs is miniscule. The reverse holds for the one-factor GDFM model. These results seem to run against the findings of Hofmann (2008) that factor models with money do consistently better than factor models without money in forecasting inflation over the 12-quarter horizon.

Turning to partial equilibrium models, the results in Berger and Stavrev (2008) imply little or no role for money (Fig. 3.3, second row). More specifically, the simplest P* model without money (where the price gap is the deviation of the price

---

[44] The adjustment cost results are particularly interesting because Berger and Stavrev (2008) condition the central bank's interest rate function on model-consistent expected inflation. The improvement in forecasting accuracy from incorporating monetary factors in the interest rate rule suggests that money supplies additional information. As discussed in Sect. 3.3.2, one reason could be that because of informational frictions the central bank does not fully observe the state of the economy reflected, in part, in monetary developments.

[45] Money affects inflation mainly through improving the empirical specification of the aggregate demand and aggregate supply equations, while the effects from the fact that monetary policy reacts to money balances in the generalized models (see Sect. 3.3.2) is small.

from an estimated equilibrium level) has the best-forecast performance in this class of models, with the two models incorporating money (including the money-gap P* approach in Sect. 3.3.3) lagging far behind (left panel). Similarly, among the reduced-form Phillips curve models, the standard formulation excluding money produces the best forecast among this group of models at longer horizons, with the two-pillar Phillips curves, and, in particular, the one with long-term money growth along the lines of Sect. 3.3.3 faring much worse.

An interesting observation comparing the performance of the money-based approaches across the various model classes is the seemingly "u-shaped" relationship between the degree of their theoretical underpinnings and their forecasting performance: the best empirical model and the best DSGE model do better than the best partial equilibrium model. A corollary of this is that, from a forecasting standpoint, it is clear that the information content of money is not necessarily adequately captured by money growth (or its long-term component) alone, or even by adding a thorough specification of trend values, as in the two P* models with money—instead, a more explicit modeling of the dynamics and underlying theoretical structure of the money-inflation relationship seem to be called for.[46]

Berger and Stavrev (2008) conclude that the quantitative importance of money for inflation forecasting is rather limited. The improvement in RMSE from adding money in a particular model class is often very small. In addition, in a horserace of all forecasting models—while not at the core of the empirical exercise geared toward within-modelmoney-less models class comparison—the best performers are money-less models. Even though the quantitative advantage of the is not always large, these findings, too, put the role of money in an integrated empirical setting into perspective.

3.4.3 Summary

The empirical debate on the role of money in monetary policy is ongoing. Much of the empirical literature focuses on the usefulness of money in inflation forecasting, a task that arguably is also of high interest for practitioners of monetary policy. The results overall seem to be mixed, with some papers declining that money plays a useful role in enhancing forecasting accuracy of inflation in the euro area and elsewhere, while others tend to support such a role.

A systematic comparison of these studies is difficult. One complication is that sample periods and empirical approaches vary widely. Another issue is that there is little discussion of causality. For instance, rather than focusing on the marginal contribution of money within a certain model class, comparative studies such as

[46] One possible explanation for the relatively weak performance of the money-enhanced partial equilibrium may be their particular sensitivity to money demand instability. Fischer et al. (2008) also note that, from the perspective of forecasting practitioners, simple bivariate models foregoing an explicit money demand specification are dominating other approaches.

Nicoletti-Altimari (2001), OECD (2007), or Hofman (2008) tend to focus more on overall horse races across model types. And little work has been done so far using structural general equilibrium approaches, which allow perhaps the most direct test for a causal role of money with regard to modeling present and future inflation.

Moving in this direction, recent IMF staff research suggests that money may indeed contribute to forecasting accuracy within a number of model classes. Evaluating the relative out-of-sample inflation forecasting performance of models with and without money for a uniform sample period, the results show, for instance, that money-enhanced structural New Keynesian DSGE models outperform their cashless counterpart, signaling both a causal and an informative role for money. A positive marginal contribution of money to forecasting accuracy is also found for some of the purely empirical models. However, partial equilibrium models with money often perform worse than their money-less counterparts. In addition, there is an interesting "u-shaped" relationship between the degree of the theoretical underpinnings of the inflation models and their forecasting performance: the best non-structural empirical model and the best DSGE model are doing better than the best quantity-theory inspired partial equilibrium models.

This research also shows, however, that the quantitative contribution of money to inflation forecasting accuracy is often small. Depending on the model class, the marginal improvement in terms of the RMSE of the forecasting error can be miniscule. What is more, in an all-out horserace money-enhanced models tend to be dominated by non-monetary models. While not at the core of the empirical exercise (which is geared toward within-model class comparison) and even though the quantitative advantage of the money-less models is not always large, this also warns against overestimating the role of money in an integrated empirical setting.

3.5 Disaggregated Monetary Analysis

Since the inception of the ECB, the evolution of M3 has posed a challenge for the ECB's monetary analysis. M3 growth has continuously exceeded its reference value of 4.5% since June 2001, often by a wide margin, but inflation has hovered around 2%, close to the ECB's definition of price stability. The apparent decoupling of money growth and inflation occurred against a background of surging financial innovation, deregulation, as well as increasing use of internet banking, which lowered financial transaction costs significantly. At the same time, many financial assets, including money market funds and equities, turned into close substitutes to money, as measured by M3, and, as a consequence, the impact of shifts in domestic or internationally diversified asset portfolios on M3 has increased. Although the precise repercussions and links between these developments and M3 growth are subject to some debate, it seems likely that they have contributed to distorting the relation between money growth and inflation (Fig. 3.4).

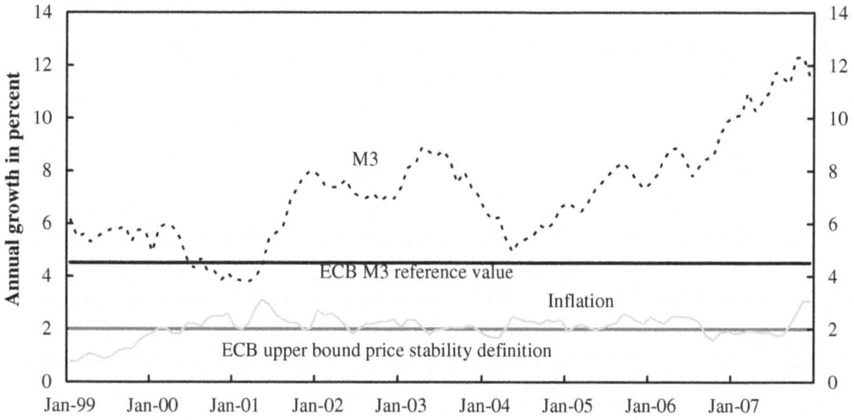

Fig. 3.4 Euro area money growth and inflation. Source: ECB

Partly in reaction to these developments, in 2003 the ECB adjusted its monetary strategy framework, broadening its monetary analysis to explicitly account for changes in the institutional features of the monetary and financial sector (see Sect. 3.2). Disaggregated monetary analysis, including the close monitoring of M3 components, is seen as a natural starting point for the assessment whether M3 variations are broad based and a useful indicator of future price trends, or may need to be adjusted—for instance because they reflect preference shocks to financial portfolios including elements of M3.

This section will provide a brief discussion of the ECB's monetary analysis framework focusing on its disaggregate aspect. In particular, it will discuss the ECB's judgmental analysis and adjustments to M3 in response to financial innovation and integration, including international portfolio shifts and securitization.

3.5.1 The Background of the ECB's Disaggregated Monetary Analysis

The ECB has repeatedly pointed to the observation that money and inflation are closely related over the medium- to long-run horizon in the euro area, with money leading inflation by as much as 3 years. Implicit in its assessment of the particular importance of money for medium- to long-term price trends is the presumption that money affects inflation and not vice versa. While a structural or causal relationship between money and inflation can be modeled in a number of ways (see Sect. 3.3), the economic concept most closely related to the ECB's reference value approach is certainly the quantity theory of money.

Consider the quantity identity

$$m_t + v_t \equiv p_t + y_t, \tag{3.14}$$

where p_t denotes the price level, m_t the nominal stock of money, y_t real output (all in logs) and v_t is the (log) income velocity of money at period t. After rearranging this equation, real balances or real money demand equal real output corrected for velocity

$$m_t - p_t = y_t - v_t. \tag{3.15}$$

If prices were fully flexible, velocity constant and the available nominal money supply modeled as an exogenous (policy) variable, any change in the nominal stock of money would result in a proportional change in prices and (real) money demand would, again, equal the supply of real money balances. With these assumptions the quantity identity becomes a simple quantity theory of the price level that implies that any change in the nominal stock of money (or its growth rate) will—at least over the longer run—result in a proportional change in prices (or inflation) and, in that sense, inflation would mainly be a monetary phenomenon.

But there are two important objections or caveats to the hypothesis that there should be a stable and causal relationship from money to prices. First, velocity is not constant, and, second, money is not fully exogenous. We will discuss these issues in turn.

3.5.1.1 Velocity is not Constant

In most empirical studies, velocity is characterized by large swings or trends over time while also exhibiting high short-run volatility. To illustrate, Fig. 3.5 shows income velocity of various monetary aggregates in the euro area (left panel) and the G7 (right). These empirical features are at odds with the idea of a constant velocity underlying a simple and stable relationship between money and prices. Any objection to the existence of such relationship on the basis of variable velocity could be rectified, however, if there were nevertheless a stable functional demand for real money that in turn would imply a systematic and stable relationship between velocity and other endogenous variables, including the interest rate.

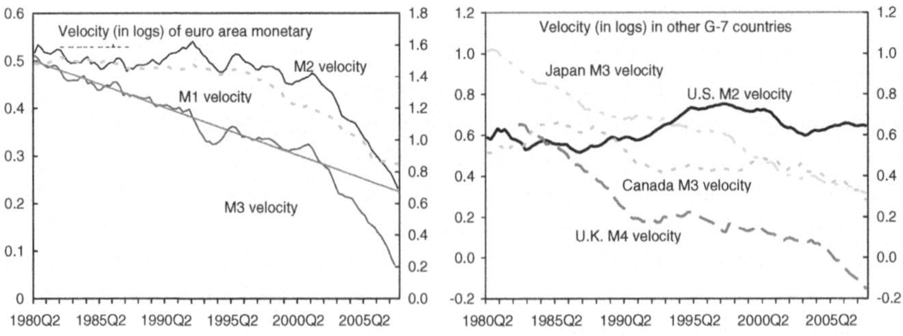

Fig. 3.5 Income velocity in the euro area and other G-7 countries. Sources: ECB and IMF. Note: Velocity is defined as $v_t = p_t + y_t - m_t$ along the lines of Eq. 3.14. The *left-hand panel* also shows a linear trend for M3-based velocity over the full sample period

Money demand and, thus, velocity, can take various forms. A straightforward cash-in-advance constraint implies constant velocity and, accordingly, interest inelastic demand for money. Simple opportunity cost considerations imply interest elastic money demand and variable velocity. But money demand may also be determined in a complex portfolio calculation where households trade off the expected returns and risks of a multitude of assets, taking account the transaction costs of portfolio adjustments. For example,

$$v_t = f\left(i_t, s_t^1, s_t^2, s_t^j \ldots, s_t^n; \sigma_t^1, \sigma_t^2, \sigma_t^j \ldots, \sigma_t^n; t_t^1, t_t^2, t_t^j, \ldots, t_t^n\right), \qquad (3.16)$$

where i_t denotes the nominal interest rate of a risk-free one-period bond, s_t^j denotes the spread between i_t and the return of some other asset j, σ_t^j the risk associated with that return and t_t^j the transaction costs associated with selling asset j. In such a model, any change in spreads, risks or in the perception of risks and in transaction costs may induce portfolio shifts that affect velocity and the real demand for money and, accordingly, blur any simple one-to-one link between the nominal stock of money and prices. And the variability in velocity and real money demand would be the higher the lower the level of transaction costs and, therefore, the higher the degree of substitutability between money and other assets.

Conceptually, a broadly defined money demand function based on a sufficiently general concept of velocity as in Eq. 3.16 may well be able to account for and predict velocity shifts while preserving the link between money and prices. However, financial innovation, technological progress and financial integration or deregulation are prone to change the functional form of $f(.)$ in Eq. 3.16 or change the set of relevant assets n in an unpredictable and erratic manner. Since the 1970s, when cash and demand deposits were the predominant means of most economic transactions, there has been a host of financial innovations including credit cards, electronic money, money market accounts and internet banking. Transaction costs of trading most financial assets fell rapidly and many became close substitutes to cash and overnight deposits. These developments, by nature hard to predict, have seriously undermined the concept of stable velocity or real money demand. Friedman and Kuttner (1996) argue that the problem of instability is especially severe in a modern financial system that offers any number of assets, of which only an arbitrary subset will be included in a given definition of a monetary aggregate.

There is still a lively empirical debate on the stability of conventional money demand functions in the euro area, with some studies finding money demand functions in the euro area to be, while not without problems, more stable than in other regions, in particular the US.[47] A number of factors might explain this

---

[47] For instance, Bruggeman, Donato and Warne (2003) find long-run euro area money demand consistently related to real GDP. Dreger and Wolters (2006) also argue that standard money demand functions are well capable of explaining the recent surge in euro area liquidity provided that the short-run homogeneity restriction on money and prices is dropped. See, among others, the surveys by Calza and Sousa (2003), Golinelli and Pastorello (2002), and Ericsson (1998).

finding. First, financial deregulation in the euro area was less rapid than in the US. Second, due to differences in the financial system, the type of financial innovation may have been different. Third, monetary euro area data prior to 1999 are a composite of national data and averaging helps stabilizing euro area money demand through potentially offsetting national demand shocks and the implicit inclusion of foreign aggregate explanatory variables. Finally, the well-known historical stability of German money demand comes to bear in euro area-wide estimates of money demand models.

Others maintain that the stability of euro-area money demand requires taking into account the influence of asset markets, reflecting the spirit of Eq. 3.16. For example, Greiber and Lemke (2005) show that stable money demand functions can be estimated if measures of uncertainty are included in the model, which help to explain what are considered portfolio or preference shifts in liquidity demand. Fererro, Nobili and Passiglia (2007) also argue that there is evidence that the recently observed increase of euro-area M3 growth may be due to portfolio choices and the acceleration of non-bank financial intermediaries' money demand. And, in related work, Greiber and Setzer (2007) show that housing prices systematically influence money demand both in the US and the euro area. One explanation could be a higher transaction volume through wealth effects on consumption or increasing construction activity. They argue that this relationship can help explain signs of instability in standard money demand function. Along similar lines Boone, Mikol and van den Noord (2004) include proxies for wealth (house and stock prices) to allow empirical money demand function to capture the post-2000 euro area money surge.

But there are a number of indications that despite these efforts, a stable money demand will prove elusive even in the euro area. For instance, Faruqee (2005) and Bordes, Clerc and Marimoutou (2007, pp. 2-5) identify structural breaks in the log velocity of money even after correcting for portfolio shifts and the influence interest rates, ultimately rejecting the "existence of a strong, stable, and predictable relation between money and prices in the euro area", which "may call for some adjustments in the conduct of the ECB's monetary policy." Along similar lines, Fischer et al. (2008, p. 111) also stress that, while the ECB has found portfolio-enhanced money demand functions helpful in explaining M3 behavior during certain periods, these models tend to produce "anomalies" during other times.

Most importantly, however, there is reason to suspect that the relative stability of euro area compared to US money demand functions will eventually disappear once euro-area financial deregulation and integration has reached US levels. Many countries in the euro area had relatively closed and heavily regulated financial markets during most of the 1970s and 1980s, and financial progress occurred at a much slower pace than in the US. With the introduction of a common currency, together with a sharp acceleration in financial deregulation and integration, however, it appears very likely that the recent instability of velocity and money demand in the euro area will persist or even increase over time. For the US, at least, there is broad consensus that financial innovation and technological progress contributed greatly to the instability of velocity and money demand. In response, the US Federal Reserve significantly downgraded its monetary analysis in the early 1990s.[48]

3.5.1.2 Money is not Fully Exogenous

Another threat to a simple causal relationship between money and prices is the endogeneity of the nominal stock of money. When fiat money was first introduced and central banks defined the initial value of account, money was widely considered a (exogenous) policy instrument under the control of the monetary authorities. Nowadays, central banks are still controlling the issuance of legal currency and exert significant direct influence over some bank deposits, including overnight or demand deposits. But other components of money, such as the amount of money market funds and debt securities that are part of the ECB's concept of broad money M3 (see Table 3.2) are largely determined by markets.

The way the concept of money has evolved over time is closely related to the discussion of stable money demand above. The introduction of near perfect substitutes to currency and zero interest yielding demand deposits, which were considered the main components of money in the past, has led to a broader definition of money that has been used for monetary analysis and specifications of money demand. Shifts between currency, zero interest yielding demand deposits and other forms of deposits largely reflect technical constraints, such as the amount of time involved in the clearing of checks and wiring balances, or finding and accessing an ATM for cash, instead of measurable variation in returns.[49] As a consequence, many central banks, rather than augmenting money demand or velocity functions

Table 3.2 Definitions of euro area monetary aggregates

Liabilities[a]	M1	M2	M3
Currency in circulation	×	×	×
Overnight deposits	×	×	×
Deposits with an agreed maturity up to 2 years		×	×
Deposits redeemable at a period of notice up to 3 months		×	×
Repurchase agreements			×
Money market fund (MMF) shares/units			×
Debt securities up to 2 years			×

Source: ECB

[a] Liabilities of the money-issuing sector and central government liabilities with a monetary character held by the money-holding sector

[48] See, for example, the discussion in Friedman and Kuttner (1996) and Kahn and Benolkin (2007).

[49] The demand for cash also depends on the size of an economy's informal sector and its use abroad.

based on a narrow money concept such as M1, instead expanded the concept of money to M2, M3, or beyond.

But the ECB's choice of M3 as key monetary aggregate for gauging inflationary pressures is not beyond dispute. For example, Reynards (2007) argues that narrower money measures, such as M2 that are more closely related to the transactions demand for money, may be preferable. Also, the ECB's current broad money M3 concept includes most liabilities of the banking sector, while other, non-bank issued financial assets are becoming relatively close substitutes to M3 components. Any inclusion of these—moving from inside money to outside money that includes net assets of the private nonbank sector—would significantly alter further the concept and meaning of money.

As monetary aggregates such as the ECB's M2 or M3, considered relevant for gauging inflation pressures, are largely endogenous and outside the control of central banks, money targeting as the operational framework for monetary policy has been abandoned by most central banks.[50] Instead, most monetary authorities set a policy target for the interest rate in the interbank overnight market and conduct their monetary operations, including repurchase agreements and outright asset purchases, to steer this rate close to the policy target, while even narrow money is determined endogenously.[51] This move is supported by the advent of "cashless" New Keynesian general equilibrium models, where, with endogenous money and inflation, there is no clear direction of causality (Svensson, 2003a). Against this background, many have argued that a stable money demand or velocity function, if it existed, would not be very helpful in gauging inflationary pressures as movements in money would mainly reflect structural shocks to other variables, or financial innovations.

3.5.2 Judgmental Adjustments to M3

In the ECB's view, the failure of standard money demand equations to systematically account for a significant part of variation in M3 in the euro area over the past decade has created a need for judgmental analysis and associated adjustments to M3.[52] Its 2003 clarification of the "monetary pillar" emphasized that structural

---

[50] For instance, according to Friedman and Kuttner (1996), the Federal Reserve targeted money mainly during 1975–1982, in the sense that it varied either the federal funds rate or non-borrowed reserves (whichever, was the policy instrument at the time) in response to observed fluctuations or either M1 or M2 that departed from the corresponding stated targets.

[51] Some argue that money remains important for central banks to control the overnight interbank interest rate, but Woodford (2003) maintains that the achievement of the central bank's interest target does not require any quantity adjustments through open-market operations in response to deviations of the market rate from the target rate.

[52] According to ECB staff, augmenting money demand equations after they have proven unstable over time should be seen as providing ex post support for the judgmental adjustment of M3 rather than a plausible alternative framework for making that judgmental assessment in real time (Fischer et al., 2008).

changes in financial markets and in the composition of wealth due to the increased sophistication of private investors may constitute a source of uncertainty regarding the definition of the monetary aggregate relevant for inflation. The ECB also highlighted that gaining a thorough understanding of the interdependencies between M3 and its counterparts in the consolidated balance sheet of the monetary financial institutions (MFI) sector was seen as instrumental in judging whether observed changes in money growth may, or may not bear implications for price trends later on. Accordingly, the ECB expanded its detailed component-based monetary analysis and offered further insight into some of the tools and frameworks used to conduct monetary analysis.[53] Adjustments to M3 may reflect statistical, technical or economic changes or developments and rely on a detailed analysis of the monetary aggregates, their components and counterparts, as recorded in the consolidated balance sheet of the euro area MFI sector.

3.5.2.1 M3 Adjustments due to Statistical and Technical Factors

M3 adjustments due to statistical and technical factors mainly reflect changes in the monetary operations framework and improvements in measurement of the M3. For example, non-resident holdings of money market funds issued by euro-area MFIs were initially included in M3 because they are difficult to measure. M3 was subsequently revised to exclude these holdings after sufficiently reliable estimation methods for this component had been developed. The introduction of remunerated reserve requirements in several countries at the start of Stage III of EMU meant a technical adjustment to the monetary operations framework that may have led to repatriation of funds and temporarily elevated levels of M3 growth. While some of these adjustments may have temporarily complicated monetary analysis and its communication to the public, most were small and the transition to corrected measures of M3 was smooth.

3.5.2.2 Portfolio Shifts

During 2001–2003, there was a broad-based slowdown in economic growth in advanced economies. Sentiment was depressed further following the terrorist attacks that occurred in the US in September 2001. In the US, economic output fell in early 2001 and subsequently in the euro area in 2003. At the same time, broad money growth accelerated markedly in the euro area and peaked at about 9% in May 2003. Interestingly, broad money growth in the US decelerated sharply after reaching its peak in November 2001 (see Fig. 3.6).

The ECB staff provided several discussions of the elevated M3 growth rates observed during 2001–2003, concluding that portfolio shifts reflecting euro area

[53] See, the ECB's Monetary Bulletins from October 2004 and July 2007.

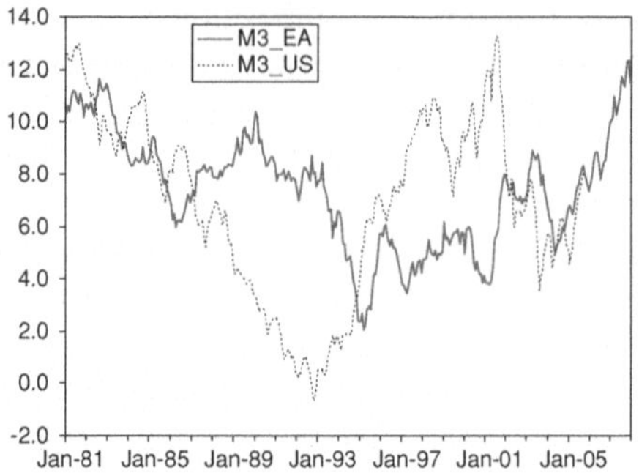

Fig. 3.6 Annual broad money growth in the US and in the euro area. Source: IMF

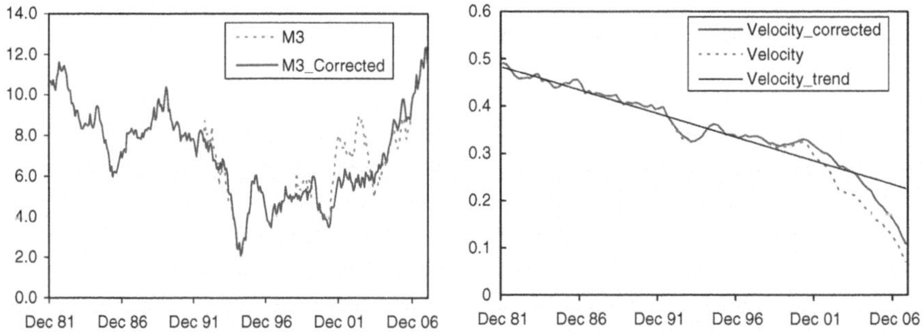

Fig. 3.7 Annual M3 growth and M3 velocity (in logs) and its trend, with and without portfolio adjustment. Sources: ECB, IMF calculations

residents' strong demand for highly liquid domestic assets were mainly responsible for the temporary surge in M3 growth.[54] According to the ECB (Monthly Bulletin January 2005, p. 13), the period of exceptional economic and financial uncertainty between 2001 and 2003 led to a strong preference by investors for liquid assets. The associated portfolio shifts were reflected in high M3 growth (Fig. 3.7).

While this assessment appears perfectly reasonable, there are a number of competing explanations (Faruqee, 2005)—and it remains unclear how to discriminate among them on the basis of a disaggregated monetary analysis alone. First, there is the question of why M3 growth in the US, where much of the economic and financial uncertainty during this period had originated, sharply decelerated during 2002–2003, following a surge that started in 1993 (Fig. 3.6). Second, the fact that the euro dollar exchange rate fell to its all time low during

[54] See, for example, ECB Monthly Bulletins May 2003, October 2004, and January 2005.

this period but has since appreciated strongly may indicate a link between US liquidity and money and price developments in the euro area.[55] Third, as Faruqee (2005) points out, the increasingly important international role of the euro could also have had implications for velocity and money demand. Finally, according to the ECB's own analysis, M3 dynamics during 2001–2003 were associated in large part with transactions involving non-residents, thereby focusing attention on international financial flows.[56] But if there had been a change in the home bias for financial assets, M3 developments should have been symmetric across advanced countries. Possibly, a change in exchange rate expectations may have played a role. In the end, a detailed discussion of banks' balance sheet items with little attention paid to prices, including exchange rates, or other variables may not be very helpful in adding structure to this analysis.

That portfolio-shifts were but one of the factors driving the post-2001 surge in M3 growth is also obvious from the limited impact of the ECB's judgmental adjustments on velocity. As Fig. 3.7 reveals, M3 growth corrected by the ECB for portfolio shifts was lower during 2001–2003 than unadjusted figures suggested and the adjustments smoothed the sharp deviation from the steady downward trend in velocity. Fischer et al. (2008) and Pill and Rautanen (2006) have stressed the importance of these corrections, in particular during 2001–2003, for improving the inflation forecasting properties of simple, single equation models that feature money and inflation. However, over the past years no further adjustments have been publicly discussed by the ECB, and eventually the corrected M3 growth and velocity have shown the same structural break as the uncorrected data.[57]

3.5.2.3 Securitization

Another recent topic featuring with some prominence in the ECB's disaggregated analysis is securitization—but its overall impact on monetary analysis has been low so far. During 2004–2007, when M3 surged, securitization growth also accelerated dramatically (see Box 3.1).[58] While it is not immediately clear as to why developments that primarily affect the composition of banks' assets should have any impact on money demand or income velocity of money, securitization may have contributed to increasing further the distortions of the empirically small signal from money to prices. The ECB (ECB 2008, p. 91) concludes that "the overall impact of loan securitization on money and credit aggregates is not

[55] Berger and Harjes (2009) find a potential link between global liquidity, primarily determined by US liquidity, and euro area inflation.

[56] See ECB (2004b), p.49.

[57] See Faruqee (2005) for a more formal treatment of the question of structural breaks in euro area velocity.

[58] Securitization may broadly be defined as the process of converting a pool of designated financial assets into tradable securities backed by cash flows of the assets and their underlying collateral (see European Securitization Forum, 1999; ECB, 2008).

Box 3.1 Securitization and the bank lending channel

Securitization has likely affected the role money may play in the economy and may have increased further the distortions of the empirically small signal from money to prices. The bank-lending channel asserts a direct link between central bank money and bank loan supply, which in turn affects demand, output and prices (see Sect. 3.3.3).[59] Diamond and Rajan (2006) highlight the three key assumptions usually underlying the bank lending channel: (a) binding reserve requirements that limit the issuance of bank deposits; (b) banks cannot easily replace deposit funding with other sources, such as new equity issues or other forms of short-term debt; (c) some borrowers cannot substitute bank loans with other forms of finance. The virtual elimination of reserve requirements has led many to believe that the importance of the bank lending channel has likely diminished over time. Diamond and Rajan (2006) show, however, that even without reserve requirements money may play an important role in the banking sector but assumptions (b) and (c) remain critical.

In the euro area, deposit funding, on average, remains the main funding source for banks, but other funding sources seem to become more important. From December 1998 to December 2007, the ratio of overnight deposits and short-term deposits with a maturity of less than 3 months to other financial bank liabilities against the private sector fell from 64 to 52%. In particular, the issuance of short-term debt securities rose sharply, albeit from a low level.

Securitization has also affected the business model of commercial banks and has likely lowered the share of bank-dependent borrowers in some countries. Banks can now securitize and sell some of their loans on to the market and rather originate and distribute loans instead of engaging in maturity transformation and credit creation. Accordingly, securitization is raising the degree of substitutability of bank loans with other forms of finance. ECB staff and others estimate that, in 2007, the annual growth rate of total loans originated by MFIs may have been 1–2 percentage points higher than the growth rate of traditional bank loans (about 11% in 2007) which were not sold on to the market.[60]

Over time, financial innovation, including securitization, is likely to further diminish the relative importance of the bank lending channel. As already emphasized by Romer and Romer (1992), it has become much easier for banks to raise funds other than deposits over the past decades. Loutskina and Strahan (2008) find that in the US securitization has weakened the link from bank funding conditions to credit supply. Bernanke (2007) states that in the US today the traditional bank-lending channel seems unlikely to be quantitatively important but may still be operative in economies that remain relatively more bank-dependent. However, recent research by Altunbas, Gambacorta and Marques (2007) found that securitization has also significantly reduced the importance of the bank lending channel in the euro area.

easy to quantify…Many different financing and investment transactions are presumably occurring simultaneously and may cancel each other out in terms of their impact on M3, but, if they take place at different points in time, they may lead to some short-term volatility in M3 developments". As a consequence, possible effects of securitization on M3 have not been captured in the ECB's corrected M3 series.

[59] It is important to reiterate that money does not affect prices directly according the bank lending channel but through its impact on demand and output (see Bernanke and Gertler, 1995).

[60] ECB (2008, p. 91) and Altunbas et al. (2007). Gross euro area securitization issuance of about euro 300 billion amounts to roughly 2 percentage points but not all of this was passed on by banks via "true sales", or sold on to the market at all.

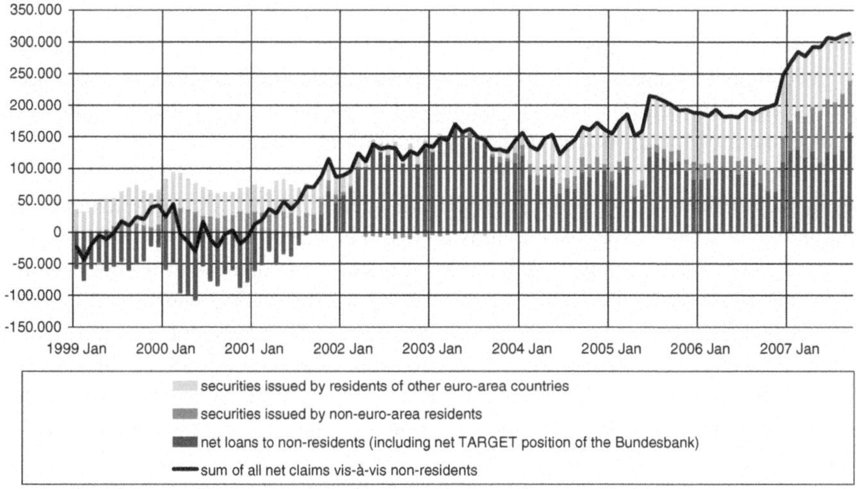

Fig. 3.8 Decomposition of net-assets of German banks vis-à-vis non-residents (annual flows, billion of euros). Source: Reischle (2007)

However, the discussion of securitization points to another possible function of a disaggregate perspective on monetary developments outside the realm of the core monetary strategy: disaggregate monetary analysis may provide useful input into the ECB's assessment of financial stability. The recent financial turmoil surrounding the so-called subprime crisis is predominantly reflecting problems with assets securitized in the US, but it is possible that a disaggregated analysis of M3 and its counterparts may have provided some early warning signs of potential problems at euro-area banks.

For example, in late 2006/early 2007 the amount on German banks' balance sheets of securities issued by non-euro-area residents suddenly rose sharply (Fig. 3.8). A plausible conjecture is that this surge also reflected the increasing inability of some German banks to hold these securities in off-balance sheet vehicles due to rising funding pressure. This example and its hypothesis may prove wrong at closer inspection but it illustrates the potential use of disaggregated monetary analysis for financial stability considerations.

3.5.3 Summary

Secular changes in the economy due to financial innovation and integration seriously complicate the systematic use of the ECB's M3-based reference value concept. Empirical specifications of money demand or the income velocity of money have become increasingly unstable over time and that trend, already highly visible in the US, is likely to continue in the euro area as well. The ECB, which seems to share this assessment, has turned to judgmental adjustments of M3 to preserve any information M3 growth might hold with regard to future price developments. These adjustments have played a crucial role in the ECB's disaggregated monetary analysis, which encompasses a detailed analysis of monetary aggregates, their components and counterparts, as recorded in the consolidated balance sheet of the euro area monetary financial institutions.

Not unlike the stability of money demand functions, however, reliable judgmental adjustment of monetary aggregates is increasingly difficult to achieve. In principle, one should expect such adjustments to be targeting obvious, unique, and relatively short lived technical or behavioral phenomena that either do not require or do not allow structural modeling. But financial innovation and integration as well as technological advance—which are among the likely forces underlying recent surges in M3 growth—are unlikely to satisfy these requirements. Moreover, their unpredictable and erratic character and their, often complex, effects on monetary aggregates make real time adjustments to these aggregates a formidable task.

A case in point is the judgmental ECB correction of portfolio shifts in the euro area during 2001–2003 and the absence of further corrections afterwards. While the ECB may indeed have corrected portfolio effects on M3 in a timely and accurate fashion, these adjustments did little to alter the medium-run instability of velocity. It remains unclear, for example, to which degree more recent financial phenomena like securitization are behind the more recent surge in euro-area M3 growth and decline in velocity. In the absence of any such adjustments, however, the indicator quality of M3 growth for medium- to long-term inflation remains doubtful.

That said, in particular the ongoing debate on the role of securitization points to a separate (or possibly alternative) function of a disaggregate perspective on monetary developments. The detailed analysis of monetary components and counterparts in the consolidated balance sheet of euro area monetary banks and other financial institutions may provide useful input into the ECB's assessment of financial stability.

3.6 How Time Path Dependent Should the ECB's Monetary Strategy Be?

Economic theory suggests that a central bank's reputation is crucial to anchor private sector inflation expectations.[61] In the presence of nominal rigidities, firms will set relative prices under uncertainty about the development of the general price level, which (at least in part) depends on monetary policy. If the central bank

---

[61] See, among others, Kydland and Prescott (1977) and Fudenberg and Maskin (1986) for important contributions to the literature on reputation and the so-called inflation bias. Clarida et al. (1999), and Woodford (2003) discuss the related problem of a stabilization bias.

is credible in its commitment to keep inflation low, the price setting of the private sector will reflect this commitment and equilibrium inflation will be low as well. In a repeated game (and in reality price setting certainly qualifies as a repeated activity) the credibility of the central bank will critically depend on its own past actions or reputation—and here a certain institutional time-path dependency can be an advantage.

For the ECB, quickly establishing high inflation-fighting credentials may have been particularly important—and linking its monetary strategy to that of the German Bundesbank proved helpful in this regard. Speed was critical simply because the ECB was a new institution without an established track record or reputation. Further urgency was added by the fact that the ECB stepped on the stage during a time of intensive structural change caused by the transformation of euro area institutions before 1999 and the introduction of the common currency (ECB, 1999; Jaeger, 2003). As a result, the uncertainties about typical shocks hitting the area, their propagation, and the monetary transmission mechanism increased. As Issing (2006, p. 3) emphasizes, this type of uncertainty was among the arguments behind the ECB's decision to stress the continuity of its policy framework with "the best performers of national central banks participating in monetary union, and especially with the Bundesbank".[62]

To that end, the ECB's monetary strategy announced in late 1998 included a strong reference to the German central bank's monetary targeting framework. While the ECB stopped well short of establishing announcing an intermediate money growth target (see Sect. 3.2), it did little to downplay the importance of the "monetary pillar" in its communication with the public. For example, answering a question on the relative importance of the "two pillars", ECB President Duisenberg noted that "it is not a coincidence that I have used the words that money will play a prominent role. So if you call it the two pillars, one pillar is thicker than the other is, or stronger than the other, but how much I couldn't tell you".[63]

The question is, however, whether fidelity to Bundesbank principles is still required on reputational grounds. There are no compelling arguments that support such a case. Clearly, the ECB's own reputation as an inflation-averse central bank is now well established, with long-run inflation expectations in the euro area more firmly anchored than in the United States (Beechey, Johannsen, & Levin, 2008), and there is reason to suspect that the ECB's credibility does not rest

[62] It is interesting to note that the Bundesbank was in a similar situation at the onset of the European Monetary System (EMS) in 1979, when several of members of its council were initially directly in favor of abandoning monetary targeting strategy. However, as von Hagen (1999) writes, later on they acknowledged the importance of "the high reputation the strategy had gained the Bank abroad" and supported the strategy, recognizing that its abandoning "the time when the new EMS was beginning to operate would create the impression that the Bundesbank was giving up on its efforts to maintain price stability and would fuel inflation expectations".

[63] See Issing (2006, p. 2) and Jaeger (2003). A certain overplaying of the importance of monetary targeting in actual decision-making was also part of the Bundesbank's monetary strategy (see, for instance, Posen, 2000).

predominantly on the "monetary pillar." In fact, since 1998, the ECB decreased the weight it attached to money in its monetary strategy along a number of dimensions. At an institutional level, the subtle downgrading of the importance of money in the ECB's monetary strategy after the 2003 monetary policy evaluation has markedly increased the difference between the ECB's and the Bundesbank's monetary strategy (see Sect. 3.2). In addition, Berger, De Haan and Sturm (2010) provide evidence that the ECB has paid continuously less attention to the monetary analysis in its words and deeds. Based on a content-analysis of the Governing Council's introductory statements for its post-meeting press conferences, they show that the overall policy inclinations communicated by the Governing Council became increasingly less correlated with the monetary analysis contained in the statements. The same holds with regard to interest rate decisions.

As a consequence, ECB observers and financial markets have stopped to attach much weight to the ECB's monetary analysis. For example, Geraats, Giavazzi and Wyplosz (2008, p.13) point out that, despite the 2003 modification in the monetary strategy, "there remains much uncertainty regarding the role of the long-term, monetary pillar," and, in light of the noisiness of the monetary analysis, many ECB watchers and the media seem to focus more on the economic analysis. Other studies show that financial markets have ceased paying attention to Governing Council's communications regarding monetary analysis and react mostly to price news, or the economic analysis. In particular, based on the analysis of high-frequency interest rate data for horizons of up to 12 months, Lamla and Rupprecht (2006) find that the ECB's comments on price developments—which tend to be based on its economic analysis—during the press conference after Governing Council meetings are strongly reflected in financial market activity controlling for other determinants, while there is no discernible reaction whatsoever to the ECB's interpretation of developments in monetary aggregates.[64] Conrad and Lamla (2007) show that, based on the high-frequency response of the euro–US dollar exchange rate, ECB information on price developments are considered news by forex market participants, but that the ECB's assessments of developments in the monetary sector are not.

According to recent ECB research, a broadly similar picture emerges from the financial market reaction to the monthly release of M3 data. On the one hand, looking at intraday market reactions across the yield curve, Coffinet and Gouteron (2007) report that market rates between a horizon of 1 and 5 years react significantly to M3 growth surprises over their full sample period from November 2000 to November 2006. However, as in Lamla and Rupprecht (2006) there is no significant impact on interest rates at shorter horizons and, somewhat unexpectedly perhaps given the longer-run nature of the ECB's monetary analysis framework, at horizons beyond 5 years. And, even more importantly, Coffinet and Gouteron (2007) show

[64] Their basic setup is a regression of the change in the Euribor rate on the post-meeting policy rate surprise (i.e., the difference between the actual post-meeting policy rate and the expected rate) and a communication indicator based on Berger et al. (2010).

that across all interest rate horizons the impact of M3 news has dramatically decreased over time, essentially becoming insignificant before or around the time of the ECB's monetary strategy clarification in 2003. The authors explain the fact that financial markets stopped listening to M3 announcements, in part, by a learning process, arguing that by 2003 market participants had understood that per ECB strategy changes in M3 had no immediate and mechanical impact on present policy rates. Of course, the results also imply that, in addition, markets concluded that there was little systematic information to be extracted from M3 about medium- or longer-term ECB actions and their impact on interest rates either.[65]

In summary, there is little reason to expect that among sophisticated investors and observers further changes in the role of the monetary analysis within the ECB's wider monetary strategy will have significant impact on the ECB's reputation as a price-stability oriented central bank. Whether it might have an impact among the broader public in countries that prior to EMU also ran on a two-pillar system is a question that has not been addressed in the literature. But there are few reasons to believe that it would, provided the transition is well managed and takes place during a period of price stability. The bottom line is that institutional time path dependency should matter less today than in 1998 or even 2003.

3.7 Conclusions

Money plays an important role in the ECB's monetary policy strategy. The prime function of monetary analysis today is to provide a so-called cross-check of the outcome of the economic analysis. The continued explicit reliance on money to guide monetary policy is a distinguishing feature of the ECB's framework compared to that of other central banks.

In practice, the implementation of the money-based element of the ECB's policy strategy has been challenging. In particular, the repeated surges of nominal M3 growth beyond the ECB's reference value have made it increasingly difficult for outside observers to understand the transmission of monetary analysis into policy action. The problem is that velocity is not constant and money is not fully exogenous. As a result, financial markets appear to put less and less weight on the signals from the monetary analysis, focusing mostly on the economic analysis. Providing a clear, consistent, and unified narrative about the role of money in the economy seems essential to improve on this state of affairs.

The analysis in this chapter suggests that there is a strong case for presenting monetary and economic analysis using a unified framework, thereby affording monetary analysis a continued role in the ECB's overall monetary strategy. An

[65] In a related result, Bulíř, Čihák and Šmídková (2008) report that there are indications that information on the ECB's policy inclination based on the "monetary pillar" is frequently out of sync with other signals send by the ECB, including the staff's inflation forecast, press releases, or monthly bulletins.

exclusive focus on non-monetary (or "economic", in ECB parlance) factors alone may leave euro-area policy makers with an incomplete picture of the economy. However, treating monetary factors as a separate matter, using potentially inferior partial-equilibrium tools to cross-check the implications of the "economic pillar", is a second-best solution to this problem. Instead, a general-equilibrium inspired analytical framework that merges the two "pillars" of the ECB's monetary strategy appears the most promising way forward. Of course, just as the current "monetary pillar" is not explicitly linked to a particular partial equilibrium model, the merged framework will not be reduced to a specific general equilibrium model either. However, it would provide a better framework to study the interaction of money with other economic variables, including, for example, asset prices or financial sector variables, and their relations with consumer prices.

However, the evidence presented in this chapter suggests that the role played by money in such unified framework may be rather limited. From a forecasting viewpoint, for example, money contains relevant information for inflation but its value-added is often small. In addition, non-monetary models generally provide better inflation forecasts than money-based models. This, of course, is not to deny that disaggregate monitoring of monetary/financial variables may be very helpful with regard to other economic or financial stability issues.

Overall, the current state of affairs could, over time, gradually detract from the credibility of the ECB and undermine potential benefits from improved monetary analysis in the future. While there is potentially much to be gained from further work on monetary analysis, it appears more productive to refine the monetary strategy in the context of a unified framework.

References

Alesina, A., Blanchard, O., Galí, J., Giavazzi, F., & Uhlig, H. (2001a). *Defining a macroeconomic framework for the euro area*. Monitoring the European Central Bank No. 3. London: CEPR.

Alesina, A., Blanchard, O., Galí, J., Giavazzi, F., & Uhlig, H. (2001b). *MECB update*. London: CEPR.

Altunbas, Y., Gambacorta, L., & Marques, D. (2007). Securitization and the bank lending channel. ECB Working Paper No. 838.

Andrés, J., López-Salido, D., & Nelson, E. (2007). Money and the natural rate of interest: structural estimates for the UK, the US and the euro area. Federal Reserve Bank of St. Louis Working Paper Series No. 2007–05A.

Andrés, J., López-Salido, D., & Vallés, J. (2006). Money in an estimated business cycle model of the euro area. *The Economic Journal, 116*, 457–477.

Angeloni, I., Kashyap, A., Mojon, B., & Terlizzese, D. (2002). Monetary transmission in the euro area: where do we stand? ECB Working Paper No. 114.

Aoki, K. (2006). Optimal commitment policy under noisy information. *Journal of Economic Dynamics and Control, 30*(1), 81–109.

Ashley, R., Granger, C. W. J., & Schmalensee, R. (1980). Advertising and aggregate consumption: an analysis of causality. *Econometrica, 48*, 1149–1167.

Assenmacher-Wesche, K., & Gerlach, S. (2006a). Interpreting euro area inflation at high and low frequencies. BIS Working Paper No. 195.

Assenmacher-Wesche, K., & Gerlach, S. (2006b). Understanding the link between money growth and inflation in the euro area. mimeo.

Assenmacher-Wesche, K., Gerlach, S., & Sekine, T. (2007). Monetary factors and inflation in Japan. mimeo.

Backhus, D., & Kehoe, P. (1992). International evidence of the historical properties of business cycles. *American Economic Review, 82*(4), 864–888.

Beck, G., & Wieland, V. (2007a). Money in monetary policy design under uncertainty: a formal characterization of ECB-style cross-checking. *Journal of the European Economic Association, 5*(2–3), 524–533.

Beck, G., & Wieland, V. (2007b). Money in monetary policy design under uncertainty: the two-pillar Phillips curve versus ECB-style cross-checking. mimeo.

Beechey, M. J., Johannsen, B. K., & Levin, A. T. (2008). Are long-run inflation expectations anchored more firmly in the euro area than in the United States? Finance and Economics Discussion Series, Federal Reserve Board, Washington, DC.

Benati, L. (2005). Long-run evidence on money growth and inflation. *Bank of England Quarterly Bulletin*, Autumn, 349–355.

Benhabib, J., Schmitt-Grohe, S., & Uribe, M. (2001a). Monetary policy and multiple equilibria. *American Economic Review, 91*(1), 167–186.

Benhabib, J., Schmitt-Grohe, S., & Uribe, M. (2001b). The perils of Taylor rules. *Journal of Economic Theory, 96*(1), 40–69.

Berger, H., De Haan, J., & Sturm, J.-E. (2010). Does money matter in the ECB strategy? New evidence based on ECB communication. *International Journal of Finance and Economics*, forthcoming.

Berger, H., & Harjes, T. (2009). Does global liquidity matter for monetary policy in the euro area? *International Finance, 12*(1), 33–55.

Berger, H., & Österholm, P. (2008a). Does money growth granger-cause inflation in the euro area? Evidence from out-of-sample forecasts using Bayesian VARs. *Economic Record*, forthcoming.

Berger, H., & Österholm, P. (2008b). Does money matter for U.S. inflation? Evidence from Bayesian VARs. IMF Working Paper No. 08/76.

Berger, H., & Stavrev, E. (2008). The information content of money in forecasting euro area inflation. IMF Working Paper No. 08/166.

Bernanke, B. (2007). The financial accelerator and the credit channel, speech at the credit channel of monetary policy in the twenty-first century conference. Federal Reserve Bank of Atlanta, June 15. Available at: http://www.federalreserve.gov/newsevents/speech/bernanke20070615a.htm.

Bernanke, B., & Blinder, A. (1988). Credit, money, and aggregate demand. *American Economic Review, 78*, 435–439.

Bernanke, B., & Gertler, M. (1995). Inside the black box: the credit channel of monetary policy transmission. *Journal of Economic Perspectives, 9*(4), 27–48.

Bernanke, B., Gertler, M., & Gilchrist, S. (1996). The financial accelerator in a quantitative business cycle framework. *Review of Economics and Statistics, 78*(1), 1–15.

Bernanke, B., Laubach, T., Mishkin, F. S., & Posen, A. S. (1999). *Inflation targeting: lessons from the international experience*. Princeton: Princeton University Press.

Beyer, A., & Reichlin, L. (2008). The role of money—money and monetary policy in the twenty-first century. In: A. Beyer, L. Reichlin (Eds.), *Proceedings of the 4th ECB central banking conference*, 9–10 November 2006. Frankfurt: ECB.

Bini-Smaghi, L., & Gros, D. (2000). *Open issues in European central banking*. London: Macmillan Press.

Bloomberg (2007). Trichet, Noyer split over money supply clouds ECB rate outlook. Online News Report, 4 June. Available at: http://www.bloomberg.com/apps/news?pid=20601109&sid=a.JaL_23jXV0&refer=home#.

Boone, L., Mikol, F., & van den Noord, P. (2004). Wealth effects on money demand in EMU: econometric evidence. OECD Economics Department Working Paper No. 411.

Bordes, C., & Clerc, L. (2007). Price stability and the ECB's monetary policy strategy. *Journal of Economic Surveys, 21*(2), 268–325.

Bordes, C., Clerc, L., & Marimoutou, V. (2007). Is there a structural break in equilibrium velocity in the euro area. Notes D'Études Et De Recherche, NER–E165.

Brand, C., Reimers, H., & Seitz, F. (2003). Forecasting real GDP: what role for narrow money? In O. Issing (Ed.), *Background studies for the ECB's evaluation of its monetary policy strategy* (pp. 302–333). Frankfurt: European Central Bank.

Bruggeman, A., Donato, P., & Warne, A. (2003). Is the demand for euro area M3 stable? In O. Issing (Ed.), *Background studies for the ECB's evaluation of its monetary policy strategy* (pp. 246–300). Frankfurt: European Central Bank.

Bulíř, A., Čihák, M., & Šmídková, K. (2008). Writing clearly: ECB's monetary policy communication. IMF Working Paper No. 08/252.

Bundesbank. (2005). The relationship between money and prices. Monthly report, 13–24 Jan 2005. Deutsche: Bundesbank.

Calza, A., Gerdesmeier, D., & Levy, J. (2001). Euro area money demand: measuring the opportunity cost appropriately. IMF Working Paper No. 179/01.

Calza, A., & Sousa, J. (2003). Why has broad money demand been more stable in the euro area than in other economies? A literature review. In O. Issing (Ed.), *Background studies for the ECB's evaluation of its monetary policy strategy* (pp. 229–243). Frankfurt: European Central Bank.

Carlstrom, C., & Fuerst, T. (2002). Taylor rules in a model that satisfies the natural-rate hypothesis. *American Economic Review, 92*(2), 79–84.

Christiano, L., Eichenbaum, M., & Evans, C. (1998). Monetary policy shocks: what have we learned and to what end? In J. Taylor, M. Woodford (Eds.), *Handbook of macroeconomics* (pp. 65–148), Vol. 1. Amsterdam: Elsevier.

Christiano, L., Eichenbaum, M., & Evans, C. (2005). Nominal rigidities and the dynamic effects of a shock to monetary policy. *Journal of Political Economy, 113*(1), 1–45.

Christiano, L., & Fitzgerald, T. (2003). Inflation and monetary policy in the 20th century. Economic perspectives (Federal Reserve Bank of Chicago) 1Q, 21–45.

Christiano, L., Motto, R., & Rostagno, M. (2008). Two reasons why money and credit may be useful in monetary policy. In: A. Beyer, L. Reichlin (Eds.), *The role of money—money and monetary policy in the twenty-first century. Proceedings of the 4th ECB central banking conference* (pp. 28–55), 9–10 November 2006. Frankfurt: ECB.

Christiano, L., & Rostagno, M. (2001). Money growth monitoring and the Taylor rule. NBER Working Paper No. 8539.

Clarida, R., Galí, J., & Gertler, M. (1999). The science of monetary policy: a New Keynesian perspective. *Journal of Economic Literature, 37*(4), 1661–1707.

Coenen, G., Levin, A., & Wieland, V. (2005). Data uncertainty and the role of money as an informational variable for monetary policy. *European Economic Review, 49*(4), 975–1006.

Coffinet, J., & Gouteron, S. (2007). Euro area market reactions to the monetary developments press release. ECB Working Paper No. 792.

Conrad, C., & Lamla, M. J. (2007). The high-frequency response of the EUR-US dollar exchange rate to ECB monetary policy announcements. KOF (Swiss Economic Institute) Working Paper No. 07-174.

Cukierman, A. (2001). Accountability, credibility, transparency, and stabilization in the eurosystem. In C. Wyplosz (Ed.), *The impact of EMU on Europe and the developing countries* (pp. 40–75). Oxford: Oxford University Press.

D'Agostino, A., Giannone, D., & Surico, P. (2006). (Un)Predictability and macroeconomic stability. ECB Working Paper No. 605.

De Grauwe, P., & Polan, M. (2005). Is inflation always and everywhere a monetary phenomenon? *Scandinavian Journal of Economics, 107*(2), 239–59.

De Haan, J., Eijffinger, S. C. W., & Waller, S. (2005). *The European Central Bank credibility, transparency, and centralization*. Cambridge, MA: MIT Press.

Diamond, D., & Rajan, R. (2001). Liquidity risk, liquidity creation, and financial fragility: a theory of banking. *Journal of Political Economy, 109*(2), 287–327.

Diamond, D., & Rajan, R. (2006). Money in a theory of banking. *American Economic Review, 96*(1), 30–53.
Dotsey, M., & Hornstein, A. (2003). Should monetary policy makers look at money? *Journal of Monetary Economics, 50*(3), 547–579.
Dow, J. (2007). Weber warnt vor Aufgabe der monetären Säule in EZB-Strategie. Online News Report, 29 May. Available at: http://www.djnewswires.de/news.php?id=11134.
Dreger, C., & Wolters, J. (2006). Investigating M3 money demand in the euro area—new evidence based on standard models. DIW Berlin Discussion Papers No. 561.
Ehrmann, M., Gambacorta, L., Martinez-Pages, J., Sevestre, P., & Worms, A. (2003). Financial systems and the role of banks in monetary policy transmission in the euro area. In I. Angeloni, A. Kashyap, B. Mojon (Eds.), *Monetary policy transmission in the euro area: a study by the eurosystem monetary transmission network* (pp. 235–269). Cambridge: Cambridge University Press.
Ericsson, N. (1998). Empirical modeling of money demand. *Empirical Economics, 23*(3), 295–315.
European Central Bank. (1998). A stability-oriented monetary policy strategy for the ESCB. Press release, 13 October 1998. Available at: http://www.ecb.int/press/pr/date/1998/html/pr981013_1.en.html.
European Central Bank. (1999). The stability-oriented monetary policy strategy of the eurosystem. *Monthly Bulletin*, January, 39–50.
European Central Bank. (2001). The monetary policy of the ECB. ECB: Frankfurt.
European Central Bank. (2003a). The outcome of the ECB's evaluation of its monetary policy strategy. *Monthly Bulletin*, June, 79–90.
European Central Bank. (2003b). The ECB's monetary policy strategy. Press release, 8 May 2003. Available at: http://www.ecb.int/press/pr/date/2003/html/pr030508_2.en.html#.
European Central Bank (2004a). *The monetary policy of the ECB*, 2nd edn. ECB: Frankfurt
European Central Bank. (2004b). Monetary analysis in real time. *Monthly Bulletin*, February, 43–66.
European Central Bank. (2008). Securitisation in the euro area. *Monthly Bulletin*, February, 81–94.
European Securitization Forum. (1999). european securitization: a resource guide. Available at: http://www.europeansecuritisation.com/esfPubs.shtml.
Faruqee, H. (2005). Declining money velocity in the euro area: implications for the ECB's monetary analysis (pp. 32–61). IMF Country Report No. 05/266.
Fatás, A., Mihov, I., & Rose, A. (2007). Quantitative goals for monetary policy. *Journal of Money, Credit, and Banking, 39*(5), 1163–1176.
Ferrero, G., Nobili, A., & Passiglia, P. (2007). The sector distribution of money supply in the euro area. Banca D'Italia, Temi Di Discussione Del Servizio Studi No. 627.
Fischer, B., Lenza, M., Pill, H., & Reichlin, L. (2008). Money and monetary policy: the ECB experience 1999–2006. In A. Beyer, L. Reichlin (Eds.), *The role of money—money and monetary policy in the twenty-first century. Proceedings of the 4th ECB central banking conference* (pp. 102–175), 9–10 November 2006, ECB: Frankfurt.
Friedman, B. M., & Kuttner, K. N. (1996). A price target for U.S. monetary policy? Lessons from the experience with money growth targets. *Brookings Papers on Economic Activity,* 1:77–146.
Fudenberg, D., & Maskin, E. (1986). Folk theorems for repeated games with discounting or incomplete information. *Econometrica, 54*(3), 533–54.
Fuhrer, J. (2000). Habit formation in consumption and its implications for monetary—policy models. *American Economic Review, 90*(3), 367–90.
Galí, J. (2008). Comment. In: A. Beyer, L. Reichlin (Eds.), *The role of money—money and monetary policy in the twenty-first century. Proceedings of the 4th ECB central banking conference* (pp. 182–189), 9–10 November 2006. ECB: Frankfurt.
Galí, J., Gerlach, S., Rotemberg, J., Uhlig, H., & Woodford, M. (2004). *The monetary policy strategy of the ECB reconsidered.* Monitoring the European Central Bank No. 5. CEPR: London.
Galí, J., & Gertler, M. (2007). Macroeconomic modeling for monetary policy evaluation. Universitat Pompeu Fabra Department of Economics and Business Working Papers No. 1039.

Geraats, P., Giavazzi, F., & Wyplosz, C. (2008). *Transparency and governance*. Monitoring the European Central Bank No. 6. CEPR: London.
Gerlach, S. (2004). The two pillars of the European Central Bank, *Economic Policy,* 40, October, 389–439.
Gerlach, S., & Svensson, L. (2003). Money and inflation in the euro area: a case for monetary indicators? *Journal of Monetary Economics, 50*(8), 1649–1672.
Golinelli, R., & Pastorello, S. (2002). Modeling the demand for M3 in the euro area. *European Journal of Finance, 8*(4), 371–401.
Goodfriend, M. (2000). Overcoming the zero bound on interest rate policy. *Journal of Money, Credit, and Banking, 32*(4), 1007–1035.
Goodfriend, M., & McCallum, B. (2007). Banking and interest rates in monetary policy analysis: a quantitative exploration. *Journal of Monetary Economics, 54*(5), 1480–1507.
Greiber, C., & Lemke, W. (2005). Money demand and macroeconomic uncertainty. Deutsche Bundesbank Discussion Paper No. 26/2005.
Greiber, C., & Setzer, R. (2007). Money and housing—evidence for the euro area and the US. Deutsche Bundesbank Discussion Paper No. 12/2007.
Hallman, J., Porter, R., & Small, D. (1991). Is the price level tied to the M2 monetary aggregate in the long run? *The American Economic Review, 81*(4), 841–58.
Hofmann, B. (2008). Do monetary indicators lead euro area inflation? ECB Working Paper No. 867.
Ireland, P. (2001). The real balance effect. NBER Working Paper No. 8136.
Ireland, P. (2004). Money's role in the monetary business cycle. *Journal of Money, Credit, and Banking, 36*(6), 969–983.
Issing, O. (2001). The euro area and the single monetary policy. Österreichische Nationalbank Working Paper No. 44.
Issing, O. (2003). In I. Angeloni, V. Gaspar, H. Klöckers, K. Masuch, S. Nicoletti-Altimari, M. Rostagno, F. Smets (Eds.), *Background studies for the ECB's evaluation of its monetary policy strategy*. ECB: Frankfurt.
Issing, O. (2006). The ECB's monetary policy strategy: why did we choose a two pillar approach? Available at: www.ecb.int/events/pdf/conferences/cbc4/Issing.pdf.
Issing, O., Gaspar, V., Angeloni, I., & Tristani, O. (2001). *Monetary policy in the euro area, strategy and decision-making at the European Central Bank.* Cambridge: Cambridge University Press.
Jaeger, A. (2003). The ECB's money pillar: an assessment. IMF Working Paper No. 03/82.
Jones, B., & Stracca, L. (2006). Are money and consumption additively separable in the euro area? A non-parametric approach. ECB Working Paper No. 704.
Kahn, G., & Benolkin, S. (2007). The role of money in monetary policy: why do the Fed and the ECB see it so differently? *Federal Reserve Bank of Kansas City Economic Review,* Third Quarter, 5–36.
Kremer, J., Lombardo, G., & Werner, T. (2003). Money in a new-Keynesian model estimated with German data. Deutsche Bundesbank Discussion Paper No. 15/2003.
Kydland, F., & Prescott, E. (1977). Rules rather than discretion: the inconsistency of optimal plans. *Journal of Political Economy, 85*(3), 473–91.
Lamla, M., & Rupprecht, S. (2006). The impact of ECB communication on financial market expectations. KOF (Swiss Economic Institute) Working Paper No. 06–135.
Leeper, E., & Roush, J. (2003). Putting "M" back in monetary policy. *Journal of Money, Credit, and Banking, 35*(6), 1217–57.
Leeper, E., Sims, C., & Zah, T. (1996). What does monetary policy do? *Brookings Papers on Economic Activity, 2*, 1–78.
Loutskina, E., & Strahan, P. (2008). Securitization and the declining impact of bank finance on loan supply: evidence from mortgage originators. mimeo.
Lubik, T., & P. Surico (2006). The Lucas critique and the stability of empirical models. Federal Reserve Bank of Richmond Working Paper No. 06–05.
Lucas, R. (1980). Two illustrations of the quantity theory of money. *American Economic Review, 70*(5), 1005–1014.

Lucas, R. (1986). Adaptive behavior and economic theory. *The Journal of Business, 59*(4), 401–426.
Masuch, K., Nicoletti, S., Altimari, S., Rostagno, M., & Pill, H. (2003). The role of money in monetary policymaking. In O. Issing (Ed.), *Background studies for the ECB's evaluation of its monetary policy strategy* (pp. 187–228). Frankfurt: European Central Bank.
Masuch, K., Pill, H., & Willeke, C. (2001). Framework and tools of monetary analysis. In H. Klöckers & C. Willeke (Eds.), *Monetary analysis: tools and applications* (pp. 117–144). Frankfurt: European Central Bank.
McCallum, B. (1981). Price level determinacy with an interest rate rule and rational expectations. *Journal of Monetary Economics, 8*(3), 319–329.
McCallum, B. (2001). Monetary policy analysis in models without money. NBER Working Paper No. 8174.
McCallum, B. (2003). Multiple-solution indeterminacies in monetary policy analysis. *Journal of Monetary Economics, 50*(5), 1153–1175.
Meltzer, A.H. (2001). The transmission process. In Deutsche Bundesbank (Ed.), *The monetary transmission process: recent developments and lessons for Europe* (pp. 112–130). London: Palgrave.
Nelson, E. (2002). Direct effects of base money on aggregate demand: theory and evidence. *Journal of Monetary Economics, 49*(4), 687–708.
Nelson, E. (2003). The future of monetary aggregates in monetary policy analysis. *Journal of Monetary Economics, 50*(5), 1029–1059.
Nelson, E. (2007). Comment on: Samuel Reynard, ''Maintaining Low Inflation''. *Journal of Monetary Economics, 54*(5), 1472–1479.
Neumann, M. (1997). Monetary targeting in Germany. In I. Kuroda (Ed.), *Towards more effective monetary policy* (pp. 176–210). London: Macmillan.
Neumann, M., & Greiber, C. (2004). Inflation and core money growth in the euro area. Deutsche Bundesbank Discussion Paper No. 36/2004.
Nicoletti-Altimari, S. (2001). Does money lead inflation in the euro area? ECB Working Paper No. 63.
Noyer, C. (2007). Financial innovation, monetary policy, and financial stability, speech, 17 Apr 2007. Available at: http://www.banque-france.fr/gb/instit/telechar/discours/20070428.pdf.
OECD (2007). *Economic survey of the euro area 2007: the role of monetary aggregates in monetary policy*. OECD: Paris.
Orphanides, A. (2003). Historical monetary policy analysis and the Taylor rule. *Journal of Monetary Economics, 50*(5), 983–1022.
Orphanides, A., & Porter, R. (2000). P* revisited: money-based inflation forecasts with a changing equilibrium velocity. *Journal of Economics and Business,52*(1/2), 87–100.
Papademos, L. (2006). The role of money in the conduct of monetary policy. In *The 4th ECB central banking conference "the role of money: money and monetary policy in the twenty-first century"*, Frankfurt am Main, November, 2006. Available at: http://www.ecb.int/press/key/date/2006/html/sp061110.en.html.
Pill, H., & Rautanen, T. (2006). Monetary analysis: the ECB experience. mimeo, Frankfurt.
Posen, A. (2000). Lessons from the Bundesbank on the occasion of its early retirement. In L. Mahadeva & G. Sterne (Eds.), *Monetary policy frameworks in a global context* (pp. 393–421). London: Routledge.
Reischle, J. (2007). Recent developments in the net external asset position of German Banks. In *ECB workshop "the external dimension of monetary analysis"*, Frankfurt/Germany, December 2007.
Reuters. (2007). Papademos tritt Zweifeln an EZB-Strategie entgegen. *Online News Report*, 12 Jun 2007. Available at: http://de.today.reuters.com/news/newsArticle.aspx?type=economicsNews&storyID=2007-06-12T173253Z_01_HUM263163_RTRDEOC_0_EZB-STRATEGIE-PAPADEMOS.xml.
Reynard, S. (2007). Maintaining low inflation, money, interest rates, and policy stance. *Journal of Monetary Economics, 54*(5), 1441–1471.

Roffia, B., & Zaghini, A. (2007). Excess money growth and inflation dynamics. ECB Working Paper No. 749.

Romer, C., & Romer, D. (1992). New evidence on the monetary transmission mechanism. *Brookings Papers on Economic Activity,* 149–198.

Rudebusch, G., & Svensson, L. (2002). Eurosystem monetary targeting: lessons from U.S. data. *European Economic Review, 46*(3), 417–442.

Sargent, T., & Wallace, N. (1975). 'Rational' expectations, the optimal monetary instrument, and the optimal money supply rule. *Journal of Political Economy, 83*(2), 241–254.

Scharnagl, M., & Schumacher, C. (2007). Reconsidering the role of monetary indicators for euro area inflation from a Bayesian perspective using group inclusion probabilities. Deutsche Bundesbank Discussion Paper No. 09/2007.

Smets, F. (2003). Discussion "Putting 'M' back in monetary policy". *Journal of Money, Credit, and Banking, 35*(6), 1257–1264.

Stavrev, E. (2006). Measures of underlying inflation in the euro area: assessment and role for informing monetary policy. IMF Working Paper No. 06/197.

Svensson, L. (2000). Does the P* model provide any rationale for monetary targeting? *German Economic Review, 1*, 69–81.

Svensson, L.E.O. (2003a). Monetary policy and real stabilization. NBER Working Paper No. 9486.

Svensson, L. (2003b). Comment on: Nelson (2003), The future of monetary aggregates in monetary policy. *Journal of Monetary Economics, 50*, 1061–1070.

Tödter, K., & Reimers, H. (1997). P-star as a link between money and prices in Germany. *Weltwirtschaftliches Archiv, 130*, 273–289.

Uhlig, H. (2008). Comment. In: A. Beyer, L. Reichlin (Eds.), *The role of money—money and monetary policy in the twenty-first century. Proceedings of the 4th ECB central banking conference* (pp. 87–96), 9–10 November 2006, ECB: Frankfurt.

Van den Heuvel, S. (2007). The bank capital channel of monetary policy. mimeo. Pennsylvania: University of Pennsylvania.

von Hagen, J. (1999). Money growth targeting by the Bundesbank. *Journal of Monetary Economics, 43*, 681–701.

Woodford, M. (2003). *Interest and prices: foundations of a theory of monetary policy*. Princeton: Princeton University Press.

Woodford, M. (2007). How important is money in the conduct of monetary policy? NBER Working Paper No. 13325.

Woodford, M. (2008). Does a "Two-Pillar Phillips Curve" justify a two-pillar monetary policy strategy? In: A. Beyer, L. Reichlin, L. (Eds.), *The role of money—money and monetary policy in the twenty-first century. Proceedings of the 4th ECB central banking conference* (pp. 56–82), 9–10 November 2006, ECB: Frankfurt.

Chapter 4
Euro Area Monetary Policy in Uncharted Waters

Martin Čihák, Thomas Harjes and Emil Stavrev

4.1 Introduction

European economies are in the most severe and protracted economic and financial crisis in many decades. The crisis, which originated in the global financial sector, has spread to economic activity and resulted in significant output declines and growing unemployment. To contain the crisis, and to put the economy on a sustained recovery path, policy makers have used a combination of fiscal, financial sector, and monetary policy measures.

This chapter focuses on the effectiveness of the policies undertaken by the European Central Bank (ECB 2009) in response to the financial crisis. This topic

We thank Luc Everaert for guidance. We are also very grateful to Brian Sack and Eric Swanson for providing us with their Matlab codes for estimating the macro-finance model of term structure. We used a modified version of the codes that fine-tune the nonlinear optimization method of the Bernanke, Reinhart, and Sack (2004). Finally, we thank for useful comments to F. Hammermann, S. Sauer, C. Kamps, R. Adalid, P. Moutot, other ECB staff, and participants in seminars at the IMF and the ECB. Any remaining errors are ours. The views expressed in this chapter are those of the authors and should not be attributed to the IMF, its Executive Board, or its management. The analysis is based on information available upto August 2009.

M. Čihák
Monetary and Capital Markets Department, International Monetary Fund,
700 19th Street NW, Washington, DC, USA
e-mail: mcihak@imf.org

T. Harjes (✉)
European Department, International Monetary Fund, 700 19th Street NW,
Washington, 20431 DC, USA
e-mail: t.harjes@imf.org

E. Stavrev
Research Department, International Monetary Fund, 700 19th Street NW,
Washington, 20431 DC, USA
e-mail: estavrev@imf.org

J. de Haan and H. Berger (eds.), *The European Central Bank at Ten*,
DOI: 10.1007/978-3-642-14237-6_4,

comprises a range of policy-relevant questions. In particular, how effective have been the conventional and non-standard monetary policy measures implemented by the ECB? Have these measures helped maintain price stability and reduce tensions in the interbank market? Given the significant problems in the financial system, how effective is monetary policy in forestalling strong disinflationary pressure, particularly when policy rates are very low?

We find, first, that the functioning of the traditional transmission channels (interest rate, bank lending, broad credit, and expectations) has been impaired by the crisis. There is some evidence that policy rate transmission has weakened: the cost of credit to both businesses and households declined much less than the policy rates, as credit spreads initially increased and only recently eased somewhat. Examining the efficacy of the transmission channels in detail, we find that even during the crisis, policy rate changes have still been transmitted to market rates, but the efficiency of the transmission has been disrupted. The transmission has slowed down (the lags have become longer), and has become noisier; the policy reaction needed to stabilize the economy has become stronger.

Our second finding is that the non-standard monetary policy measures implemented so far had some measurable effects on money market spreads and the yield curve. The non-standard measures included a major lengthening of the maturity of the ECB's refinancing operations and resulted in a sizeable increase in the ECB's balance sheet. We find some evidence that the yield curve for euro area government bonds has been somewhat lower and flatter than predicted by standard macro variables since September 2008, indicating that the policy measures may have had some beneficial effects on government bond term spreads.

The structure of this chapter is as follows. Section 4.2 discusses the evolution of the ECB's policy response since the beginning of the crisis. Section 4.3 then examines the effectiveness of the monetary transmission, focusing on the impact of the crisis. Section 4.4 analyzes the effectiveness of the non-standard policy measures in countering deflationary risks. Section 4.5 concludes.

4.2 ECB's Policy Response to the Crisis

In the beginning of the financial crisis, characterized by a sudden eruption of stress in interbank money markets in the second half of 2007, the ECB responded promptly with significant adjustments in its liquidity management operations (soon followed by other central banks). It provided liquidity in large amounts, including at term maturities, and since October 2008 the ECB eased collateral requirements to prevent them from becoming a constraint for increased funding from the ECB. On average, the overnight rate remained close to the policy rate target, but term spreads surged, reflecting sharp increases in both counterparty default risk and liquidity risk, due to severe funding pressure at longer term maturities (Čihák & Harjes 2008).

Meanwhile, the ECB emphasized in its communications the distinction between its two core functions[1]: (1) liquidity management with the primary goal to mitigate as much as possible the risk that protracted liquidity shortages turned into bank solvency problems, and (2) pursuit of price stability by choosing an appropriate monetary policy stance. However, the stress in money markets, characterized by sharp spikes in spreads between unsecured and secured rates for term funds, led to a significant rise in money market yields, including the 1-year Euribor rate, which also affected the transmission of monetary policy in a crucial way. Nonetheless, the ECB insisted that its liquidity provision would not interfere with monetary policy objectives.[2]

When interbank trading came to a virtual halt in mid-September 2008, the ECB started to engage in a new mode of liquidity provision, calling it "enhanced credit support." This approach focuses primarily on banks, as they are the main source of credit in the euro area economy, and seeks to enhance the flow of credit above and beyond what could be achieved through policy interest rate reductions.

There are five main building blocks of the enhanced credit support[3]: (1) unlimited provision of liquidity through "fixed rate tenders with full allotment"; (2) extension of the (already long) list of collateral assets, so that the share of private sector assets increased to 56% of the nominal value of securities on the list[4]; (3) extension of the maturity of long-term refinancing operations, initially to 6 months, and then, in late June 2009, to 12 months, aiming to decrease uncertainty in commercial banks' liquidity planning; (4) liquidity provision in foreign currencies, particularly U.S. dollars, through swap lines with the Federal Reserve; and (5) outright purchases of covered bonds (for an amount of 60 billion euros) in order to revive that market, which is important for banks' funding.

There is some indication that the ECB's measures helped to improve functioning of the money market. Liquidity premia in term euro money market spreads seem to have declined (see Fig. 4.1), primarily as a result of the ECB's proactive liquidity management. Last year's sharp rise in money market term premia

---

[1] See, for example, the speech by José Manuel González-Páramo on "Financial market failures and public policies: a central banker's perspective on the global financial crisis", January 2009.

[2] As argued by Berger, Harjes, and Stavrev in Chap. 3, the ECB's two-pillar approach (which includes a monetary pillar which gives high prominence to monetary aggregates in determining the appropriate policy stance) may have made communication more challenging. Bulíř, Čihák, and Šmídková (2008) arrive at a similar conclusion.

[3] For a description of the ECB's enhanced credit support, see in particular the speech by Jean-Claude Trichet, President of the ECB, at the University of Munich on July 13, 2009, and "Governing Council decisions on non-standard measures," *ECB Monthly Bulletin*, June 2009, pp. 9–10.

[4] Meanwhile, the (already large) number of counterparties participating in ECB's refinancing operations increased from 1,700 before the crisis to 2,200, as refinancing through money markets became more difficult. The number of *active* counterparties before the crisis was about 450 (compared to 20 in the United States), and increased to 750 during the crisis; also, the number of counterparties that participated in the 1-year longer term refinancing operation was more than 1,100.

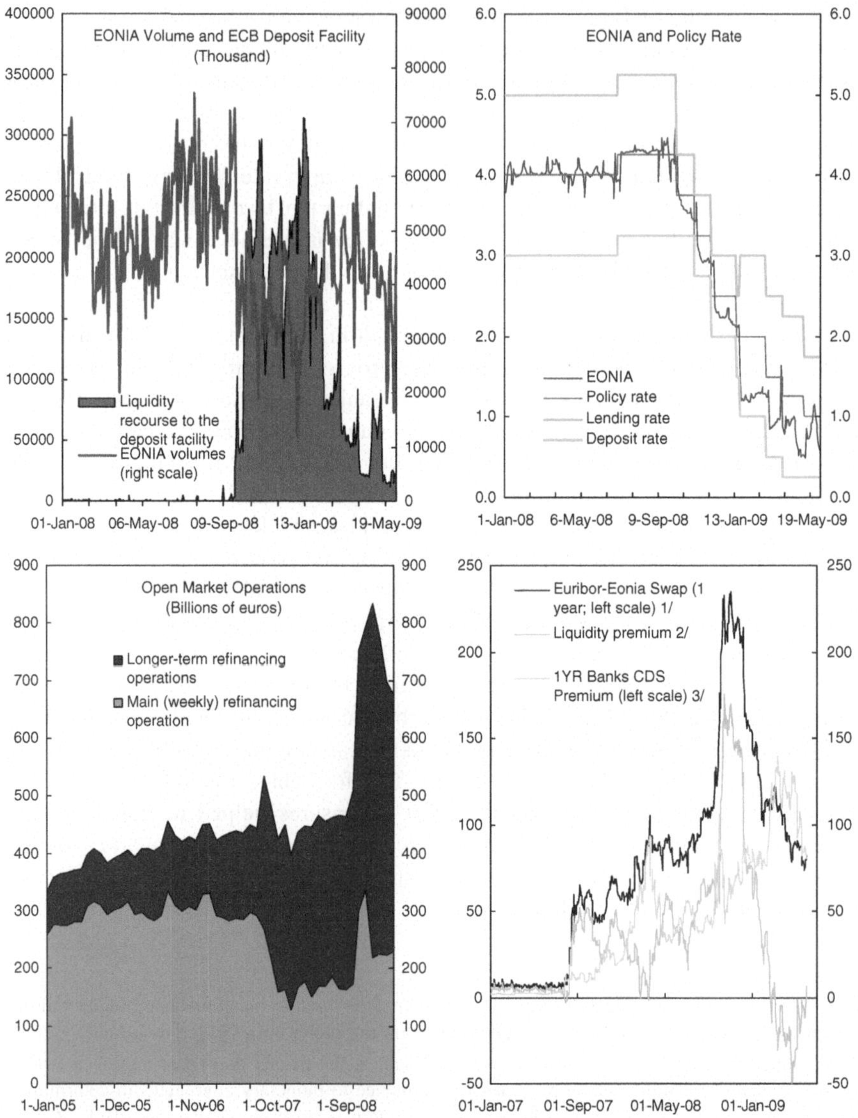

Fig. 4.1 Euro area: recent developments of the ECB's liquidity operations (%, or in units as indicated) *Sources*: DataStream; and Bloomberg. 1/ Euribor refers to "the best price between the best banks" provided by Euribor panel members. 2/ The liquidity premium is the difference between the Euribor - Eonia Swap spread and the CDS premium. 3/ The one-year banks CDS premium is the average of premia for the "best" five Euribor panel banks out of 24 with the lowest premium

reflected both increased counterparty and liquidity risks as banks were confronted with mounting losses and liquidity funding pressure, especially at term maturities. Following unlimited provision of longer term funds at fixed-rates by the ECB, which began at the end of October 2008, term money market spreads dropped sharply and now correspond closely to measures of counterparty risk, while liquidity premia have virtually been eliminated. Spreads are still at elevated levels but are not likely to fall much further until perceptions of counterparty risk in the banking sector normalize.

Following the intensification of the financial turmoil in September 2008, the ECB effectively intermediated liquidity flows among banks in order to ease funding liquidity tensions in money markets.[5] In January 2009, to encourage the resumption of normal interbank trading activity, the ECB restored the interest rate corridor (the difference between the rates charged on lending to banks and paid on deposits) from ±50 basis points to ±100 basis points around the policy rate. Also in January 2009, the ECB decided to tighten risk control measures for newly issued asset-backed securities and uncovered bank bonds to reduce credit risk and encourage resumption of activity in these markets. So far during 2009, bank deposits at the ECB have declined sharply, and overnight interbank market volumes have stabilized at around 40–60 billion euros, indicating some revival of private interbank activity.

4.3 Has the Transmission Been Impaired?

The reduction of the policy rates has been transmitted to market rates, although the pass-through was less than full, and varied across market segments and maturities. For example, from September 2008 to February 2009, bank lending rates on new loans declined by: (1) 20–60 bps for consumer loans; (2) 50–180 bps for house purchase loans; and (3) 70–250 bps for loans to non-financial corporations (Fig. 4.2). At the same time, short-term money market rates dropped by around 300 bps, and spreads also declined but remained elevated (Fig. 4.1).

Looking just at the interest rate changes, however, provides only a partial view of the effectiveness of the transmission mechanism. It does not address the efficacy of the interest rate channel compared to previous cycles, and, more importantly, analyzing only the transmission of policy rates to market rates is insufficient for assessing the effectiveness of monetary policy in achieving its ultimate goal of price stability. In that regard, the effective functioning of all transmission channels, namely, the interest rate, the bank lending, and the broad credit channels, is key. Also, the ability of the central bank to maintain inflation expectations in line with the definition of price stability is crucial for the effective working of the transmission mechanism (see Chap. 5).

[5] The size of the ECB's balance sheet has multiplied by a factor of 1.5 between mid-2007 and early 2009. The corresponding ratios for the Bank of England's and for the U.S. Federal Reserve have been 3.0 and 2.5.

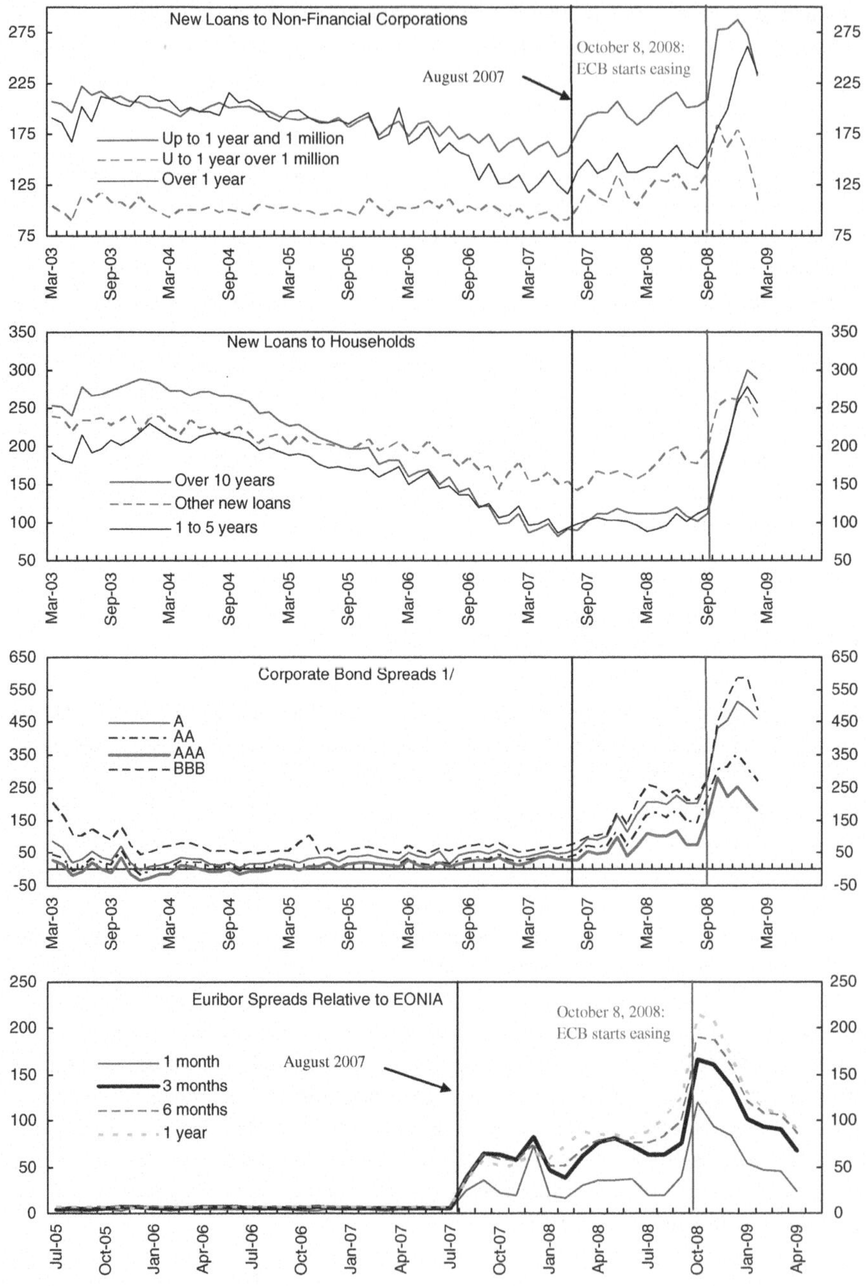

Fig. 4.2 Euro area: cost of borrowing by businesses and households (spreads relative to the ECB policy rate, basis points) *Sources*: Haver and IMF staff calculations. 1/ Corporate bonds with 3-5 year maturity relative to the 5-year benchmark government bond index

A comprehensive analysis is needed to determine various aspects of the effectiveness of monetary transmission. Such an analysis is of particular interest in the context of the current crisis, given the strong disinflationary pressure facing the euro area and the already low level of policy rates. A combination of several bi-variate vector autoregression (VAR) models, comprising the policy rate and a set of market interest rates, and a theory-based general equilibrium framework allows for this. The bi-variate VARs are used to assess the pass-through of policy rates to several market rates, while the theory-based model is used to examine the functioning of all channels jointly in a general equilibrium framework.

4.3.1 Transmission Channels

The functioning of each channel can be summarized as follows.[6] In the *interest rate channel*, monetary policy affects short nominal interest rates, which through expectations and sticky prices feed through to long nominal and real interest rates, and thus the user cost of capital. As a result, investment, and aggregate output adjust. In addition, interest rates influence economic activity by affecting the relative prices of present and future consumption. In the *bank lending channel*, bank credit to borrowers where asymmetric information can be especially pronounced, such as small and medium size enterprises, plays an important role. A key feature of this channel is that the central bank can affect the supply of credit provided by financial intermediaries, and thus the cost of capital to bank-dependent borrowers, not only by changing interest rates but also by changing the quantity of base money. The *broad credit channel* works through the net worth of firms. In the presence of financial frictions (like imperfect information and costly enforcement of contracts), monetary policy affects not only interest rates, but also the financial position of borrowers and the relative cost of external and internal funds (external finance premium).

In addition to the above channels, expectations play an important role in achieving the goal of price stability. Expectations influence significantly the effectiveness of all other channels of monetary policy transmission to the extent that central bank policy is anticipated by the market and priced into the yield curve. In that regard, anchoring inflation expectations is a key feature. Several factors can enhance to role of the expectations channel. In particular, the degree of central bank credibility, predictability of central bank actions, and commitment by the central bank to vary its instrument consistently.

Various aspects of monetary transmission in the euro area have been analyzed in the empirical literature. Most studies have examined the effectiveness and the relative importance of transmission channels over the cycle, with some papers looking also at the asymmetric functioning of the channels during upturns and

[6] Mishkin (1995) and Bean, Larsen, and Nikolov (2002) discuss the transmission channels in detail.

downturns. However, the effectiveness of monetary transmission during significant crisis, and in particular during the current financial crises, has been much less investigated.

In a survey of studies by the Monetary Transmission Network, Angeloni, Kashyap, Mojon, and Terlizzese (2002) conclude that, while the interest rate channel is the most important for monetary policy transmission in the euro area, the other channels also play a role. The survey shows that an unexpected monetary policy tightening temporarily reduces output, with the maximum impact occurring after a year. The response of prices is much slower, with inflation barely affected in the first year and only gradually declining over the medium term. The interest rate channel, while not responsible for all of the monetary transmission, is by far the most important channel for one-sixth of the euro area countries. For the rest of the member states, the interest rate effects are sizable, and in some cases interest rates are almost the sole determinant of investment fluctuations.

The interest rate channel is complemented by financial factors in several ways. In some countries, banks are an important source of business credit supply to finance investment. However, not for all countries for which loan supply matters is it important for investment, as household lending matters as well. On the characteristics that matter for the role of banks in the transmission mechanism, Angeloni et al. (2002) find that bank liquidity positions seem to be important in virtually all EMU members, while bank capital and bank size seem to matter much less. In addition, the relative importance of the bank-lending channel differs among euro area countries—it is significant in Germany and Italy, but there are also countries where it is insignificant.

Given the short time horizon since the beginning of the current crisis, its impact on monetary transmission in the euro area has been much less studied. International Monetary Fund (2008), using a vector error correction framework comprising policy and market rates, analyzes the impact of the crisis on the interest rate transmission in the United States and the euro area. The results of the study indicate that the pass-through of policy rates onto market rates in the United States and the euro area has been disrupted, but to a different degree in the two regions and over the maturity spectrum. The disruption has been particularly evident for the long-term rates in both the United States and the euro area, while the transmission to the short rates has been less affected in the euro area.

4.3.2 Methodology

The VAR approach is used to study the first stage of the interest rate channel, namely the pass-through of policy rate changes to various market interest rates. The pass-through of policy rates to market rates is assessed by comparing the impulse responses of the models estimated over the period prior to the crisis with the impulse responses of the same models estimated including the post crisis period (through April 2009). In addition, the variation and the bias of the residuals from the VARs are used as a signal for potential malfunctioning of the pass-through since the crisis.

The theory-based framework is used to analyze in a general equilibrium setup the functioning of all channels as well as the role of expectations. The functioning and the relative importance of each channel as well as the role of expectations are assessed using the impulse responses and the variance decomposition. The functioning of the transmission mechanism prior and post-crisis is evaluated by comparing the estimated coefficients over the two sub-samples as well as impulse response to standard shocks (demand, supply, and monetary policy). The theory-based framework is particularly suited for such a comparison, because the model is estimated using Bayesian techniques, which allow for a more robust estimation of the coefficients in small samples. As in the VAR approach, the residuals from the entire sample are used to gauge the degree to which the functioning of the channels was affected by the crisis.

4.3.2.1 Bi-variate VAR Regressions

The pass-through of the policy rate is estimated with bi-variate VAR regressions using monthly data as follows:

$$\begin{aligned} pr_t &= \alpha_1 + \sum_{j=1}^{3} \beta_j pr_{t-j} + \sum_{j=1}^{3} \gamma_j mr_{t-j} + \varepsilon_t \\ mr_t &= \alpha_2 + \sum_{j=1}^{3} \delta_j mr_{t-j} + \sum_{j=1}^{3} \varphi_j pr_{t-j} + \xi_t \end{aligned} \tag{4.1}$$

where pr_t is the ECB policy rate approximated by the overnight EONIA rate, and mr_t is one of the following market interest rates: (1) 1-, 3-, 6-month, and 1 year Euribor rates; (2) corporate bond yields of 3–5-year maturity rated A, AA, AAA, and BBB; (3) new loans to non-financial corporations (up to 1 year and up to 1 million; up to 1 year and over 1 million; and over 1 year); (4) new loans to households (housing loans 1–5 years and over 10 years, and other loans); (5) consumer credit (1–5 years and over 5 years).

The sample period is January 1999–April 2009 for interbank rates and corporate bond yields, and January 2003–April 2009 for loans to non-financial corporations and households. The lag length of the VAR models is set at 3 months, based on Akaike and Schwarz information criteria. The bi-variate VARs are estimated both in levels and first differences of the variables using ordinary least squares estimator (OLS).[7]

[7] The models with the levels of the variables are also estimated using Bayesian VAR (BVAR), following Sims and Zha (1998). The BVAR results are qualitatively similar to the OLS estimates, and available upon request.

4.3.2.2 Theory-based (General Equilibrium) Framework

For a fuller assessment of the transmission channels, a theory-based general equilibrium framework is used. In the core of the framework is a New Keynesian type of model that is modified in several ways. The three main equations describe the evolution of inflation, π_t, the output gap, y_t, and the monetary policy response, captured by the policy rates, i_t (see Appendix 4.1 for the full model specification).

Specifically, inflation is determined by:

$$\pi_t = \lambda_1 \pi 12^e_{t+12} + (1 - \lambda_1)\pi 12_{t-1} + \lambda_2(y_{t-1} + y_{t-2} + y_{t-3})/3 + \varepsilon^\pi_t \qquad (4.2)$$

where π_t is monthly inflation (seasonally adjusted at annual rate), $\pi 12^e_{t+12}$ is expected year-on-year inflation, $\pi 12_t$ is year-on-year inflation, y_t is a measure of the output gap, and ε^π_t is a supply shock.[8] This specification implies that prices are set as a mark-up over marginal cost, captured by the output gap, while the degree of price flexibility and inflation inertia are both captured by the weight on the expected inflation term.

Aggregate demand evolves according to:

$$y_t = \beta_1(y_{t-1} + y_{t-2} + y_{t-3})/3 + \beta_2 y^e_{t+1} - \beta_3(r_{t-1} - r\_eq_{t-1}) + \varepsilon^y_t \qquad (4.3)$$

where y^e_{t+1} is the expected output gap next period, r_t is the actual short-term real interest rate, defined as the difference between the short-term nominal interest rate and expected inflation, r_eq_t is the equilibrium real interest rate, and ε^y_t is a demand shock.[9] In this aggregate demand specification, the lagged moving average output gap term reflects the degree of inertia in the economy, the forward looking output gap term captures inter-temporal smoothing by economic agents, and the third term, the deviation of actual from equilibrium real interest rates, represents the interest rate channel.

The monetary policy reaction function is:

$$i_t = \gamma_1 i_{t-1} + (1 - \gamma_1)(r\_eq_t + \pi 12^e_{t+12} + \gamma_2(\pi 12^e_{t+12} - \bar{\pi}_t) + \gamma_3 y_t) + \varepsilon^i_t \qquad (4.4)$$

[8] For the empirical analysis, which is done with monthly data, $\pi_t = 1{,}200(p\_sa_t - p\_sa_{t-1})$, where p_sa_t is the logarithm of the seasonally adjusted harmonized index of consumer prices (HICP), and $\pi 12_t = 100(p_t - p_{t-12})$, where p_t is a logarithm of the HICP index. Economic activity is approximated by a weighted average of industrial production (30% share) and retail sales indexes. As initial values for the output gap y_t for the Bayesian estimation, the log-difference of the actual index from its Hodrick-Prescott filtered value is used.

[9] Given that the model is estimated with monthly data, the leads and lags in Eqs. 4.2 and 4.3 are chosen so as to obtain dynamic responses that are in line with the dynamic response from models estimated with quarterly data and also reflect plausible lengths of price setting contracts as well as the lags with which capacity utilization affects inflation in reality.

where i_t is nominal policy interest rate, $\bar{\pi}_t$ is the inflation target, and ε_t^i is a monetary policy shock. The first term in this rule captures the degree of Eqs. 4.2 and 4.3 interest rate smoothing by the central bank. The second term is the natural interest rate, and the third and fourth terms represent the usual components for a forward looking Taylor rule where the central bank reacts to the deviation of expected inflation from inflation target and the output gap.

The model is extended in several ways. First, to capture market perceptions about underlying inflation, the inflation target is allowed to be time varying as in:

$$\bar{\pi}_t = \rho\pi^{ss} + (1 - \rho)\pi 12_{t-1} + \varepsilon_t^{\bar{\pi}} \tag{4.5}$$

where π^{ss} is the steady-state inflation, and $\varepsilon_t^{\bar{\pi}}$ is a shock to underlying inflation. Allowing for a time-varying inflation target also provides insights about central bank credibility (see, for example, Hördahl, Tristani, & Vestin, 2006).

Second, to test for the importance of the bank lending channel, a simple loan demand and supply block is added to the core Eqs. 4.2–4.5 of the model. In particular, loan demand is modelled as follows:

$$l_t = -\lambda_i i_{t-1}^l + \lambda_y g_{t-1} + \varepsilon_t^{ld} \tag{4.6}$$

where l_t is the growth of loans provided by the banking system, i_t^l is the interest rate on loans, g_t is the growth of output, and ε_t^{ld} is a loan demand shock. Loan supply is represented by an inverse loan supply function (determining interest rates on bank loans) as follows:

$$i_t^l = \tau_1 l_{t-1} + \lambda_m \mu_{t-1} + \varepsilon_t^{ls} \tag{4.7}$$

where μ_t is money growth, and ε_t^{ls} is a loan supply shock. To close the loan demand and supply block, a standard money demand function is used in which money growth μ_t is determined by output growth and policy interest rates.

Finally, to capture the effect of bank lending on aggregate demand, real loan rates are added to the aggregate demand Eq. 4.3 in addition to the real short-term interest rates. All of the above changes comprise a version of the model that is used to analyze the functioning of the bank-lending channel.

In a second version of the model, to examine the importance of the broader credit channel, an equation that describes the corporate bond yield spread (the difference of corporate and government bond yields) is added to the loan demand and supply block. The spread term is added to the aggregate demand Eq. 4.3. As Friedman and Kuttner (1992) show, the spread between the corporate bond yield and the government bond yield captures the external finance premium, which is in general positive due to risk and liquidity premia. To close the model, the corporate bond spread, or the external finance premium, is endogenized by modelling it to depend on overall economic conditions captured by the output gap and policy rate as follows:

$$sp_t = \sigma_1 i_{t-1} + \sigma_2 y_{t-1} + \varepsilon_t^{sp} \tag{4.8}$$

where ε_t^{sp} is a shock to corporate spread.

The above models are estimated with monthly seasonally adjusted data, using Bayesian methods over January 1995–February 2009 for the version with the bank-lending channel and January 1999–February 2009 for the version with the broader credit channel. Economic activity is approximated by a weighted average of industrial production (with a share of 30%) and retail sales. In addition, the following variables are used: short-term rates (approximated by the EONIA interest rate), an average of interest rates on new loans to euro area residents of 1–5-year maturity, AAA-, AA-, A-, BBB-rated corporate bond yields of 3–5-year maturity, the spread of corporate bond yield and government bond yield, HICP inflation, money supply (approximated by M3 aggregate), and bank loans to the euro area residents.

4.3.3 Results

4.3.3.1 Bi-variate VAR Regressions

The results from the VAR analysis (based on the full sample) show that policy rate changes have been transmitted to market rates, although the degree and the speed of pass-through vary (Fig. 4.3). The impact on the 3-month Euribor rate is close to one-for-one and the speed of adjustment is fast, with the maximum impact transmitted within a month. The initial impact on corporate bond yields and new loans to non-financial corporations is similarly quick, although the full adjustment is more protracted and the impact on higher-grade bond yields is smaller than on lower grade bond yields (0.6–0.7% point for AA- and AAA-rated bonds vs. 1.2 for BBB-rated bonds). The pass-through of the policy rates on loans to households for house purchases and the speed of adjustment are somewhat lower (notice that other consumer loans adjust faster).[10]

The results also suggest that the pass-through to all market rates has slowed down during the crisis. In particular, impulse responses from the first difference bi-variate VARs imply that the time for the full adjustment of market rates has increased to over 12 months, from 3 to 6 months before the crisis (the results from the bi-variate VARs in levels estimated both with OLS Bayesian methods show a similar picture). The transmission to lower grade corporate bonds seems to have

[10] These results are consistent with the finding by International Monetary Fund (2008) that the 3-month Euribor rates have more stable and reliable relation with the policy rate than other lender rates, and by Sørensen and Werner (2007) that bank rates on corporate loans appear to adjust most efficiently, followed by mortgage loan rates. Also, our findings are consistent with the conclusion by the ECB (2009) that "even during the current financial crisis, the bank interest rate pass-through has worked relatively well in terms of responding to developments in the EURIBOR and longer term market rates, although less well in terms of responding to developments in the EONIA."

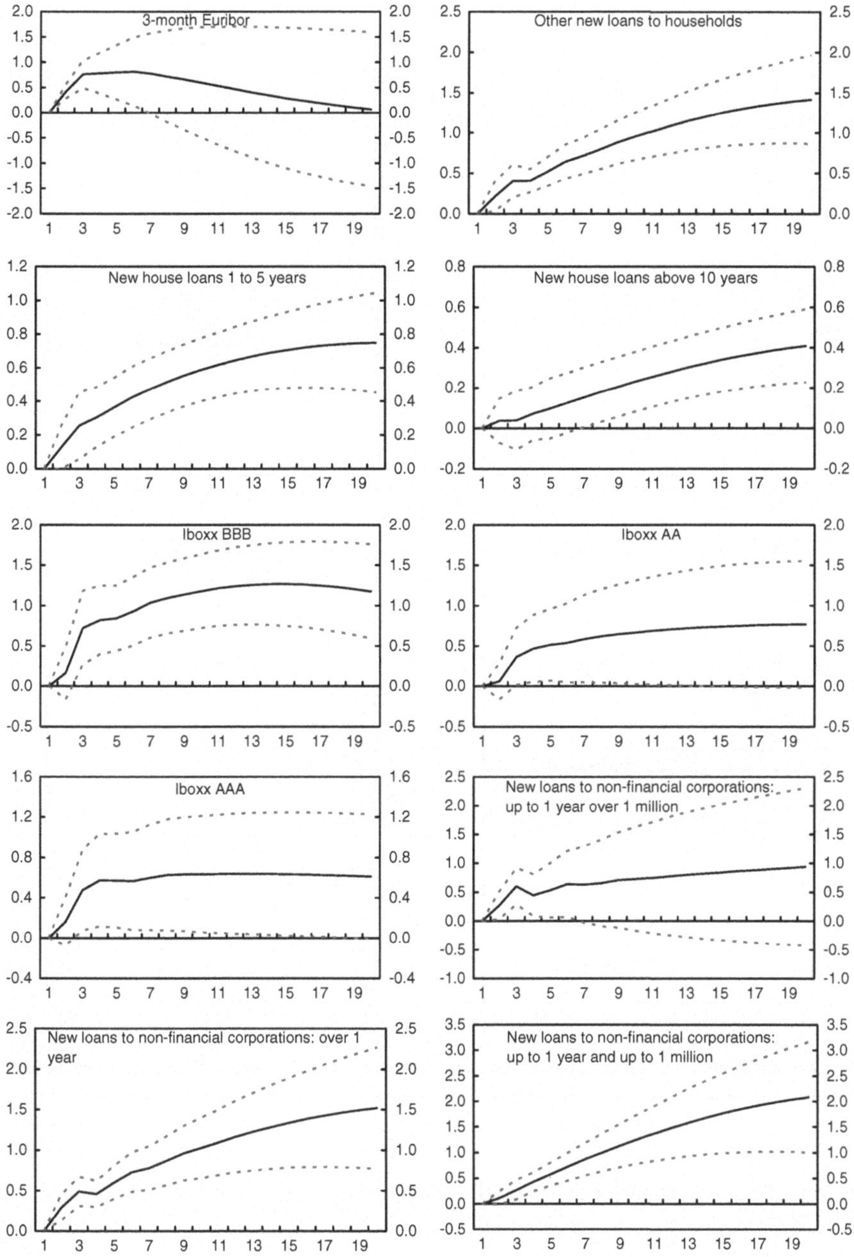

Fig. 4.3 Euro area: pass-through of the ECB policy rate changes to market rates (response to non-factorized one-unit innovations, 85% confidence interval) *Sources*: ECB and IMF staff estimates

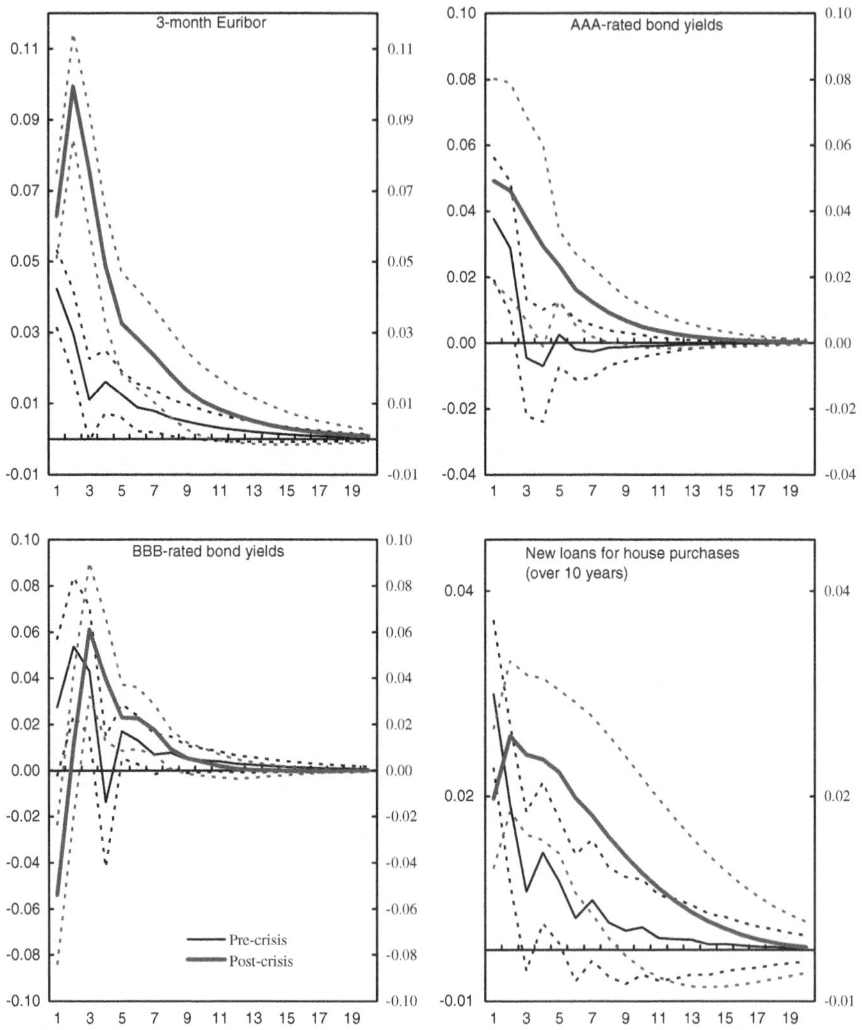

Fig. 4.4 Euro area: the impact of the crisis on policy rate pass-through (VARs in first difference, response to Cholesky one SD innovations, 85% confidence interval) *Source*: IMF staff estimates

been particularly negatively affected, following the crisis—the initial response of the BBB-rated corporate bond yields has switched from positive before the crisis to negative thereafter (Fig. 4.4).

In addition, the pass-through from the policy rates to market rates has become less reliable since the beginning of the financial crisis. Specifically, the variance of the residuals of the equations for the market rates has increased since the beginning of 2008 (Fig. 4.5), in most cases significantly. This is in line with the preliminary findings in International Monetary Fund (2008) that the pass-through

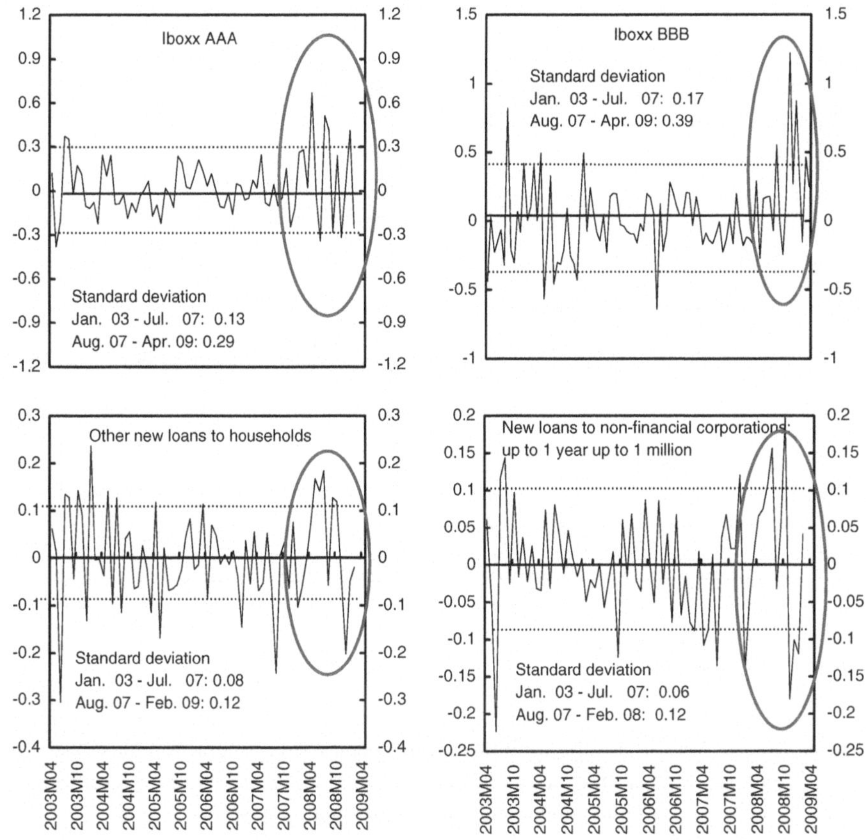

Fig. 4.5 Euro area: VAR residuals of market rates (% points) *Sources*: ECB, and IMF staff estimates

to market rates during the crisis has become less efficient, reflecting most likely the dislocation of the markets for short-term bank financing.[11]

More importantly, as bank-lending standards have tightened following the crisis, quantity effects may be at play that could further impair monetary policy effectiveness. Indeed, the role of the interest rate pass-through for monetary policy effectiveness needs to be viewed in the context of tightening lending standards. While interest rate pass-through provides an important signal for monetary policy effectiveness, in times of significant stress in credit markets quantities are also important. Indeed, the April 2009 ECB bank lending survey suggests continuing tightening of lending standards, albeit at a slower pace. In this situation, banks may have significantly reduced lending by cutting loan originations rather than raising

[11] Altunbas, Gambacorta, and Marqués (2007) suggest that the pass-through to market rates has become less efficient already before the crisis, due to increased securitization.

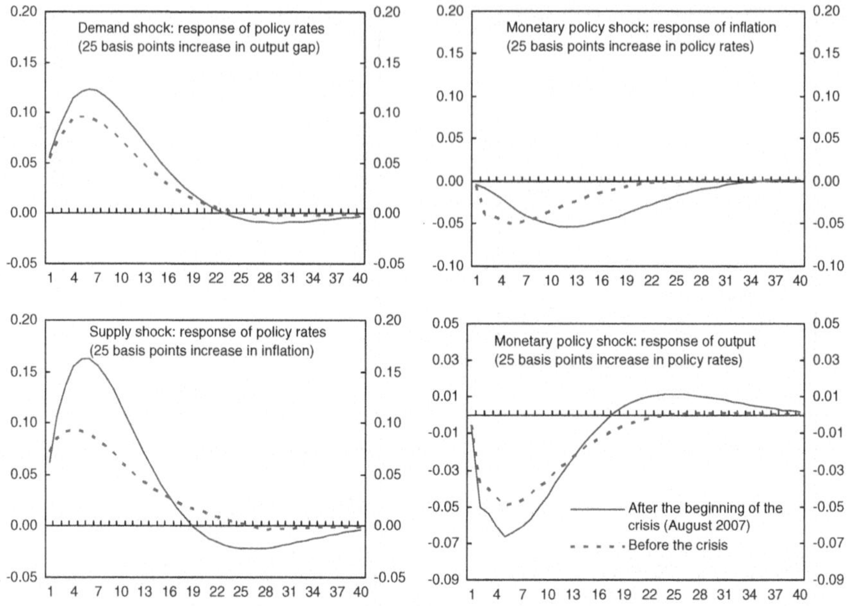

Fig. 4.6 Euro area: effectiveness of monetary policy (pre- and post-crisis in basis points) *Source*: IMF staff estimates

interest rates. Also, the shift of loans from special investment vehicles back to banks' balance sheets, the so called re-intermediation, as well as continuing funding pressures for the banks may put additional pressure on banks' capital needs, thus slowing further new credit creation.

4.3.3.2 Theory-based (General Equilibrium) Framework

A comparison of impulse responses from the theory-based model estimated before and after the beginning of the crisis indicates that after the beginning of the crisis the overall transmission has slowed (Fig. 4.6).[12] For both supply and demand shocks, the policy reaction needed to stabilize the economy is somewhat stronger, with the time needed for the policy feedback to pass-through increasing to about 2½ years, from about 1½ year before the crisis (Fig. 4.6, left column). Similarly, the time for a full transmission of monetary policy shocks to inflation has increased from about 2 years before the crisis to about 3 years during the crisis (Fig. 4.6, right column). Compared with the findings from the VAR, these results suggest

[12] The pre-crisis sample is prior to August 2007 and the crisis sample is from September 2007 to February 2009. The choice of August 2007 as a split point of the sample is supported by Chow break-point test.

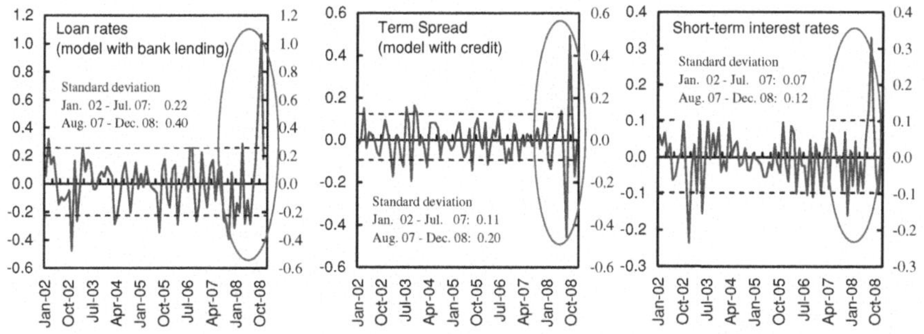

Fig. 4.7 Euro area: residuals from the structural models (percentage points) *Source*: IMF staff estimates

that not only the first stage of the transmission (i.e., the pass-through to market rates), but also the overall working of the transmission mechanism seems to have slowed down during the crisis.

At the same time, a comparison of coefficients estimated over the two samples, shows that the changes in the main structural parameters of the economy are not dramatic. The largest change took place in the coefficient capturing the reaction of policy makers to the deviation of inflation from the inflation target. This coefficient has increased from around 1.2 before the crisis to 1.4 during the crisis. The response of policy makers to fluctuations in the output gap basically remained unchanged between the two sub-samples at around 0.5.

The model residuals also confirm that shocks increased since mid-2008 (see Fig. 4.7). Indeed, the variability of the residuals from the models jumped up after mid-2008. The increased volatility of the residuals (shocks) suggests that during the financial crisis, the transmission of monetary policy has not only become subject to longer lags (i.e., slower), it has also become less predictable (i.e., subject to more noise).

Another sign of the decreased efficiency of transmission is that inflation expectations, while remaining broadly stable over the estimation period, declined significantly in the last quarter of 2008, reflecting the significant deterioration in economic activity. As shown in Fig. 4.8, inflation expectations derived from the model declined significantly in the fourth quarter of 2008, but as policies eased significantly to counter the strong disinflationary pressures, inflation expectations recovered since the beginning of 2009. This development of the model-derived inflation expectations agrees with market-based measures of inflation expectations.[13]

[13] The market-based measures of inflation expectations need to be interpreted with caution, given the problems in the markets during the crisis. Nonetheless, the measures still contained useful information, as illustrated by their high correlation (a correlation coefficient of 75%) with the model-derived inflation expectations.

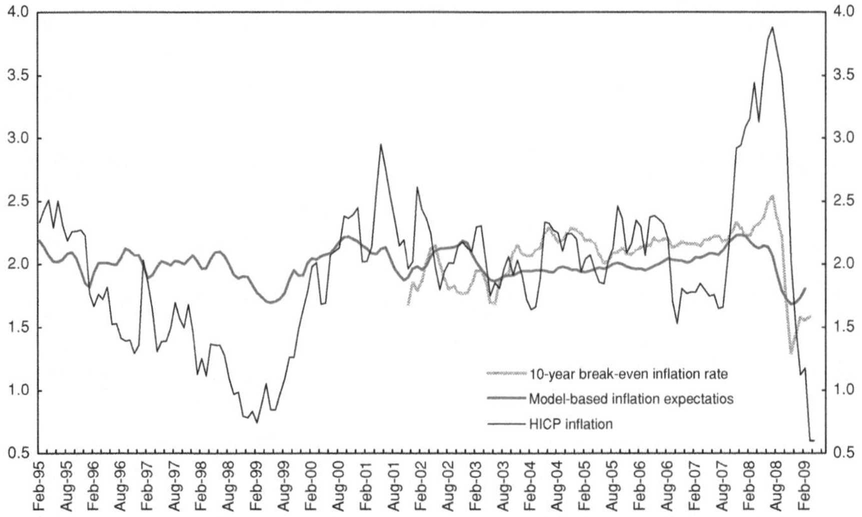

Fig. 4.8 Euro area: model and market-based inflation expectations (year-on-year, %) inflation
Sources: Eurostat, Haver, and IMF staff estimates

Going beyond the impact of the crisis on the transmission, the model results suggest that the interest rate channel is the dominant transmission channel. In particular, it accounts for over 30% of inflation variation and close to 50% of output variation. Importantly, the results imply a major role of expectations, which account for around 40% of inflation variation and about 30% of output variation. The results also suggest some role for the bank-lending and credit channels, which explain about 15 and 10% of output variation, correspondingly. These findings are broadly in line with previous literature. For example, Angeloni et al. (2002) conclude that the interest rate channel is the most important for monetary policy transmission in the euro area and that the bank-lending channel also plays a role, with different relative importance in different euro area countries.

4.4 Monetary Policy and the Return of the Liquidity Trap

The recent non-standard ECB measures have been primarily implemented to ease systemic liquidity risk in the banking sector and support the transmission of lower policy rates to money market rates, but they may have also helped in countering deflationary risks. To study this impact, we use a macro-financial model developed by Bernanke, Reinhart, and Sack (2004) to analyze the effect of the non-standard measures on the term spreads of euro area government benchmark bonds.

4.4.1 Overview

Overnight interest rates have come to record lows in many advanced economies, including in the euro area. Keynes (1936) described situations in which conventional monetary policies become constrained or ineffective, despite the need for further monetary easing, as liquidity traps. The experience of Japan in the 1990s and 2000s and the possibility of deflation in the United States in the mid-2000s reignited interest in this topic. The current economic and financial crisis and the emergence of significant deflationary risks in many economies across the globe have again brought this issue to the fore of many debates.

Krugman (1998), analyzing the Japanese experience, emphasizes the importance of inflation expectations in a liquidity trap where nominal interest rates cannot be lowered any further and additional injections of base money may have no effect if the private sector views base money and short-term (government) bonds as perfect substitutes. If the private sector expects deflation, a central bank could lower real interest rates by convincing markets that it would generate future inflation. However, Krugman's analysis is based on a two-period model. In a multi-period model, a central bank would face some difficulties to re-anchor inflation expectations after having successfully promised to be temporarily "irresponsible".

Eggertsson and Woodford (2004) present a dynamic analysis of monetary policy in a liquidity trap, emphasizing the role of expectations regarding future policy in determining the severity of the distortions that result from hitting the lower bound. They show that the creation of inflation expectations can be reconciled with maintaining the credibility of the central bank's commitment to long-run price stability through a history-dependent policy, such as price level targeting. However, price level targeting faces other challenges and such a regime change would likely require some time to implement.

There is a number of practical measures with which central banks may be able to further ease the monetary policy stance once policy rates have reached levels closer to zero: (1) shaping the expectations of the public about future settings of the policy rate; (2) increasing the money supply beyond the level needed to set the policy rate at zero; and (3) providing liquidity to specific credit markets that are considered dysfunctional (Bernanke et al. 2004).

4.4.1.1 Shaping the Public's Expectations about Future Policy Rate Settings

If a central bank can convince the markets that its policy rate will remain low for longer than markets previously expected, it may add further stimulus to the economy. Usually, central banks do not provide unconditional commitments for their policy rates, especially over the medium term.[14] In normal times, it is most

[14] In the years before the crisis, the ECB developed a system of code words that effectively pre-announced the next adjustments in policy rates. However, these pre-announcements have

common for inflation targeting central banks to conditionally commit that the central bank will set the policy rate to levels such as to maintain expected inflation close to its target. Some central banks, including the U.S. Federal Reserve and the Bank of Canada, have recently emphasized that they expect to keep rates low as long as deflationary risks persist, or inflation remains significantly below the target.[15] A much stronger signal to keep rates low as long as needed is the provision of term funds at the policy rate. The ECB's policy in this regard has initially been targeted at reducing liquidity premia in term money markets. Nonetheless, the extension of maturity and the explicit commitment to continue the refinancing operations for a clearly defined period had also a powerful impact on policy rate expectations.

4.4.1.2 Quantitative Easing

An increase in the money supply could also have a stimulating effect on the economy and raise inflation expectations. An increase in the monetary base can be brought about by open market operations, such as central bank purchases of assets, or by other (more "passive") measures, such as easing the collateral requirements for central bank lending. Additional money supply may directly lower nominal bond yields by raising demand for bonds and triggering a portfolio rebalancing. While the transmission to higher inflation expectations through the portfolio-rebalancing channel would also seem to require a subsequent increase in other broader monetary aggregates, markets may also interpret such operations as a signal that policy rates may remain low longer than anticipated and that at least some of the increase in money supply is going to be permanent. Such operations, if effective, should flatten the yield curve over the near- to medium-term.

4.4.1.3 Credit Easing

A key characteristic of the current financial crisis has been the breakdown of several specific credit markets, such as markets for asset-backed commercial paper, including for residential, commercial mortgage and credit card debt backed securities, that had increasingly become an important funding/credit source, especially in the United States but also in the euro area. Transaction costs, incomplete or asymmetric information and other financial market frictions could

---

(Footnote 14 continued)
occurred only several weeks before the policy decisions, and were arguably only a weak form of commitment (see Chap. 5).

[15] On April 30, 2009, the Fed's Federal Open Market Committee stated that "The Committee will maintain the target range for the federal funds rate at 0–¼% and anticipates that economic conditions are likely to warrant exceptionally low levels of the federal funds rate for an extended period."

drive a wedge between their prices and other financial assets. A sharp increase in credit risk for these securities, but also severe risk aversion together with a lack of transparency for these products and their pricing, virtually stopped secondary market activity. Given the importance of these markets in the United States, the Fed decided to intervene directly in these markets to restart private activity and bring down any possible liquidity premia. The ECB initially supported these markets indirectly by broadening its collateral requirements, and more recently through direct interventions in the covered bond market (as part of the "enhanced credit support"). Such measures are targeted directly at restoring the transmission of low policy rates, as pointed out above. Moreover, if successful, they should stimulate activity and lower the risk of deflation. However, they also shift credit risk to the central bank and may prove more difficult to reverse than other measures once market conditions normalize.

4.4.2 Empirical Assessment

This section studies the effects of the recent non-standard ECB measures as a means of countering deflationary risks. Although these "enhanced credit support" measures have been primarily implemented to support the flow of credit in the economy, they may have also affected term spreads and the yield curve of euro area government benchmark bonds through the channels discussed above. To investigate if such effects occurred, we use a macro-financial model as applied by Bernanke et al. (2004) to study these effects.

4.4.2.1 The Model

Most term structure studies have used latent factor models to explain movements in the term structure, and usually these factors are not given any macroeconomic interpretation. Instead, many standard finance models (such as Dai & Singleton 2000) relate the yield curve only to current and past interest rates. Following Ang and Piazzesi (2003), the model of Bernanke et al. (2004) incorporates macro variables as factors that determine the pricing kernel that prices all bonds in the economy. This approach recognizes that interest rates and other macroeconomic variables evolve jointly over time and affect each other. Contrary to the Ang and Piazzesi (2003) approach, all shocks affecting the pricing kernel are driven by observable macro factors in the Bernanke et al. (2004) model. This model is therefore best described as a vector autoregression (VAR)-based model that additionally imposes a no-arbitrage condition, which is commonly applied in affine term structure finance models. Alternatively, other studies use small-scale rational expectations models usually based on a New Keynesian Phillips curve to describe the economy, instead of a VAR (Rudebush & Wu 2003; Hördahl et al. 2006).

The model used here follows closely Rudebusch, Swanson, and Wu (2006). It comprises four macroeconomic variables as state variables, which are the factors for pricing bonds: (1) a measure of output gap obtained by detrending with a Hodrick-Prescott filter an index of economic activity that is the weighted average of seasonally adjusted industrial production (30% weight) and retail sales (70% weight); (2) year-on-year HICP inflation; (3) the monthly average of overnight interest rate (EONIA); and (4) the 1-year Euribor interest rate as a proxy for market expectations of short-term rates and inflation that may not be fully captured by the other variables, given that separate data for interest rate futures and inflation expectations in the euro area are only available very recently. Data are monthly observations from January 1999 to January 2009.

The state variables (monthly data) follow a VAR model with three lags, which can be stacked into a 12-element vector X_t and described by a VAR(1) model:

$$X_t = \mu + AX_{t-1} + \Sigma\varepsilon_t \tag{4.9}$$

where X_t is a vector of state variables, Σ is a matrix of Choleski decomposition of the VAR innovations.

The pricing kernel, or stochastic discount factor, with which bonds are priced in the model is conditionally log-normal distributed with functional form:

$$m_{t+1} = \exp(-i_t - \frac{1}{2}\lambda_t'\lambda_t - \lambda_t'\varepsilon_{t+1}) \tag{4.10}$$

where i_t is the one-period nominal interest rate and λ_t is a vector of market prices of risk associated with the innovations ε_{t+1} from the VAR.

The prices of market risk are assumed to be linear in the state variables:

$$\lambda_t = \lambda_0 + \lambda_1 X_t \tag{4.11}$$

the prices of risk are assumed to depend only on the contemporaneous state of the economy, which given the specification of the state vector X_t means that only the first four elements in the twelve-by-one vector λ_0 and the upper-left four-by-four part of the twelve-by-twelve matrix λ_t are non zero.

Bonds in the model are priced according to the standard relationship with the stochastic pricing kernel:

$$P_t^n = E_t m_{t+1} P_{t+1}^{n-1} \tag{4.12}$$

where P_t^n denotes the price of an n-period zero-coupon bond at time t. The existence of a strictly positive discount factor m_t implies that there are no arbitrage opportunities in bond markets. Let y_t^n denote the corresponding continuously compounded yield on the same zero-coupon bond. We use annualized monthly average yields for synthetic euro area government bonds with 2, 3, 5, 7, 10, 15, 20, and 30-year maturities bond yields.

As shown in Ang and Piazzesi (2003), using the above macro-finance model, the yield of a zero-coupon bond at maturity 1 to n can be expressed as a linear function of the state variables:

$$y_t^n = \frac{1}{n}(a_n + b_n' X_t), \tag{4.13}$$

where $a_0 = 0$, $b_0' = 0$ and the scalar a_n and the four-by-one vector b_n' are computed recursively as follows:

$$a_{n+1} = \delta_0 + a_n + b_n'(\mu - \Sigma\lambda_0) - b_n'\Sigma\Sigma' b_n, \tag{4.14}$$

$$b_{n+1} = \delta_1 + (A - \Sigma\lambda_1)' b_n,$$

where the scalar δ_0 (a scalar) and δ_1(a four-by-one vector) describe the one-period interest rate as a function of the state of the economy

$$y_t^1 = i_t = \delta_0 + \delta_1' X_t. \tag{4.15}$$

Since the one-period interest rate is included in the state vector, $\delta_0 = 0$ and all elements of δ_1' are zero, except for that element that picks out the current value of the one-period interest rates in the state vector, approximated by the monthly average of EONIA. The element corresponding to the policy rate (approximated by EONIA) is equal to one while the rest are zeros.

4.4.2.2 Results

The model is estimated in two stages (Rudebusch et al. 2006). First, the VAR model is estimated. Second, the coefficients from the VAR model are taken as given, and the stochastic pricing kernel factor loadings are estimated using non-linear least squares to fit the bond yield data over the period 1999M1–2009M1.

The main estimation results are presented in Tables 4.1 and 4.2 and in Fig. 4.9. The VAR coefficient estimates for the euro area have features similar to those reported by Rudebusch et al. (2006) for the United States. The sum of each variables' own lags is near unity, as is the coefficient of each variable's first lag.

The estimated risk factor loadings are similar in size. Bernanke et al. (2004) found inflation expectations 1-year ahead of particular importance. Given that such time series data (as well as data for interest rate futures for the euro area) have become available only very recently, 1-year Euribor rates are used instead. Risk factor loadings and variance of this variable are comparable to those for other variables (Table 4.1).

The yields as predicted by the model track actual bond yields very closely (Fig. 4.9, first panel). The estimates of the long-run "risk-free" yields during 1999M1–2009M1 are slightly above 3% for long-term yields. Short-term (2-year) model residuals (Fig. 4.9, second panel) do not have an obvious trend, but model residuals for long-term government bonds have been more or less consistently negative since 2004–2005. This reflects the fact that, as in the United States (where former Federal Reserve chairman Greenspan famously called it a "conundrum"),

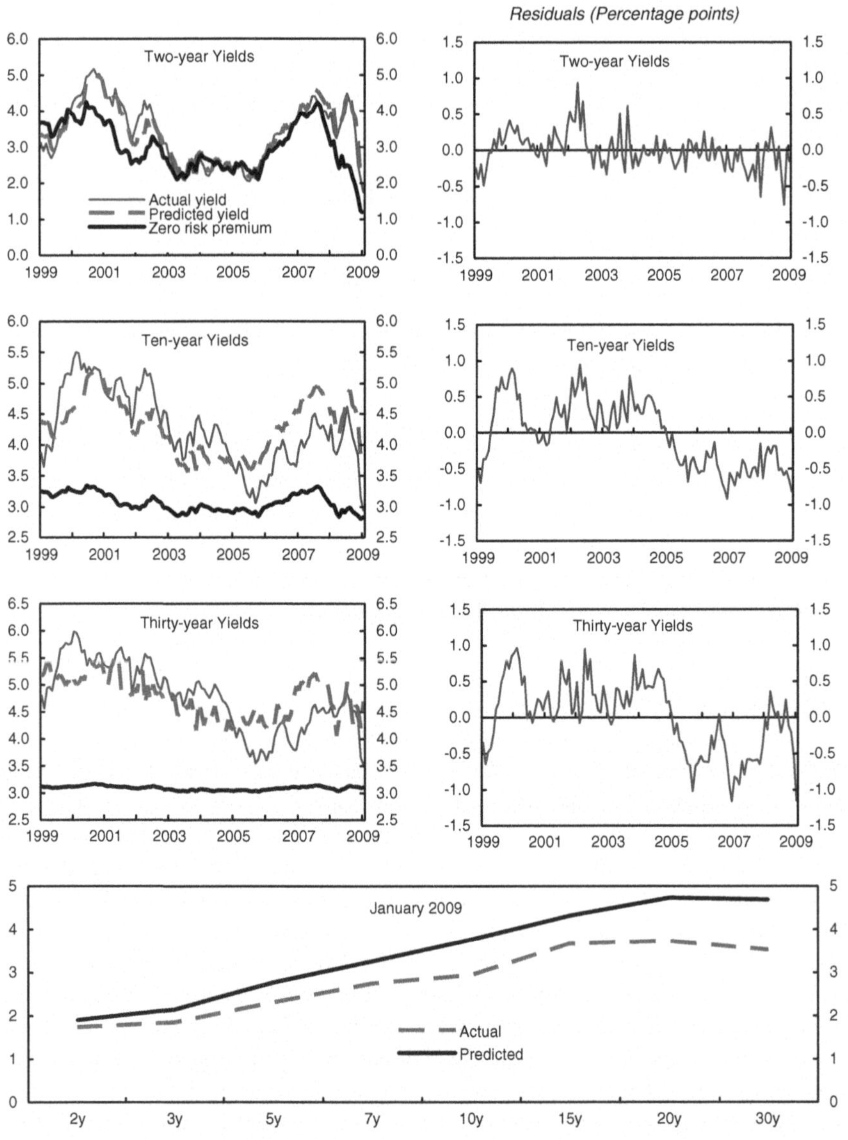

Fig. 4.9 Euro area macro-financial model: Government bond yields and model estimates (%)1/
Sources: DataStream; and IMF staff calculations1/ Euro area synthetic government bond yields

long-term rates did not increase much when the ECB raised its policy rates. The residuals have fluctuated since the onset of the crisis, but sharply turned negative in October 2008, when the ECB introduced a host of new non-standard measures. In the subsequent period, the actual yield curve has become lower and flatter than the predicted yield curve, as illustrated by the latest observation in the bottom panel of Fig. 4.9.

Table 4.1 VAR Parameter Estimates

Coefficient estimates	y_t	π_t	rs_t	rl_t
y_{t-1}	0.617	0.087	0.040	0.089
π_{t-1}	0.125	1.144	0.073	0.056
rs_{t-1}	0.247	0.086	1.141	0.230
rl_{t-1}	0.269	−0.081	0.085	0.427
y_{t-2}	0.102	−0.013	−0.011	0.032
π_{t-2}	0.232	0.371	0.005	0.036
rs_{t-2}	0.100	0.111	0.199	0.003
y_{t-3}	0.276	0.001	0.006	−0.041
π_{t-3}	0.679	0.125	−0.131	−0.016
rl_{t-3}	−0.317	−0.078	−0.004	0.014
rl_{t-3}	−0.305	−0.090	−0.070	0.026
Constant	0.802	0.339	0.326	0.086
Cholesky-factored residual variance				
	0.477	0.000	0.000	0.000
	−0.006	0.202	0.000	0.000
	0.020	0.048	0.208	0.000
	0.007	0.043	0.024	0.166

Source: IMF staff estimates

Table 4.2 Risk Factor Loadings

λ_0	λ_1			
5.8064	0.10665	0.18516	−0.75491	−0.17347
−3.4934	0.05948	−0.11369	0.41976	0.14019
1.0628	0.019663	0.030768	−0.1237	−0.04697
−0.88776	−0.01009	0.01366	0.070758	0.066151

These results provide some indication that the ECB's policy actions during the crisis had some effect on yields, although the results should be treated only as preliminary and illustrative. The lower level of the yield curve is likely to reflect the increase in the monetary base and the relative supply of money relative to bonds, as suggested by the portfolio-rebalancing channel. Moreover, the flattening of the yield curve could imply that markets interpreted the ECB's policy actions as implicit commitments to keep policy rates low longer than anticipated and the current state of the economy (as captured by the simple VAR) would suggest. This finding should be interpreted cautiously, given that the time period under investigation is short, and given that we analyze the impact of the ECB's measures only indirectly (also, the flattening has been most pronounced at the long end, while market expectations of an increase period of low policy rates should have a greater effect at the short end of the yield curve; and there are other possible explanations for the observed behaviour in the model's residuals, including capital flows associated with "flight to safety"). Despite these caveats, the fact that the level of the yield curve has been lower and the slope flatter over the past months than predicted by the macroeconomic variables can give some comfort to those concerned about deflation.

4.5 Conclusions

The analysis of the effectiveness of monetary policy in the context of the financial crisis suggests that the traditional transmission channels (interest rate, bank lending, and broad credit) have continued to operate, but at a lower efficiency. During the crisis, the transmission has slowed down (the lags have become longer), the policy reaction needed to stabilize the economy has become stronger, and the transmission has become subject to more noise (illustrated by the increased residuals in the estimates during the crisis). Also, inflation expectations, while remaining broadly stable, declined significantly in the last quarter of 2008, reflecting the major deterioration in economic activity.

The ECB's non-standard measures, such as a major lengthening of the maturity of monetary operations and a significant increase of its balance sheet, likely have contributed to reducing term spreads in money markets, although the evidence for this is only preliminary and indirect at this point. They may also have had some beneficial effects on government bond term spreads and the level of the yield curve.

4.6 Appendix: Small Theory-based Model for the Euro Area

This appendix describes the equations of the theory-based model, discusses the data that are used for its estimation, and provides the estimates of the coefficients.

The three main equations describe the evolution of inflation, π_t, the output gap, y_t, and the monetary policy response, captured by the policy rates, r_t.

4.6.1 Inflation Equation (Phillips Curve)

$$\pi_t = \lambda_1 \pi 12^e_{t+12} + \frac{(1-\lambda_1)\pi 12_{t-1} + \lambda_2(y_{t-1} + y_{t-2} + y_{t-3})}{3 + \varepsilon^\pi_t} \tag{A4.1}$$

where π_t is monthly inflation (seasonally adjusted at annual rate), $\pi 12^e_{t+12}$ is expected year-on-year inflation, $\pi 12_t$ is year-on-year inflation, y_t is a measure of the output gap, and ε^π_t is a supply shock. This specification implies that prices are set as a markup over marginal cost, captured by the output gap; and the degree of price flexibility and inflation inertia are captured by the weight on the expected inflation term.

For the empirical analysis, which is done with monthly data, $\pi_t = 1{,}200(p\_sa_t - p\_sa_{t-1})$, where p_sa_t is the logarithm of the seasonally adjusted harmonized index of consumer prices (HICP), and $\pi 12_t = 100(p_t - p_{t-12})$, where p_t is the logarithm of the HICP index. Economic activity is approximated by a weighted average of industrial production (30% share) and retail sales indexes. As initial values for the output gap y_t for the Bayesian estimation, the log-difference of the actual index from its Hodrick-Prescott filtered value is used.

4.6.2 Aggregate Demand

$$y_t = \frac{\beta_1(y_{t-1} + y_{t-2} + y_{t-3})}{3 + \beta_2 y^e_{t+1} - \beta_3(r_{t-1} - r\_eq_{t-1}) - \theta_l \hat{r}^l_{t-1} - \theta_{sp} sp_{t-1} + \varepsilon^y_t} \tag{A4.2}$$

where y^e_{t+1} is the expected output gap next period, r_t is the actual short-term real interest rate, defined as the difference between the short-term nominal interest rate and expected inflation, r_eq_t is the equilibrium real interest rate, $\hat{r}^l_t$ is the deviation of the real rate of loans from equilibrium, sp_t is the spread between corporate bonds and government bonds, and ε^y_t is a demand shock.

In this aggregate demand specification, the lagged moving average output gap term reflects the degree of inertia in the economy and the forward-looking output gap term captures intertemporal smoothing by economic agents. The third term, the deviation of actual from equilibrium real interest rates, represents the interest rate channel, while the fourth and fifth terms capture the effects of the bank lending and the broader credit channels, respectively.[16]

Given that the model is estimated with monthly data, the leads and lags in Eqs. A4.1 and A4.2 are chosen so as to obtain dynamic responses that are in line with the dynamic response from models estimated with quarterly data and reproduce plausible lengths of price setting contracts and the lags with which capacity utilization affects inflation in reality.

---

[16] Instead of loan rates, the quantity of loans could be used in the aggregate demand Eq. A4.2. In principle, having loan rates or the quantity of loans in the aggregate demand equation should be equivalent. However, in times of severe stress in the banking system rationing of borrowers may occur, which is not fully reflected in loan interest rates. Testing whether using loans instead of loan rates in the aggregate demand equation changes the results, is left for future research.

4.6.3 Monetary Policy Reaction Function

$$i_t = \gamma_1 i_{t-1} + (1-\gamma_1)(r\_eq_t + \pi 12^e_{t+12} + \gamma_2(\pi 12^e_{t+12} - \bar{\pi}_t) + \gamma_3 y_t) + \varepsilon^i_t \quad \text{(A4.3)}$$

where i_t is the nominal policy interest rate, $\bar{\pi}_t$ is the inflation target, and ε^i_t is a monetary policy shock. The first term in this rule captures the degree of interest rate smoothing by the central bank. The second term is the natural interest rate, and the third and fourth terms represent the usual components for a forward looking Taylor rule where the central bank reacts to the deviation of expected inflation from inflation target and the output gap.

The model is extended in several ways. First, to capture market perceptions about underlying inflation, inflation target is modelled as time varying.

4.6.4 Inflation Target

$$\bar{\pi}_t = \rho \pi^{ss} + (1-\rho)\pi 12_{t-1} + \varepsilon^{\bar{\pi}}_t \quad \text{(A4.4)}$$

where π^{ss} is the steady-state inflation, and $\varepsilon^{\bar{\pi}}_t$ is a shock to underlying inflation. Allowing for a time-varying inflation target also provides insights about central bank credibility (see for example Hördahl et al. 2006).

Second, to test for the importance of bank lending channel, a simple loan demand and supply block is added to the core Eqs. A4.1–A4.4 of the model.

4.6.5 Loan Demand

$$l_t = -\lambda_i i^l_{t-1} + \lambda_y g_{t-1} + \varepsilon^{ld}_t \quad \text{(A4.5)}$$

where l_t is growth of loans provided by the banking system, i^l_t is the interest rate on loans, g_t is growth of output, and ε^{ld}_t is a loan demand shock.

4.6.6 Loan Supply

Loan supply is represented by an inverse loan supply function (determining interest rates on bank loans) as follows:

$$i^l_t = \tau_1 l_{t-1} + \lambda_m \mu_{t-1} + \varepsilon^{ls}_t \quad \text{(A4.6)}$$

where μ_t is money growth, and ε^{ls}_t is a loan supply shock. To close the loan demand and supply block, a standard money demand function is used in which money growth μ_t is determined by output growth and policy interest rates.

4.6.7 Credit Spread

To examine the importance of the broader credit channel, an equation that describes the corporate bond yield spread (the difference of corporate and government bond yields) is added to the model. As Friedman and Kuttner (1992) show, the spread between the corporate bond yield and government bond yield captures the external finance premium, which is in general positive due to risk and liquidity premia. The corporate bond spread is modelled to depend on overall economic conditions captured by the output and policy rate as follows:

$$sp_t = \sigma_1 i_{t-1} + \sigma_2 y_{t-1} + \varepsilon_t^{sp} \tag{A4.7}$$

where ε_t^{sp} is a shock to the corporate spread.

4.6.8 Equilibrium Growth

$$g_t = \tau g^* + (1 - \tau) g_{t-1} + \varepsilon_{g,t} \tag{A4.8}$$

where g_t is the quarterly real GDP growth at annual rate, g^* is steady state real GDP growth and ε_g is a shock to steady state growth.

4.6.9 Equilibrium Output

$$\bar{y}_t = \bar{y}_{t-1} + \frac{g_t}{4} + \varepsilon_{\bar{y},t} \tag{A4.9}$$

where $\bar{y}_t$ is the log of the level of equilibrium real GDP, g_t is the quarterly real GDP growth at annual rate, and $\varepsilon_{\bar{y},t}$ is a shock to equilibrium output.

4.6.10 Equilibrium Real Interest Rate

$$r_t^n = \rho r^* + (1 - \rho) r_{t-1}^n + \varepsilon_{r_t^n,t} \tag{A4.10}$$

where r^* is steady state real interest rate and $\varepsilon_{r_t^n,t}$ is a shock to equilibrium real interest rates.

4.6.11 Real Interest Rate

$$r_t = i_t - \pi 12_{t+12}^e \tag{A4.11}$$

The model is estimated with monthly seasonally adjusted data, using Bayesian methods over the period January 1995 to February 2009 for the version with the

Table 4.3 Euro area: estimates of model parameters

Parameter	Estimate	Standard deviation	*t* Statistics	Prior distribution	Prior standard deviation
λ_1	0.77	0.05	16.65	Beta	0.05
λ_2	0.12	0.06	1.92	Gamma	0.10
β_1	0.74	0.10	7.57	Gamma	0.10
β_2	0.14	0.05	2.73	Beta	0.05
β_3	0.20	0.05	4.22	Gamma	0.05
θ_1	0.08	0.04	1.76	Gamma	0.05
θ_{sp} 1/	0.05	0.02	2.08	Gamma	0.05
γ_1	0.83	0.15	5.40	Beta	0.15
γ_2	1.38	0.27	5.14	Gamma	0.35
γ_3	0.47	0.15	3.20	Gamma	0.15
τ	0.04	0.02	2.10	Beta	0.05
π^{ss}	1.98	0.16	11.99	Norm	0.50
g^*	1.80	0.50	3.64	Norm	0.50
ρ	0.05	0.02	2.95	Beta	0.07
r^*	1.49	0.21	7.23	Norm	0.50
λ_i	0.34	0.12	2.91	Gamma	0.10
λ_y	0.73	0.30	2.45	Gamma	0.10
τ_i	0.15	0.04	3.89	Gamma	0.10
λ_m	0.33	0.19	1.69	Gamma	0.10
σ_1	0.48	0.07	6.45	Gamma	0.10
σ_2	1.12	0.12	9.68	Gamma	0.10

Source: IMF staff estimates
1/ The sample starts in January 1999

bank-lending channel and from January 1999 to February 2009 for the version with the broader credit channel. Economic activity is approximated by a weighted average of industrial production (30% share) and retail sales. In addition, the following variables are used: short-rates approximated by EONIA interest rate, an average of interest rates on new loans to euro area residents of 1–5-year maturity, AAA-, AA-, A-, BBB-rated corporate bond yields of 3–5-year maturity, the spread of corporate bond yield and government bond yield, HICP inflation, money supply (approximated by M3 aggregate), and bank loans to the euro area residents (Table 4.3).

References

Altunbas, Y., Gambacorta, L., Marques, D. (2007). Securitization and the bank lending channel. ECB Working Paper No. 838.

Ang, A., & Piazzesi, M. (2003). A no-arbitrage vector autoregression of term structure dynamics with macroeconomic and latent variables. *Journal of Monetary Economics,50*(4), 745–787.

Angeloni, I., Kashyap, A., Mojon, B., Terlizzese, D. (2002). Monetary transmission in the euro area: Where do we stand? ECB Working Paper No. 114.

Bean, C., Larsen, J., Nikolov, K. (2002). Financial frictions and the monetary transmission mechanism: Theory, evidence and policy implications. ECB Working Paper No. 113.

Bernanke, B., Reinhart, V., Sack, B. (2004). Monetary policy alternatives at the zero bound: An empirical assessment. Board of Governors of the Federal Reserve, Finance and Economics Discussion Series No. 2004–2048.

Bulíř, A., Čihák, M. Šmídková, K. (2008). Writing clearly: ECB's monetary policy communication. IMF Working Paper No. 08/252.

Čihák, M., Harjes, T. (2008). *Liquidity management in the euro area, IMF country report No. 08/ 263*. Washington: International Monetary Fund.

Dai, Q., & Singleton, K. (2000). Specification analysis of affine term structure models. *Journal of Finance, 55*, 1943–1978.

Eggertsson, G., & Woodford, M. (2004). Policy options in a liquidity trap. *American Economic Review, 94*(2), 76–79.

European Central Bank (2009). Recent developments in the retail bank interest rate pass-through in the euro area. *ECB Monthly Bulletin,* 93–105.

Friedman, B. M., & Kuttner, K. N. (1992). Money, income, prices, and interest rates. *American Economic Review, 82*, 472–492.

Hördahl, P., Tristani, O., & Vestin, D. (2006). A joint econometric model of macroeconomic and term structure dynamics. *Journal of Econometrics, 131*, 405–444.

International Monetary Fund (2008). Stress in bank funding markets and implications for monetary policy. *Global financial stability report*. Washington: IMF.

Keynes, J. (1936). *The general theory of employment, interest and money*. London: Macmillan.

Krugman, P. (1998). It's back: Japan's slump and the return of the liquidity trap. *Brookings Papers on Economic Activity, 29*, 137–206.

Mishkin, F. S. (1995). Symposium on the monetary transmission mechanism. *Journal of Economic Perspectives, 9*(4), 3–10.

Rudebusch G, Swanson E, Wu T (2006). The bond yield 'Conundrum' from a macro-finance perspective. Federal Reserve Bank of Dallas working paper no. 2006–2016.

Rudebush, G., & Wu, T. (2003). A macro-finance model of the term structure, monetary policy, and the economy. Federal Reserve Bank of San Francisco Working Paper No. 17.

Sims, C. A., & Zha, T. (1998). Bayesian methods for dynamic multivariate models. *International Economic Review, 39*(4), 949–968.

Sørensen, C.K., & Werner, T. (2007). Bank interest rate pass-through in the euro area: A cross country comparison. ECB Working Paper No. 580.

Chapter 5
The Communication Policy of the European Central Bank: An Overview of the First Decade

Jakob de Haan and David-Jan Jansen

5.1 Introduction

Since its inception, the European Central Bank (ECB) has regarded communication as an integral part of its monetary policy. It has communicated frequently to the public on various issues, such as its objective, its policy decisions, and the economic outlook. In doing so, the ECB has used various communication channels. For instance, the ECB extensively uses press conferences to inform the public on its decisions almost on a real-time basis. In addition, the ECB employs other communication channels, like the Monthly Bulletin, its website, as well as speeches by and interviews with prominent ECB policymakers.

This emphasis on communication is not unique to the ECB. Over the past two decades, a true revolution in thinking and practice has occurred with respect to central bank openness. For a number of reasons—including the greater independence from the political process and the related increased need for accountability—central banks have shed their previous shrouds of mystery. Most importantly, communication has become important because it has the potential to affect private sector expectations. As such, it offers central banks an additional instrument to achieve their monetary policy objectives. By now, communication has developed

---

The views expressed in this chapter are those of the authors and should not be attributed to De Nederlandsche Bank.

J. de Haan (✉) and D.-J. Jansen
Research Department, De Nederlandsche Bank, PO Box 98,1000 AB, Amsterdam, The Netherlands
e-mail: J.de.Haan@dnb.nl

D.-J. Jansen
e-mail: d.jansen@dnb.nl

J. de Haan
University of Groningen, Groningen, The Netherlands

J. de Haan and H. Berger (eds.), *The European Central Bank at Ten*,
DOI: 10.1007/978-3-642-14237-6_5,

into a key instrument in the toolbox of many central bankers (Blinder, Ehrmann, Fratzscher, De Haan, & Jansen, 2008).

This chapter describes and evaluates ECB communications during the first decade of its operation in light of this revolution in thinking and practice. According to Cecchetti and Schoenholtz (2008), the first-decade record is filled with outside complaints about ECB communication with financial markets. However, as they rightly point out, much of this criticism underestimates the challenge of communicating with so many diverse constituencies. Indeed, our assessment of the ECB's communication policies is quite favourable. We conclude that, overall, ECB communication has contributed to the effectiveness of its monetary policy. Our review of the literature shows that ECB communications affect the level and volatility of financial prices—suggesting that private sector expectations reacted to ECB communication. In addition, there is evidence that—on balance—communication has improved the predictability of interest rate decisions. Although financial market impact and predictability are important, they are not sufficient because communication should also contribute to anchoring market expectations in the long run. In this respect, the effectiveness of ECB communications seems less clear.

The chapter is structured as follows. Section 5.2 discusses why communication may offer important benefits to central banks. We also discuss some methodological challenges—in particular the need to account for context—in assessing the effects of communication. Next, Sect. 5.3 reviews the various topics on which the ECB has communicated and its communication channels. Section 5.4 examines empirical evidence on the effects of ECB communications. Finally, Sect. 5.5 offers some policy implications and outlines issues for future research.

In this chapter, we also discuss two issues concerning ECB communication that have received limited attention in previous surveys on central bank communication. First, we discuss whether dispersion in ECB communication has increased uncertainty on upcoming interest rate decisions (Sect. 5.4.2). Second, we review the effectiveness of efforts of ECB officials to affect the euro dollar exchange rate by so-called 'oral interventions' (Sect. 5.4.5).

5.2 Why Can Central Bank Communication Matter for Monetary Policy?

Central bank communication has two main objectives: first, it contributes to the accountability of the central bank and, second, it helps the central bank in managing expectations. In this chapter, we leave the first objective aside and focus upon the second objective of central bank communication (see De Haan, Eijffinger, & Waller, 2005 for a further discussion on the accountability of the ECB).

Why are expectations relevant? Nowadays, it is widely accepted that the central bank's ability to affect the economy critically depends upon the degree to which it can influence market expectations regarding the *future path* of overnight interest rates. The reason is simple: few, if any, economic decisions hinge on the overnight bank rate, which is the only market interest rate that is effectively controlled by the central bank. Long-term interest rates, reflecting expected future short-term interest rates, affect saving and investment decisions by households and firms. Therefore, the public's perception of future policy rates is critical for the effectiveness of monetary policy.

Still, from a theoretical point of view, it is not obvious that communication may help the central bank realizing its ultimate objective(s), like price stability and stable economic growth. For instance, communication has little value added if the central bank credibly commits to a policy rule. Assuming that the public has rational expectations, any systematic pattern in the way that policy is conducted should be correctly inferred from the central bank's observed behaviour (Woodford 2005). Thus, when it comes to predicting future interest rates, the public merely has to interpret (forecasts of) economic data in view of the central bank's policy rule; there is no role for central bank communication. Following Faust and Svensson's (2001, p. 373) definition of central bank transparency—i.e., how easily the public can deduce central-bank goals and intentions from 'observables'—one might say that a central bank can be fully transparent without any communication.

This example is highly stylised. Still, it points out three conditions under which central bank communication may matter: non-rational expectations, absence of commitment to unchanging policy rules, and asymmetric information.

First, the assumption that the public will understand monetary policy perfectly regardless of the efforts that are made to explain it may be unrealistic. Woodford (2005, p. 403) argues that: "Insofar as explanation of the policy rule to the public does no harm under the assumption of rational expectations, but improves outcomes under the (more realistic) assumption that a correct understanding of the central bank's policy commitments does not occur automatically, then it is clearly desirable for the central bank to explain the rule that it follows."

King (2005) goes even further and argues that the public may follow simple (but possibly fairly robust) 'heuristics' in making decisions instead of following optimising behaviour. He argues that in this case central bank communication can play an important role in leading people to choose heuristics of the right sort: "the more the central bank can do to behave in a way that makes it easy for the private sector to adopt a simple heuristic to guide expectations the better. A good heuristic from that point of view would be 'expect inflation to be equal to target'" (King 2005, p. 12). In other words, by communicating to the public the central bank may help anchoring expectations.

Second, it is unlikely that the central bank would stick to an unchanged policy rule for long. For example, according to Bernanke (2004), "specifying a complete and explicit policy rule, from which the central bank would never deviate under any circumstances, is impractical. The problem is that the number of contingencies to which policy might respond is effectively infinite (and, indeed, many are unforeseeable)." Likewise, ECB President Trichet has repeatedly emphasized that the ECB takes its decisions one step at a time, rather than following a rule. For instance, after the interest rate decision on 2 March 2006, Trichet said: "We do not engage a priori in a series of interest rate hikes…we do not pre-commit ourselves unconditionally."[1]

Third, financial-market participants generally do not have as much information as monetary-policymakers on a number of key inputs to policymaking, including the weights policymakers assign to possible objectives, or their assessment of the economic situation. If there is *asymmetric information*, so that the public and the central bank dispose of different information, it may be perfectly rational for the public to adjust their expectations if the central bank provides new information. Here it is important that we distinguish between the types of information on which asymmetries may exist.

In the first place, the central bank may provide *information about its reaction function*. This should lead, *ceteris paribus*, to an increase in the private sector's ability to forecast the central bank's policy decisions. Suppose, the central bank follows a Taylor-type rule,

$$r_t = r^* + \pi_t + \alpha y_t + \beta(\pi_t - \pi^*) \tag{5.1}$$

where r, r^*, y, π and π^* denote the interest rate, the equilibrium real interest rate, the output gap, inflation and target inflation, respectively. An improvement in the private sector's understanding of what values the central bank uses for r^*, π^*, α and β would lead to improved private sector forecasts for r_t (Swanson 2006). One possibility in countries without explicit inflation targets is that the central bank may provide information about its long-run inflation target (Kohn & Sack 2004). Likewise, central banks could also provide information on the relative weights that the central bank places on its output and inflation objectives. The parameter α is an important determinant of the speed with which policy seeks to put inflation back on target following adverse shocks. The larger is α, the larger is the 'flexibility' allowed in returning to the inflation target following a shock. Hence, it determines the period-by-period deviations of inflation from its target. Providing this kind of information may help the private sector to form more accurate expectations. According to Trichet (2005), "If the central bank is able to convince economic agents and markets participants of its analysis and assessment of the outlook, and about the policy measures that it is going to take in response to it, this mechanism of anticipation will act in self-equilibrating manner. As soon as the macroeconomic news is released, expectations of the short-term interest rates will adjust in the equilibrating direction that markets expect to see implemented by the central bank."

Bernanke (2004) refers to the recent literature on adaptive learning in explaining why communication on these issues affects monetary policy effectiveness (see Blinder et al. 2008 for a further discussion). When the public does not know but instead must estimate the central bank's reaction function, there is no

[1] http://www.ecb.int/press/pressconf/2006/html/is060302.en.html.

guarantee that the economy will converge to the optimal rational expectations equilibrium because the public's learning process *itself* affects the behaviour of the economy. The feedback effect of learning on the economy can lead to unstable or indeterminate outcomes. In such a setting, communication by the central bank may play a key role in helping improve economic performance.

Furthermore, the central bank may have better information on the economic outlook.[2] Various studies find that financial markets not only react to macroeconomic news, but also to *information on the economic outlook* provided by the central bank. Apparently investors update their own views in response to the information conveyed by the central bank. Kohn and Sack (2004) argue that private agents may lend special credence to the economic pronouncements of the central bank, particularly if the central bank has established credibility as an effective forecaster of the economy. They point out that the Federal Reserve has been broadly correct on the direction of the economy and prices over the past two decades, on occasion spotting trends and developments before they were evident to market participants. This record has enhanced its reputation and credibility.[3]

Even though there are good reasons why communication may be beneficial, it is by no means clear what constitutes an optimal communication strategy. The literature on central bank transparency has shown that full disclosure of all available information is often not optimal. Unfortunately, the theoretical literature has not come up with clear-cut conclusions regarding the optimal level of transparency (Geraats 2002; Van der Cruijsen & Eijffinger 2010), although progress is being made (van der Cruijsen, Eijffinger, & Hoogduin, 2008). In general, the central bank faces a trade-off when there are limits as to how much information can be digested effectively (Kahnemann 2003). The trade-off might become even more pronounced if the central bank communicates about issues on which it receives noisy signals itself, such as the evolution of the economy (as opposed to, e.g., its intentions regarding upcoming interest rate decisions). This has been stressed by Amato, Morris, and Shin (2002) who argue that central bank communication can co-ordinate the actions of financial market participants away from fundamentals, in the sense that they attach too much weight to the central bank's views, not taking into account that they reflect a noisy signal. However,

[2] Another difference may be the asymmetry in the treatment of macroeconomic information. Market participants have a monitoring horizon biased toward short-term movements of financial markets, while the central bank analyses every kind of economic development and their short to medium-term impact on inflation and economic activity. As a consequence, market participants have a limited ability to build proper data-driven economic scenarios consistent with the central bank's view of future inflation. Communication may help them forming a better view.

[3] Romer and Romer (2000) provide statistical evidence that the Federal Reserve staff forecasts for output and inflation have been more accurate than private sector forecasts over the past several decades. Gamber and Smith (2009) find that the Fed's forecast errors remain significantly smaller than the private sector's but the gap has narrowed considerable since the mid-1980s, especially after 1994.

Blinder et al. (2008) discuss some of the arguments casting doubts on the validity of this conclusion.[4]

Before turning to the empirical evidence regarding ECB communication, we want to highlight some methodological challenges in measuring communication. Central bank communication does not appear out of thin air, but is a reflection of economic reality. Any comment made by a policymaker is, therefore, also a specific interpretation of economic reality made in a particular context. It is crucial to account for this context when assessing the effectiveness of communication.

A first way to do so is by explicitly labelling the various elements of the communication process itself. One useful tool is the analytical framework proposed by Lasswell (1948) which analyses communication by answering the following five questions: '*Who* says *what* to *whom* in *what* channel, with *what* effect?' Or, to put it slightly different, to study communication one should identify the sender of the message, the receiver, the message itself, the channel through which the message is sent and the effect that the message produces (Graber 2004). It is important, for instance, to identify the intended audience. In many cases, the literature has focused on the reaction of financial market participants. Recently, however, the general public has moved into focus. For example, recently van der Cruijsen, Jansen, and De Haan (2010) conducted an internet survey to establish through which channels the general public obtains information on monetary policy.

Second, the economic environment is a crucial element of the context in which communication takes place. The credibility of statements on the economic outlook will probably depend on the state of the economy. In an economic trough, positive statements may be less likely to be believed than at the peak of the cycle. To account for the economic environment, researchers use various types of data as control variables. In a study on the day-to-day reactions of financial markets, it is standard to use announcements of macroeconomic data as controls (see, for instance, Jansen & de Haan 2007a, b). In other cases, researchers have used macroeconomic projections or real-time figures on economic growth and inflation as control variables (Jansen 2008).

Finally, it is important to account for the institutional environment in which communication occurs. There are important differences between central banks with regard to the nature of its decision making process, and the structure of its monetary policy committee. For example, the Bank of England has a committee of nine members who are individually accountable, while both the FOMC and the ECB Governing Council are larger committees with group accountability, while the Reserve Bank of New Zealand has a single decision maker. Central banks need to tailor their communication strategies to these and other institutional features. For a proper analysis of the effectiveness of central bank

[4] For instance, Svensson (2006) argues that the assumptions underlying the Morris and Shin result are not likely to hold in practice. See also Gosselin, Lotz, and Wyplosz (2007).

communication, researchers have to carefully account for these institutional differences.

5.3 ECB Communication: Topics and Channels

5.3.1 Communication on Objectives

Independent central banks often benefit from a clearly defined mandate given by government. The Maastricht Treaty did not provide for a quantitative target for the ECB's main objective of price stability but the ECB defined price stability as 'inflation close to but below 2% in the medium run for the euro area as a whole'. Quantitative targets have two benefits. First, numerical targets facilitate accountability, enabling the performance of the central bank to be assessed against its mandated yardstick. Second, a quantitative objective (or objectives) helps to anchor the expectations of economic agents. Often, and through various channels, the ECB has informed the public on its definition of price stability.

5.3.2 Communication on Decisions: the ECB Press Conferences

Most central banks nowadays inform the public about their monetary policy decisions on the day they are taken. Many central banks do so by releasing short press statements. The ECB has been rather unique in detailing the motives behind a particular policy decision at elaborate press conferences after policy meetings. So far, it has refrained from releasing minutes of the policy meeting. Press conferences may provide less detail than minutes, but they are timelier and more flexible, if they allow the media to ask questions.

Policy meetings of the ECB Governing Council typically take place on the first Thursday of each month. Following these meetings, the ECB announces the monetary policy decisions at 13:45 CET. Some 45 minutes later, at around 14:30, the ECB President and Vice-President hold a press conference that comprises two elements: a prepared introductory statement containing the background considerations for the monetary policy decision, and a Questions & Answers (Q&A) part during which the President and the Vice-President are available to answer questions by the attending journalists. The introductory statement is understood to reflect the position and views of the Council, agreed upon on a word-by-word basis by its members. While providing background information on the rationale for its decision, the ECB press conference is generally less detailed than the minutes of the Bank of England or the Federal Reserve (Blinder et al. 2008). In particular, it does not provide information on voting. However, the press conference avoids the substantial time delay of the minutes. Furthermore, the Q&A session allows the press to ask follow-up questions and thus can help clarify open issues (Ehrmann & Fratzscher 2009).

5.3.3 Communication through other Channels

A second important communication device for the ECB is its *Monthly Bulletin*, which is published 1 week after each monetary policy meeting and contains both the assessment of economic developments and information on its analytical framework—such as models, methods, and indicators—used in the decision-making process. The editorial of the Bulletin contains a short explanation of the previous interest rate decision and frequently includes a summary statement of the Governing Council's view of the economy.

The testimonies of the ECB President to the European Parliament (EP) offer a third opportunity to communicate. Four times a year, the President appears before the EP's Committee on Economic and Monetary Affairs and explains the ECB's policy decisions and its economic outlook. Subsequently, he answers questions posed by Committee members. These testimonies are open to the public and the transcripts of the presentations are published on the websites of both the EP and the ECB.

Finally, ECB officials often give speeches or interviews on monetary policy. Communications by individual central bankers offer greater flexibility in timing than pre-scheduled events. Speeches and interviews by individual committee members between meetings offer a way to communicate changes in views rapidly, if so desired (Blinder et al. 2008). Furthermore, in the case of the ECB, national central banks feel they are responsible for explaining ECB policies to their respective national audiences. However, inter-meeting comments may be a potential source for confusion. For example, Ehrmann and Fratzscher (2007a) report that only 62.2% of communications on the monetary policy inclination by individual ECB central bankers were in line with the ECB policy decision taken at the Governing Council meeting following the communication.

Ehrmann and Fratzscher (2007b) have also analysed the timing of communication by individual ECB Governing Board members. Figure 5.1, which is reproduced from their study, shows that except for days surrounding the monetary policy meetings, there is a somewhat higher level of activity before than after meetings (which is statistically significant at the 5% level), stressing the attempt of the ECB to prepare markets for the upcoming meeting. Ehrmann and Fratzscher also find that when a policy surprise is large (i.e., when its absolute value is above the average absolute surprise) ECB officials are more talkative. Whereas the members of the Governing Council normally talk to the public roughly every 7 (business) days, they do so more than every 5 days if there has been a large surprise at the previous meeting.

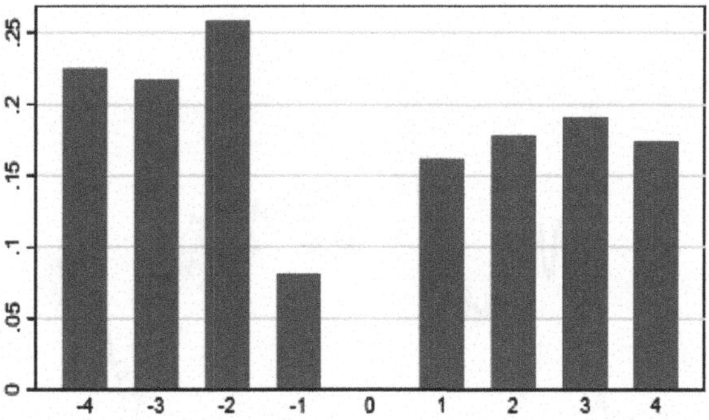

Fig. 5.1 Timing of ECB communication. Source: Ehrmann and Fratzscher (2007a)

5.3.4 Communication on Future Policy Decisions

When it comes to future policy decisions, many central banks provide some sort of forward guidance, albeit in very different ways. A few central banks (like those of New Zealand, Norway, and Sweden) even provide *quantitative* guidance by publishing the numerical path of future policy rates that underlies their macroeconomic forecasts.

The ECB has so far refrained from giving explicit information on future interest rate decisions. However, the use of key words and phrases to signal views on monetary policy has played an important role throughout the years. For example, euro area central bankers have used phrases such as 'interest rates are appropriate', which can readily be interpreted as a neutral comment on interest rates.

During some time, the term 'vigilance' and variations thereof played an important role in ECB communication (Jansen & De Haan 2007b). Between June 2003 and December 2005, the ECB maintained its main refinancing rate at a level of 2%, but frequently voiced its concern about inflation. One worrisome development was that inflation expectations at the time sharply increased, which led the ECB to signal that it was 'vigilant' regarding upward risks to price stability. In 2006, ECB President Trichet (2006, p. 9) described this strategy as follows: "Importantly, signalling vigilance proved instrumental in reaching a common understanding with the markets: the ECB, though observationally inactive, was at any time ready to start action". At another occasion, Trichet (2005) noted: "Over time, our communication became increasingly 'alert', signalling our vigilance to the upside risks to inflation which grew at the time." According to ECB Board member Bini Smaghi (2005), "Vigilance can thus be communicated … even if policy rates remain unchanged[.] … If the communication strategy is successful, expectations converge over time back to the level of unchanged policy rates."

To illustrate the role of 'vigilance', Fig. 5.2 shows 10-year euro area break-even inflation (solid line) and the occurrence of 'vigilance' (the grey diamonds) between June 2003 and March 2007. The dotted line denotes the ECB's main refinancing rate. Starting in March 2004, the term 'vigilance' is used on 114 trading days.

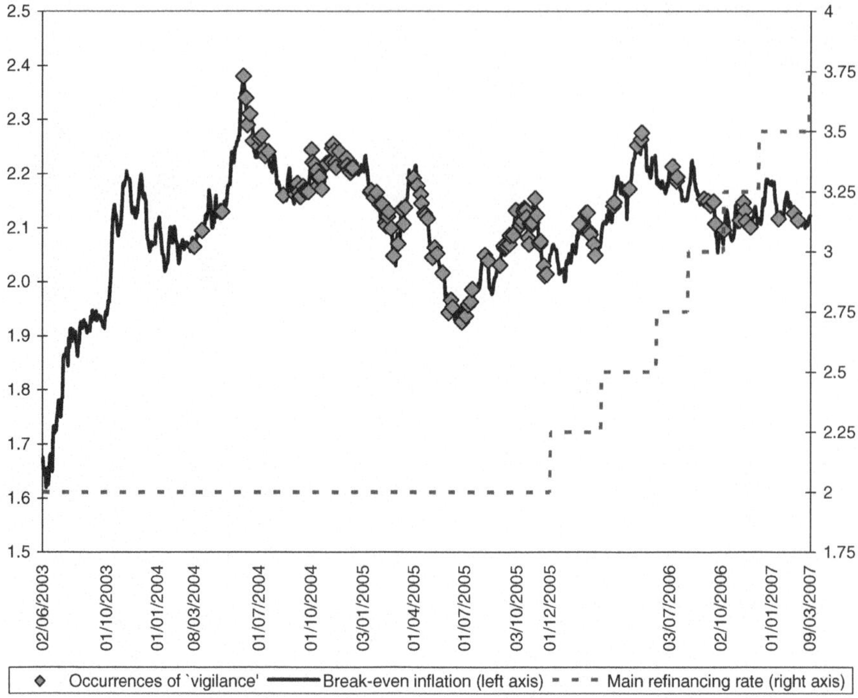

Fig. 5.2 'Vigilance' in ECB communication between 2003 and 2007. The *solid line* shows euro area break-even inflation between June 2003 and March 2007. The *grey diamonds* indicate that on a particular day 'vigilance' was used in ECB communications. The *dotted line* denotes the ECB main refinancing rate. Dates are denoted in DD/MM/YYYY. *Source*: Jansen and De Haan (2007b)

After December 2005, the term 'vigilance' only occurs on 32 trading days. Figure 5.2 also shows how from that point onwards, the ECB tightened monetary policy in a number of consecutive steps. Interestingly, after 2005, the interpretation of 'vigilance' changed as market participants saw the phrase as an indicator of upcoming policy changes. For example, according to Bloomberg, "ECB President Jean-Claude Trichet has used the word 'vigilant' to flag each of the six rate increases since late 2005" (Bloomberg News, 15 February 2007). Likewise, according to UBS: "Trichet has made a practice of effectively pre-announcing hikes at the prior meeting with the use of the key 'vigilant' phrase" (UBS FX Trade and Research, 9 January 2007).

The use of 'vigilance' seems to have ended abruptly as the liquidity crisis started over the summer of 2007. At a press briefing on 2 August, Trichet noted "The existence of upside risks to price stability at medium to longer-term horizons is confirmed by the strength of the underlying rate of monetary expansion: *strong vigilance* is therefore of the essence to ensure that risks to price stability over the medium term do not materialise."(italics added).[5] However, at the subsequent Governing Council meeting in September, interest rates were left unchanged, and there was no mentioning of 'vigilance'. When asked about the absence of 'strong vigilance' during the Q&A session, Trichet replied: "... I would say that you have noted that I did not say the words 'strong vigilance', and I don't want to comment any further on that. It is up to you, observers and the market to make your own judgement on the overall statement I have just given on behalf of the Governing Council."[6] When the credit crisis further unfolded in 2008 and 2009, 'vigilance' did not reoccur in the ECB's communications.

The use of code words may contribute to short-term predictability, but there may be drawbacks. Cecchetti and Schoenholtz (2008, p. 12) are rather critical about the use of code words by the ECB: "Codes are imperfect signals at best, and typically relate only to near-term policy prospects, which may be of least importance in the formulation of critical long-run market expectations. Rather, these expectations depend sensitively on the transparency and reliability of the central bank's reaction function, along with an understanding of the evolution of prices and the economy."

5.3.5 Communication on Economic Developments

Central bankers often communicate their views on the current economic situation and likely future developments. This can be done qualitatively—for instance, by stating that economic growth will pick up—or by providing quantitative guidance. In December 2000, the ECB began publishing so-called 'projections' on a biannual basis. The projections, which are published in the June and December issues of the ECB Monthly Bulletin, consist of forecast ranges for inflation, GDP growth, and main expenditure components. The projections are prepared by experts from euro area national central banks and from the ECB, and serve as important input to the deliberations of the Governing Council (European Central Bank 2001). The ECB President makes the projections public at the press conference, following a Governing Council meeting. This could create some confusion, as the Governing Council does not necessarily endorse the projections. Each release of the projections is accompanied by a short note detailing the main assumptions underlying the forecasts, followed by a short description of the economic rationale behind the projection itself. Since 2004, the ECB also releases the ECB staff projections, which are constructed in the spring and fall of each year.

One economic variable that received a lot of attention during the early years of the EMU was the exchange rate. Before its introduction, the euro was widely expected to be a strong currency. Some even hoped (or feared) that the euro would

[5] Available at http://www.ecb.int/press/pressconf/2007/html/is070802.en.html.

[6] Available at http://www.ecb.int/press/pressconf/2007/html/is070906.en.html.

compete with the dollar in its role of most important international currency. As the new currency was an important symbol for the EMU, its decline against the dollar led some observers to question the overall success of the EMU. Moreover, the strong depreciation of the euro was a serious threat to price stability in the euro area. In the end, the ECB reacted by intervening in the foreign exchange market in 2000. Apart from interventions, the ECB has been very active to support the euro verbally (a strategy known as 'talking up the currency'). ECB officials have often expressed the view that the euro was undervalued during the period under consideration. Once the euro started to appreciate against the dollar, the exchange rate has figured less prominently in ECB communications.

Now that we have described the ECB communications, we will analyze to what extent these communications have contributed to the effectiveness of ECB monetary policy making.

5.4 What has ECB Communication Contributed?

5.4.1 Effects of ECB Communication on Predictability of Interest Rate Decisions

One perceived benefit of central bank transparency is that it will contribute to predictability of monetary policy. Indeed, the empirical evidence points out that ECB monetary policy generally has been quite predictable. Also, predictability of ECB policy decisions has increased over time (see Blattner, Catenaro, Ehrmann, Strauch, & Turunen, 2008, for an overview). For instance, Bernoth and Von Hagen (2004) find that the money markets were able to predict short-term rates well, suggesting that ECB communication has worked well during the first years of EMU. Also, Rosa and Verga (2007) conclude that the forecasting ability of communication by the ECB (measured on the basis of the introductory statements of the ECB President) is similar to the one implied by market-based measures of monetary policy expectations. Ehrmann and Fratzscher (2007a) also find that financial markets have been able to anticipate ECB decisions well. In fact—using changes in short term interest rates on meetings days as a measure of predictability—they find that the ECB has been as predictable as the Federal Reserve, and that both have been somewhat more predictable than the Bank of England.

It is less clear which pieces of communication contribute in particular to predictability. Several papers analyse whether communication adds information compared to the information contained by variables typically included in a Taylor-rule model. As we argued in Sect. 5.2, this is one area where communication could make a difference.[7] Heinemann and Ullrich (2007) find that their communication

[7] As Bernanke and Boivin (2003) point out, most empirical analyses of monetary policy have been confined to frameworks in which the central bank is implicitly assumed to exploit only a

index, based on the wording of the introductory statements by the ECB President at the press conference following Governing Council meetings, adds information not provided by Taylor-rule variables. Also Rosa and Verga (2007) conclude that words and data on macroeconomic variables are essentially complements, rather than substitutes. However, Jansen and De Haan (2009) conclude that communication-based models do not outperform models based on macroeconomic data in predicting decisions, although they find that statements on the main refinancing rate and future inflation are significantly related to interest rate decisions.

5.4.2 Dispersion in ECB Communication

Clear communication requires that the various communication tools send signals that are mutually consistent and well coordinated, and that different central bankers communicate in a consistent way. In the first part of this section we discuss recent research on the consistency among different ECB communication channels, while in the second part we discuss whether ECB officials communicated in a consistent way.

With a variety of communication tools available, coordination of the message across these tools is crucial. For example, if the ECB President identifies risks for price stability, while the published inflation projection indicates that inflation is expected to stay below the target, the public may become confused as to the course of future monetary policy. Bulíř, Čihák, and Šmídková (2008) analyze the various measures of forecast risk that the public can obtain from ECB communication. The basic idea is that it is much easier for the public to understand monetary policy if all communications send the same message, pointing to the same type of forecast risk. The authors compare the signals from various ECB communication tools, namely inflation forecasts, inflation targets, and verbal assessments of the inflation risks contained in the ECB's press releases, and monthly bulletins. Their main finding is that during 1999–2007, the ECB's communication was clear in about 95% and that the clarity improved in 2003–2007 as compared to 1999–2002. This compares favourably with communication clarity in other central banks.

We will now discuss whether ECB officials communicated in a consistent way. Decision-making in the ECB Governing Council is often described as 'collegial' (see Blinder 2007). Also the communication strategy of the ECB has been

(Footnote 7 continued)
limited amount of information, like in the Taylor-rule model. In practice, the central banks' approach to data analysis typically mixes the use of large macro-econometric models, smaller statistical models, heuristic and judgmental analyses, and informal weighting of information from diverse sources. One way of interpreting central bank communication may be that it summarizes the central bank's assessment of all the information it employs. In that case, models using central bank communication should outperform those that rely only on a limited number of macro variables.

characterized as 'collegial'; in comparison to the Federal Reserve, the communication of individual central bankers of the ECB is less diverse (Ehrmann & Fratzscher 2007a). Still, at times, there has been quite some dispersion in ECB communication. A potential problem is that too many disparate voices might confuse rather than enlighten the public—especially if the messages appear to conflict. If done poorly, uncoordinated group communication might actually lower the signal-to-noise ratio.

To examine this hypothesis, we analyze the effects of dispersed communication during the initial years of the EMU.[8] We performed a content analysis of comments by leading euro area central bankers on the main refinancing rate, the outlook for euro area inflation, and the outlook for euro area economic growth. Per topic, we classified each comment on a ternary scale (−1, 0, +1). For example, statements suggesting a tightening of monetary policy are coded +1, whereas statements hinting at interest rate cuts are coded −1. We measure dispersion in communication by computing the standard deviation of the coded statements. As shown in Fig. 5.3, notably ECB statements on the outlook for inflation and economic growth were dispersed, with the degree increasing over time.

We evaluate the effects of dispersion on predictability by using survey data on interest rate expectations.[9] Following the approach by Ehrmann and Fratzscher (2005), Table 5.1 shows tobit estimation results where the dependent variable is either the absolute prediction error (column 1), the fraction of incorrect predictions (column 2) or the standard deviation of expected interest rates (column 3). We control for the fact that communication is not the only factor that influences predictability by using the standard deviation of a daily series of one-month Euribor rates in the week before the one in which the interest rate decision is made to control for macroeconomic uncertainty.[10]

We find that dispersion on the inflation outlook negatively influences predictability as measured by the absolute prediction error. Inconsistencies in statements on the main refinancing rate and the outlook for economic growth are not related to the absolute prediction error (column 1). We also find a positive relationship between dispersion in comments on inflation and the degree of incorrect interest rate predictions (column 2). The marginal effect in this case is equal to 0.21 ($p = 0.03$), which implies a sizeable effect of dispersion on predictability. Finally, there is a strong indication that dispersion leads to higher levels of uncertainty as the

[8] The sample period is 6 May 1999 to 2 May 2002. This period is interesting as both the ECB and financial markets had to learn how to deal with communication by a newly created international organisation. Further details are given in Jansen and De Haan (2006).

[9] These expectations are taken from the Reuters poll of forecasters. Before each ECB interest rate decision, Reuters polls key economists on their views on the main refinancing rate after the upcoming meeting. The use of these data instead of market-based expectations allows us to examine the impact of communication dispersion on market uncertainty as reflected in the dispersion of the views of the forecasters.

[10] We also estimated specifications with a linear trend as, over the years, the ECB may have become more predictable. This did not affect the results.

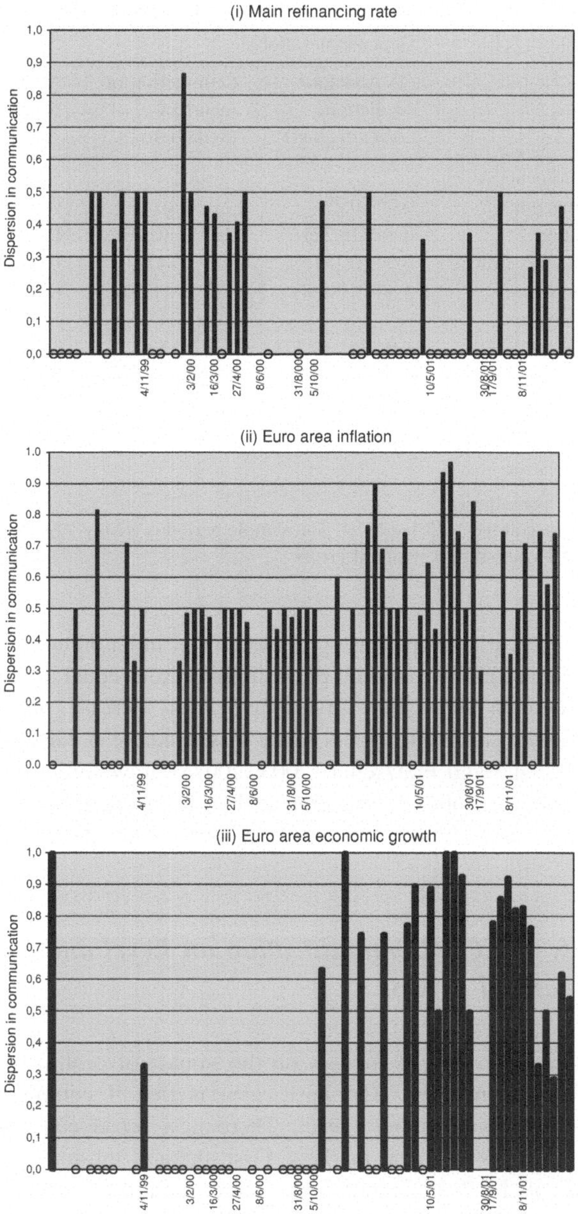

Fig. 5.3 Dispersion in comments by euro area central bankers. The figures show the degree of dispersion in comments on (*i*) the ECB main refinancing rate, (*ii*) euro area inflation and (*iii*) euro area economic growth. Dispersion is measured as the standard deviation of the coded statements. The sample period is 6 May 1999 to 2 May 2002. The dates correspond to the occurrence of ECB interest rate changes (DD/MM/YY). The *circles* on the *x*-axis indicate that there was more than one comment on a specific topic during the event window, but no inconsistency between the comments. Source: Jansen and De Haan (2006)

Table 5.1 Dispersion in communication made interest rate decisions less predictable

	Dependent variable		
	(1) Absolute prediction error (median)	(2) Fraction of incorrect predictions	(3) Standard deviation of expected rates
Dispersion in comments on			
Main refinancing rate	0.06 (0.29)	−0.01 (0.25)	0.02 (0.04)
Euro area inflation	0.44* (0.22)	0.41** (0.20)	0.11*** (0.03)
Euro area economic growth	0.07 (0.18)	0.17 (0.15)	0.03 (0.03)
Standard deviation 1-month Euribor	3.88** (1.84)	4.50** (1.79)	0.88*** (0.31)
Constant	−0.67** (0.17)	−0.28** (0.13)	−0.04** (0.02)
Chi^2 LR-test	6.1	12.2**	19.4***
Number of observations	65	65	65
Percentage of censored observations	70.5	43.1	41.5

Standard errors in parenthesis
*/**/*** Significance at the 10/5/1% level. The sample period is 6 May 1999 to 2 May 2002. All results use robust Huber–White standard-errors

coefficient for the variable measuring dispersion in inflation comments is highly significant (column 3). The marginal effect in this case is equal to 0.07 ($p = 0.00$).

These regressions show that diverging views increase uncertainty about upcoming decisions, and that agents make less accurate predictions. Using different data, Ehrmann and Fratzscher (2005, 2007a) draw similar conclusions for the ECB. Overall, the policy implication is that, from the perspective of predictability, central bankers should take care that their statements are consistent.

5.4.3 Effects of ECB Communication on Level and Volatility of Financial Prices

An important line of research focuses on the impact of central bank communications on financial markets. The basic idea is that if communications steer expectations, asset prices should react. There is a broad consensus that ECB communication affects financial markets. First, there is substantive evidence that various forms of ECB communication affect volatility, which implies that expectations changed (De Haan 2008). This holds true for short-term interest rates (Sebestyén & Sicilia 2005), the bond market (Andersson, Overby, & Sebestyén, 2009), the stock market (Andersson 2007), and the swap markets (Coffinet & Gouteron 2007). The strongest effects are generally found for the President's introductory statements at the ECB press conference following the Governing Council's meeting (Connolly & Kohler 2004 and Sebestyén & Sicilia 2005). Ehrmann and Fratzscher (2009) analyse whether the press conferences provide *additional* information, beyond that explaining a given decision. If a policy decision contains all relevant information for market participants, markets should not show any systematic movement during press conferences. The separation of the release of the decision from its explanation allows separating the effect of monetary policy decisions from the accompanying communication. These authors find that the size of the market reaction to the press conference is, on average, substantially larger than the reaction to the policy decision itself, while the press conference at the same time exerts lower effects on market volatility. The market reaction to the press conference is related to the characteristics of the decision: the more a decision surprised the market, the stronger is the reaction to the introductory statement. Especially statements containing a reference to inflationary developments and responses to questions regarding interest rate discussions at the Governing Council meeting have substantial effects on markets.

While studies focusing on volatility can only establish whether or not markets react (Blinder et al. 2008), studies that have coded ECB communication yield evidence that financial markets also moved in the intended direction.[11] For instance, Ehrmann and Fratzscher (2007a) find that statements suggesting tighter monetary policy lead to higher rates, while statements suggesting easing lead to lower rates. Statements on monetary policy inclinations move interest rates by 1.5–2.5 basis points. Musard-Gies (2006) finds similar results, although the short end of the yield curve reacts more sharply to statements than the long end. Using tick-by-tick data on Euribor futures, Rosa and Verga (2008) show that the unexpected component of ECB comments has a sizable impact on futures prices. More importantly, they analyze whether ECB comments moved markets in the intended direction. Table 5.2, which is based on their study, shows how the response of financial markets seems to be in accord with the tone of ECB communication: hawkish statements lead to higher futures rates, while dovish statements lead to the opposite reaction. Interestingly, ECB communications apparently have long-term implications, in particular if the comments are dovish.

5.4.4 Effects of ECB Communications on Inflation Expectations

Predictability and market impact are necessary, but not sufficient conditions for successful and effective communication. In addition, communication policy

[11] In this line of research, communication is quantified in order to assess both the direction and magnitude of its effects on asset prices. Communications must be classified according to their content and/or likely intention, and then coded on a numerical scale. Negative (positive) values are assigned to communications that are perceived as dovish (hawkish), and zero to those that appear to be neutral. Whereas some researchers restrict the coding to directional indications by using a scale between -1 and $+1$ (e.g., Jansen & De Haan 2005; Ehrmann & Fratzscher 2007a), others assign a finer grid that is at least suggestive of magnitude (Berger, De Haan, & Sturm, 2010; Rosa & Verga 2007, 2008, 2008; Heinemann & Ullrich 2007; Musard-Gies 2006), e.g. by coding statements on a scale from -2 to $+2$.

Table 5.2 Does ECB communication have the intended effects?

	Hawkish statements	Dovish statements
Effects on futures rates after		
1 day	0.022**	−0.014*
2 days	0.022*	−0.017
3 days	0.019*	−0.023*
5 days	0.016	−0.022
10 days	0.041*	−0.067***
15 days	−0.013	−0.098***

Source: Rosa and Verga (2008), Table 8. The numbers in the table are changes in futures rates over various event windows following ECB meetings
***/**/* Significance at the 10/5/1% level

should also aim at anchoring and guiding market expectations over the medium to long run (Issing 2005). As the main objective of the ECB is price stability, an important issue is to what extent communication can help anchoring inflation expectations.

Only four studies that we are aware of have examined the impact of the ECB's communication on inflation expectations. Ehrmann and Fratzscher (2007a, b) examine the impact of communication on 5-year inflation expectations derived from indexed bonds and find that their measures of communication are not significantly related to inflation expectations. Jansen and De Haan (2007b) find evidence that communication by the ECB regarding risks to price stability (measured by the frequency and strength of the key word 'vigilance') between June 2003 and December 2005—a period during which the ECB did not change its policy rates—reduced high-frequency inflationary expectations slightly in the second half of 2005, when a change in the ECB's policy stance became increasingly likely. To some extent, their results lend support to Trichet's (2005) claim that communication has helped stabilize inflation expectations without a policy change. However, the reported impact is quite small so that it is clear that other factors also played a crucial role in stabilizing these expectations. Furthermore, the impact is only significant for the period when an interest rate hike became more likely. In other words, communication apparently works best when supported by (a credible likelihood of) deeds.

Finally, Ullrich (2008) examines whether the updated Heinemann-Ulrich ECB communication indicator is related to expected inflation. To proxy expectations, she uses data from the ZEW Financial Markets Test in which qualitative answers of experts from banks, insurance, investment, and industrial companies with regard to the development of inflation in the following 6 months are transformed into quantitative inflation expectations. Her results suggest that when the ECB communicates concern about inflation risks, this induces financial market experts to adjust inflation expectations with a 6-month horizon upwards. Our reading of this result, however, is that communication does not have the desired impact. If the ECB were credible, financial markers would believe that ECB policies would ensure that inflation does not deviate too much from target.

5.4.5 Effects of ECB Communication on Exchange Rates

A recent strand in the literature studies the effects of central bank communication on the exchange rate. Various studies have focused on the effects of comments regarding monetary policy and the economic outlook. Conrad and Lamla (2007) investigate the impact of the ECB's policy announcements on the euro-dollar exchange rate. They find that surprise interest rate changes explain exchange rate movements immediately after the press release, and that, during the introductory statement, communication with respect to future price developments is most relevant. However, Ehrmann and Fratzscher (2007a) find no evidence that ECB communication has affected the exchange rate, although they do find that ECB comments have affected interest rates and equity markets.

One difference between these two studies is that the latter uses daily data. The daily frequency may be too low to pick up any effects of communication. This suggestion is also present in studies that focus on the effects of comments regarding the exchange rate. The central question in those papers is to what extent different communication strategies influence the level or volatility of the exchange rate. These strategies include intervention "threats" (suggestions or rejections of actual interventions in currency markets), "verbal" or "oral" intervention (comments on the currency intended to create positive or negative momentum) or a combination of words and actions (actual interventions closely followed by comments).

During the early years of the EMU, the ECB made frequent use of oral interventions to support the euro. At the time, central bankers were particularly worried about the potential pass-through effects of the decline in the euro-dollar exchange rate. This prompted them to make numerous comments in an apparent attempt to create positive momentum for the new currency. Jansen and De Haan (2005) have analyzed oral interventions by the ECB in their study on the period of prolonged depreciation of the euro against the dollar between 1999 and 2002. Using daily data, these authors find that the euro-dollar exchange rate did not react to ECB oral interventions. For the same sample period, but now using intraday-data, Jansen and De Haan (2007a) find that there were effects of oral interventions, but these effects were small and short-lived. In contrast, Fratzscher (2006) finds strong evidence that ECB communications affected the euro-dollar exchange rate. His analysis focuses on a longer period, however, and includes also oral interventions by the Bundesbank. Still, he finds that exchange rate comments have affected spot as well as forward exchange rates with an estimated impact on the conditional mean of up to 0.21%.

5.5 Concluding Comments, Future Research, and Policy Recommendations

A substantial body of research has examined the effects of communications by the European Central Bank. On the basis of our review of empirical studies, we conclude that, on balance, ECB communication has contributed to the effectiveness of ECB monetary policy. The literature finds that communication has influenced developments in financial markets, suggesting that the ECB has succeeded in affecting private sector expectations. In addition, there is evidence that communication has improved predictability of interest rate decisions. Still, predictability and market impact are important, but not sufficient, as communication should also aim at anchoring long run inflation expectations. In this area, the effects of ECB communication turn out to be less clear, and this remains an important point of attention.

In some respects, ECB communications seem less successful. First, the dispersion in ECB communication has increased uncertainty on upcoming interest rate decisions during the initial years of the EMU. The policy implication is that central bankers, from the perspective of predictability, should take care that their statements are consistent. Second, there is only mixed evidence that the ECB's efforts to talk up the euro have had lasting effects on the euro-dollar exchange rate.

As to future research, in our view there are some important issues to be put high on the agenda. First, as Blinder et al. (2008, p. 941) point out, "virtually all the research to date has focused on central bank communication with the financial markets. It may be time to pay some attention to communication with the general public." According to Cecchetti and Schoenholtz (2008), public support of the ECB is critical to ensuring the independence of the ECB over the long term. Although the Maastricht Treaty provides the ECB with a very strong foundation, the ECB lacks the natural constituency that the most credible national central banks typically enjoy (like the Bundesbank in the past), especially when confronted by politicians with a shorter horizon. The ECB's efforts to communicate also to the public at large may help to build that popular support, but this process may take many years.

Second, the role of intermediaries needs to be examined. Until now, studies have paid little attention to the specific way in which communication reaches market participants. Most studies have assumed that the media do not play an independent role in interpreting and transmitting central bank comments. Berger, Ehrmann, and Fratzscher (2006) are among the few who explicitly study the media channel. They find that euro area financial markets have yet to converge on a homogeneous view of the ECB, to overcome locational and national biases, and to adopt a common expectation-formation process. They suggest that there is a scope for the ECB to guide this convergence process by a careful and targeted communication policy.

Also some other improvements in ECB communication have been suggested. For instance, Cecchetti and Schoenholtz (2008) argue that the ECB's tendency to describe its decisions as unanimous may understate the nature and vigour of important Governing Council debates, thereby diminishing the ability of observers to make an informed judgment about policy and sustaining scepticism about ECB communications more generally. However, the drawback may be that dispersed views hamper predictability of interest rate decisions, as shown by our empirical analysis.

Finally, the future enlargement of the euro area will be particular challenging for ECB communication. Even today, no other central bank faces the task of communicating with the general public in so many different countries. On the one hand, the task of explaining ECB policy to this diverse audience will helped by the presence of governors of national central banks. At the same time, the diversity may create new challenges. As Cecchetti and Schoenholtz (2008) point out, speaking to local governments or populations is fundamentally different than communicating with financial markets. Diverse national histories may prompt different constituencies to view identical policy statements in very different ways. If the ECB wants to secure a popular base, then enlargement only intensifies that challenge.

References

Amato, J. D., Morris, S., & Shin, H. S. (2002). Communication and monetary policy. *Oxford Review of Economic Policy, 18*(4), 495–503.

Andersson, M. (2007). Using intraday data to gauge financial market responses to Fed and ECB monetary policy decisions. ECB Working Paper No. 726.

Andersson, M., Overby, L.J. & Sebestyén, S. (2009). Which news moves the Euro area bond market? *German Economic Review*, 10(1), 1–31.

Berger, H., Ehrmann, M., & Fratzscher, M. (2006). Monetary policy in the media. ECB Working Paper No. 679.

Berger, H., De Haan, J., & Sturm, J.-E. (2010). Does money matter in the ECB strategy? New evidence based on ECB communication, *International Journal of Finance and Economics*, forthcoming.

Bernanke, B. (2004). Fedspeak, remarks at the meetings of the American Economic Association, San Diego. The Federal Reserve Board. http://www.federalreserve.gov/boarddocs/speeches/2004/200401032/default.htm.

Bernanke, B., & Boivin, J. (2003). Monetary policy in a data-rich environment. *Journal of Monetary Economics, 50*(3), 525–546.

Bernoth, K., & von Hagen, J. (2004). The Euribor futures market: Efficiency and the impact of ECB policy announcements. *International Finance, 7*(1), 1–24.

Bini Smaghi, L. (2005). Inflation, expectations and current challenges to monetary policy. Speech at 'The European Inflation-Linked Conference' in Rome, 10 October. http://www.ecb.int/press/key/date/2005/html/sp051010_1.en.html.

Blattner, T., Catenaro, M., Ehrmann, M., Strauch, R., & Turunen, J. (2008). The predictability of monetary policy. European Central Bank Occasional Paper No. 83.

Blinder, A. S. (2007). Monetary policy by committee: Why and how? *European Journal of Political Economy, 23*(1), 106–123.

Blinder, A. S., Ehrmann, M., Fratzscher, M., De Haan, J., & Jansen, D. (2008). Central bank communication and monetary policy: A survey of theory and evidence. *Journal of Economic Literature, 46*(4), 910–945.

Bulíř, A., Čihák, M., & Šmídková, K. (2008). Writing clearly: ECB's monetary policy communication. IMF Working Paper No. 08/252.

Cecchetti, S. C., & Schoenholtz, K. L. (2008). How central bankers see it: The first decade of ECB policy and beyond. NBER Working Paper 14489.

Coffinet, J., & Gouteron, S. (2007). Euro area market reactions to the monetary developments press release. ECB Working Paper No. 792.

Connolly, E., & Kohler, M. (2004). News and interest rate expectations: A study of six central banks. In C. Kent & S. Guttman (Eds.), *The future of inflation targeting* (pp. 108–134). Sydney: Reserve Bank of Australia.

Conrad, C., & Lamla, M. J. (2007). The high-frequency response of the EUR-US dollar exchange rate to ECB monetary policy announcements. KOF (Swiss Economic Institute) Working Paper No. 07-174.

De Haan, J. (2008). The effect of ECB communication on interest rates: An assessment. *Review of International Organizations, 3*, 375–398.

De Haan, J., Eijffinger, S. C. W., & Waller, S. (2005). *The European Central Bank: Credibility, transparency, and centralization*. Cambridge: MIT Press.

Ehrmann, M., & Fratzscher, M. (2005). How should central banks communicate? ECB Working Paper No. 557.

Ehrmann, M., & Fratzscher, M. (2007a). Communication by central bank committee members: Different strategies, same effectiveness? *Journal of Money, Credit, and Banking, 39*(2-3), 509–541.

Ehrmann, M., & Fratzscher, M. (2007b). The timing of central bank communication. *European Journal of Political Economy, 23*(1), 124–145.

Ehrmann, M., & Fratzscher, M. (2009). Explaining monetary policy in press conferences. *International Journal of Central Banking, 5*(2), 41–84.

European Central Bank. (2001). A guide to eurosystem staff macroeconomic projection exercises. http://www.ecb.int/pub/pdf/other/staffprojectionsguideen.pdf.

Faust, J., & Svensson, L. E. O. (2001). Transparency and credibility: Monetary policy with unobservable goals. *International Economic Review, 42*(2), 369–397.

Fratzscher, M. (2006). On the long-term effectiveness of exchange rate communication and interventions. *Journal of International Money and Finance, 25*(1), 146–167.

Gamber, E. N., & Smith, J. K. (2009). Are the fed's inflation forecasts still superior to the private sector's? *Journal of Macroeconomics, 31*(2), 240–251.

Geraats, P. (2002). Central bank transparency. *The Economic Journal, 112*(483), 532–565.

Gosselin, P., Lotz, A., Wyplosz, C. (2007). Interest rate signals and central bank transparency. CEPR Discussion Paper No. 6454.

Graber, D. A. (2004). Methodological developments in political communication research. In L. L. Kaid (Ed.), *Handbook of political communication research* (pp. 45–67). Mahwah, New Jersey: Lawrence Erlbaum Associates.

Heinemann, F., & Ullrich, K. (2007). Does it pay to watch central bankers lips? The information content of ECB wording. *Swiss Journal of Economics and Statistics, 143*(2), 155–185.

Issing, O. (2005). Communication, transparency, accountability—monetary policy in the twenty-first century. *Federal Reserve Bank of St. Louis Review, 87*(2), 65–83.

Jansen, D. (2008). Has the clarity of Humphrey–Hawkins testimonies affected volatility in financial markets? De Nederlandsche Bank Working Paper No. 185.

Jansen, D., & De Haan, J. (2005). Talking heads: The effects of ECB statements on the Euro-Dollar exchange rate. *Journal of International Money and Finance, 24*(2), 343–361.

Jansen, D., & De Haan, J. (2006). Look who's talking: ECB communication during the first years of EMU. *International Journal of Finance and Economics, 11*(3), 219–228.

Jansen, D., & De Haan, J. (2007a). Were verbal efforts to support the euro effective? A high-frequency analysis of ECB statements. *European Journal of Political Economy, 23*(1), 245–259.

Jansen, D., & De Haan, J. (2007b). The importance of being vigilant: Has ECB communication influenced euro area inflation expectations? CESifo Working Paper No. 2154.

Jansen, D., & De Haan, J. (2009). Has ECB communication been helpful in predicting interest rate decisions? An evaluation of the early years of the economic and monetary union. *Applied Economics, 41*(16), 1995–2003.

Kahnemann, D. (2003). Maps of bounded rationality: Psychology for behavioral economics. *American Economic Review, 93*(5), 1449–1475.

King, M. (2005). Monetary policy: practice ahead of theory, Mais Lecture, delivered at Cass Business School, London. http://www.bankofengland.co.uk/publications/speeches/2005/speech245.pdf.

Kohn, D. L., & Sack, B. (2004). Central bank talk: Does it matter and why? In: *Macroeconomics, Monetary Policy, and Financial Stability* (pp. 175–206), Ottawa: Bank of Canada.

Lasswell, H. D. (1948). The structure and function of communication in society. In L. Bryson (Ed.), *The communication of ideas* (pp. 37–51). New York: Institute for Religious and Social Studies.

Musard-Gies, M. (2006). Do ECB's statements steer short-term and long-term interest rates in the Euro-zone? *The Manchester School, 74*(supplement), 116–139.

Romer, C., & Romer, D. (2000). Federal Reserve information and the behavior of interest rates. *American Economic Review, 90*(3), 429–457.

Rosa, C., & Verga, G. (2007). On the consistency and effectiveness of central bank communication: Evidence from the ECB. *European Journal of Political Economy, 23*(1), 146–175.

Rosa, C., & Verga, G. (2008). The impact of central bank announcements on asset prices in real time. *International Journal of Central Banking, 4*(2), 175–217.

Sebestyén, S., & Sicilia, J. (2005). Is the external communication of the European central bank effective? mimeo.

Svensson, L. E. O. (2006). Social value of public information: Morris and Shin (2002) is actually pro transparency, not con. *American Economic Review, 96*(1), 448–451.

Swanson, E. T. (2006). Federal reserve transparency and financial market forecasts of short-term interest rates. *Journal of Money, Credit, and Banking, 38*(3), 791–819.

Trichet, J. C. (2005). Monetary policy and 'Credible Alertness', intervention at the panel discussion "Monetary Policy Strategies: A Central Bank Panel", at the Symposium sponsored by the Federal Reserve Bank of Kansas City, Jackson Hole, Wyoming, 27 August 2005. http://www.ecb.int/press/key/date/2005/html/sp050827.en.html.

Trichet, J. C. (2006). Activism and alertness in monetary policy, lecture at the conference on 'Central banks in the 21st Century' organised by the Banco de Espana, 8 June. http://www.ecb.int/press/key/date/2006/html/sp060608_1.en.html.

Ullrich, K. (2008). Inflation expectations of experts and ECB communication. *North American Journal of Economics and Finance, 19*, 93–108.

van der Cruijsen, C. A. B., & Eijffinger, S. C. W. (2010). The economic impact of central bank transparency: A survey, forthcoming. In P. Siklos, M. Bohl, & M. Wohar (Eds.), *Challenges in central banking: The present institutional environment and the forces affecting the conduct of monetary policy*. Cambridge: Cambridge University Press.

van der Cruijsen, C. A. B., Eijffinger, S. C. W., Hoogduin, L. H. (2008). Optimal central bank transparency, De Nederlandsche Bank Working Paper No. 178. *Journal of Economic Psychology*, forthcoming.

van der Cruijsen, C. A. B., Jansen, D., De Haan, J. (2010). How much does the public know about the ECB's monetary policy? Evidence from a survey of Dutch households. De Nederlandsche Bank Working Paper No. 252.

Woodford, M. (2005). Central-bank communication and policy effectiveness. In *The Greenspan era: Lessons for the future* (pp. 399–474). Kansas City: Federal Reserve Bank of Kansas City.

Chapter 6
Governance and Monetary Policy Decision-Making at the ECB

Peter Stella and Jérôme Vandenbussche

6.1 Introduction

A long debate about the appropriate reform of the Governing Council (GC), the European Central Bank (ECB)'s decision-making body, took place earlier this decade in the context of the imminent enlargement of the European Union (EU) and the Eurozone. Since its creation, the ECB GC has been composed of six Executive Board (EB) members and all of the Eurozone national central bank (NCB) governors. Each has the same de jure voting weight in monetary policy decisions. The pros and cons of various voting proposals were discussed in light of enlargement in academic and policy circles as reflected, inter alia, in Baldwin et al. (2001), Berger (2002), Gros (2003) and Heisenberg (2003). Following an ECB recommendation, the Council of the EU decided in March 2003 to introduce a rotation system in the GC once the number of governors (or, equivalently, Eurozone countries) reached 15, wherein countries would receive voting weights as a function of their economic and demographic significance. In December 2008, the ECB decided to postpone the actual implementation of the reform until the number of governors reaches 18.

Reformers of the GC aimed to strike a balance between legitimacy and efficiency. In the context of a supra-national political institution such as the ECB, legitimacy can be gauged along at least three dimensions. The first is the level of delegation from elected policy-makers to non-elected bureaucrats. The second is

The views expressed in this chapter are those of the authors and should not be attributed to the IMF, its Executive Board, or its management.

P. Stella
Stellar Consulting LLC, Virginia, USA
e-mail: pstellaconsult@gmail.com

J. Vandenbussche (✉)
European Department, International Monetary Fund, 700 19th Street NW, Washington, 20431, DC, USA
e-mail: jvandenbussche@imf.org

J. de Haan and H. Berger (eds.), *The European Central Bank at Ten*,

DOI: 10.1007/978-3-642-14237-6_6,

the level of centralization, i.e., the relative weight of national representatives (such as NCB governors) versus ECB representatives permanently based in ECB headquarters. The third is, fixing the degree of delegation and centralization, the relative weight of each national representative. Legitimacy concerns required that each national representative be granted some decision-making power, while efficiency concerns called for fixing an upper bound both on the number of GC members (to put a limit on coordination costs) and on the power of governors relative to non-governors (to make sure that the GC maintains a euro area-wide perspective).

Two important and highly relevant sets of events have taken place since then. First, the Dutch and French voters rejected the European Constitution in 2005 and Irish voters later rejected the Lisbon Treaty in 2008, putting a brake on the European political integration process and adding grist to the mill of those who give prime importance to legitimacy concerns in the design of European institutions, including the ECB. Second, the writing of this book comes at a time when the ECB has been facing by far the most challenging macro-financial environment since its creation and where most major central banks have resorted to unconventional monetary policy tools and operations in the face of a global financial crisis and recession (see Chap. 4). The GC debate took place in a far more benign political and economic environment, which may have blurred some of the fundamental ECB governance design issues.

Against this background, we aim to put in perspective and assess the effectiveness of current ECB governance arrangements. This assessment is mostly qualitative in nature as very little hard data is publicly available on the details of collective decision-making in central banks, including the ECB. Still, reforming central bank governance remains a hot topic for policy-makers and legislators beyond the particular case of the ECB, as witnessed by the recent publication of a BIS report on the subject (BIS 2009).

In Sect. 6.2, we first leave all legitimacy questions aside and analyze the lessons that can be drawn from the recent and burgeoning literature on monetary policy committees (MPCs), and on group decision-making more generally. There we try to assess whether the most salient characteristics of the GC, i.e., its size, composition and decision rule might need to be modified to enhance the efficiency of monetary policy decision-making, essentially focusing on its interest rate setting function.

We then reflect in Sect. 6.3 on how the three types of legitimacy concerns described above might lead to various types of decision-making schemes within a central bank. That officials making monetary policy should be independent of political influence once they are appointed is well accepted. But this acceptance makes the a priori specification of the decision process all that more important. Ironically, the legitimacy of monetary policy authorities may be criticized both when it is perceived as divorced from political considerations and when it is perceived to be too close to what the political authorities desire.[1] Hence the design

[1] The US Federal Reserve has been criticized from both sides of this spectrum during the current crisis.

and choice of the decision process and the appointment process must incorporate a delicate balance of interests.

We then focus more explicitly in Sect. 6.4 on the issue of the appropriate level of centralization of a supra-statal central bank by discussing the experience of the Federal Reserve System from 1913 through the Banking Act of 1935. During that period, two decades of iterative shifts in the balance of power between semi-autonomous Federal Reserve District Banks and the Board of Governors in Washington was resolved in favour of centralization during the reforms launched during the Great Depression. The current crisis might similarly lead to an accretion of power to the ECB and to the EB. In this vein, the EU Commission endorsed a recommendation made in the De Larosiere report (2009) and proposed in September 2009 the establishment of the European Systemic Risk Board (ESRB) responsible for macro-prudential supervision in the EU. The ECB's President and Vice-President would be members of the ESRB's General Board, while the ESRB's Secretariat would be fully entrusted to the ECB (see Chap. 7). Finally, Sect. 6.5 offers our conclusions.

6.2 A Few Lessons from Academic Studies on Group and MPC Decision-Making

6.2.1 Preliminary Remarks

Three main concerns have been expressed with respect to ECB decision-making in the context of the Eastern enlargement of the Eurozone. The first concerns the over-dilution of the power of economic heavyweights and of relative loss of control of the core of the institution (Frankfurt) relative to the periphery (the NCBs). The second one is that of the large increase of the size of the GC, already the largest MPC in the world, and the associated loss of efficiency related to the rise of coordination costs. The third is the increased risk of cacophony in ECB communication (see also Chap. 5), which is directly related to the increased size of the GC.[2] These three concerns point to three fundamental dimensions of MPC design, i.e., the aggregation of heterogeneous preferences, judgment, and voice.

This chapter focuses on the first two dimensions only. As to the third issue, we just remark that relatively little has been written so far on the interaction between governance and communication issues in committees. In particular, it seems to us that one positive aspect of having the ability to use different voices is the enrichment of the set of messages that a central bank can send to the public. Too often the literature on central bank communication assumes that policymakers

[2] See for example M. Brockett, "ECB Policy-Makers Clash after Trichet Engineers Truce", Bloomberg, May 14, 2009, which documents the publicly expressed diverging views of the German, Slovak and Slovene Governors on unconventional monetary operations.

follow individual strategies and ignores the possibility that they may follow a collective one whereby various MPC members would have an assigned role in a coordinated communication strategy.

To analyze the costs and benefits of having policy-makers with heterogeneous preferences and judgment decide on monetary policy, this section of the chapter draws on Vandenbussche (2006), which contains a comprehensive review of the relevant theoretical and empirical literature on group decision-making and discusses implications for the question of optimal MPC design.[3] As most ECB commentators and observers, we are primarily interested in three key and salient aspects of the GC structure: its size, its composition, and its decision rule. However, even if we focus on these three dimensions only, we need to recognize at the outset that we will not be able to provide firm and definitive answers on the question of the optimal structure of the GC, even as we leave completely aside questions of legitimacy discussed later in Sects. 6.2 and 6.3. Rather, this brief review will highlight a few important considerations and trade-offs to be taken into account when thinking about GC design and performance looking forward.

In particular, theoretical and empirical studies of decision-making by committees face the challenging task of specifying proper behavioural assumptions, such as policy-makers' social preferences as well as processes of social interaction and group dynamics. This point was emphasized by Yellen (2005) who remarked that many experts on MPCs are likely to be motivated by a sense of the public good and a spirit of cooperation, to be concerned by the quality of the atmosphere within the committee, and to respect the authority of the chairman. In a similar vein, Issing et al. (2001, p. 132) insisted that "[monetary policy] decisions are the outcome of a *process of collective reasoningwhich is more than a mere exchange of views*. This collective process can shape the final outcome more than each single vote." These remarks from famous practitioners motivate our adopting an eclectic approach to analyze the determinants of MPC members' behaviour and our devoting a part of this section to a discussion of the social psychology literature on group decision-making.

6.2.2 General Considerations Regarding the Design of a MPC

Papers written about the reform of the Governing Council tended and still tend to focus on a few selected and salient aspects and have tended to consider them only one at a time. These aspects are: (i) the Governing Council's size; (ii) its composition (i.e., the appropriate combination of Board members versus national governors, or insiders versus outsiders); (iii) its rule for making decisions (consensus versus voting); and (iv) its level of transparency and accountability

---

[3] Other recent surveys on the same topic include Berger (2006), Blinder (2007), Fujiki (2005), Gerling et al. (2003), and Sibert (2006).

Table 6.1 Main characteristics of selected MPCs

Country	MPC size	Number of outsiders	De jure decision rule	Non-voting MPC members
Eurozone	22	16	Simple majority	0
US	19	12	Simple majority	7
Japan	9	6	Simple majority	0
UK	9	4	Simple majority	0

Note Data as of August 2009. "Outsider" means committee member without full-time managerial position within the central bank

(see Buiter 1999). As comparisons are often made with other G-7 central banks, Table 6.1 provides a summary comparison of the ECB's GC with other major central banks' MPC as of August 2009.[4] Both the GC's size and the proportion of outsiders indeed appear rather large, especially if one remembers that seven out of the 12 Federal Reserve Presidents do not vote as a result of the rotation system in place at the Federal Open-Market Committee (FOMC).

However, from the theoretical design point of view, all those dimensions and several others should be thought about jointly so as to capture potentially important interaction effects. For example, the effect of the release of transcripts on the quality of the debate within an MPC may depend on whether individual votes are published. Alternatively, the effect of an additional voting MPC member is likely to be different if decisions are made by majority voting or by consensus. To summarize all dimensions of MPC design and their potential interactions, Fig. 6.1 provides a simple representation of the one-shot monetary policy game, where endogenous variables (from the designer's perspective) are all in italics (while exogenous variables are not) and arrows indicate channels of influence. As shown in the figure, these include not only the size of the committee, its composition, the appointment rules and the decision mechanism, but also the contracts offered to MPC members (including their accountability), the gathering of the economic information made available to the committee, the protocol before and during meetings, the communication strategy, and—since the "game" is repeated—the frequency of meetings.

If such an exhaustive modelling and optimization exercise were feasible, all endogenous variables would be determined as a function of exogenous variables, most notably the policy objective(s) of the designer (or, presumably, designers in the case of a supra-national institution such as the ECB). The operational difficulty of choosing the appropriate course of policy is obviously not constant across MPC meetings since rather tranquil times can suddenly be interrupted by a crisis, as we have witnessed in the recent past. As will be discussed in Sect. 6.3, one could therefore very well imagine that a sophisticated central bank law might prescribe

[4] An interesting survey of decision-making structures in central banks around the world can be found in Chap. 4 of BIS (2009) while Erhart and Vasquez-Paz (2008) have compiled a useful database on MPC characteristics covering 85 countries.

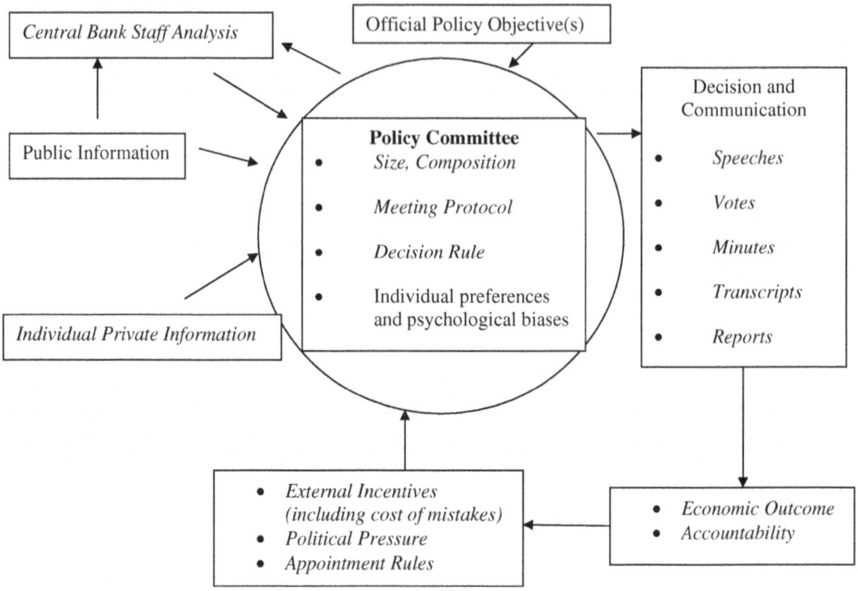

Fig. 6.1 Representation of the one-shot monetary policy game

the use of different committee structures, in particular the use of different voting rules, depending on elements of the situational context or the type of decision being contemplated.

In practice, the theoretical and empirical literature on group decision-making, whether in economics or social psychology, has examined at best two or three endogenous dimensions at a time. This means that one can expect to obtain only very partial answers from existing studies. Moreover, some important specificities of monetary policy decision making, such as its quasi-repeated game nature, are rarely considered.

6.2.3 Advantages and Disadvantages of Preference Heterogeneity in the GC

Preference heterogeneity in the GC comes in two types. The first relates to the relative weights attached by a given policy-maker to various macroeconomic or financial objectives, such as control of inflation or output stabilization. This type of heterogeneity is present in all existing MPCs and may result from ideological biases and/or sensitivity to political pressure as well as different time horizons. The second type is linked to the weight attached by a given policy-maker to euro area-wide objectives relative to national or regional objectives. This second type of heterogeneity is more likely to be present in a supra-national institution such as the

ECB where a national governor may be more sensitive to the pressure of its national government and/or public opinion. The enlargement of the GC represents an advantage to address some consequences of the first type of heterogeneity but may be a source of problems because of the second type.

6.2.3.1 Differences in the Weighting of Various Policy Objectives

Tabellini (1987) has shown theoretically how a larger MPC with appropriately staggered terms can help mitigate or solve the time-inconsistency problem of monetary policy, whereby a policymaker is tempted to produce inflation surprises in order to stimulate output in the short run and therefore is likely to generate high and costly inflation expectations. In addition to enhancing monetary policy credibility, Mihov and Sibert (2006), and Waller (2000) have demonstrated how a larger MPC also helps deliver smoother policy as the MPC acts as a mechanism to "average" policy-makers' heterogeneous preferences.

To get a better sense of the benefits brought by preference aggregation in a MPC, it would be useful to actually measure the extent of preference heterogeneity and of the influence of partisan politics on the decision-making process. Analyses of this type have been attempted by several authors using voting records or transcripts of U.S. Federal Reserve FOMC and Bank of England MPC meetings. Comparable time series of voting data or transcripts unfortunately do not seem to be available, or to have been exploited, in other countries or monetary unions such as the Eurozone, where preference heterogeneity and/or political influence could be expected to be greater on average.

Numerous studies of FOMC voting have examined monetary policy votes cast by Board members, Reserve Bank presidents, or both. These studies have typically found that policy makers with an academic or banking profile tend to dissent on the side of tightening while those with a long experience as Fed staff tend to dissent on the side of easing, and that Board members are more sensitive to political and bureaucratic influences than Reserve Bank presidents. However, these studies often suffer from serious econometric problems, such as omitted variables bias or truncation of the data (see Gildea 1990; Havrilesky & Schweitzer 1990; Krause 1996).

Chappell et al. (2005, Chap. 4) use dissent-voting data at the FOMC over 1966–1996 to estimate monetary policy reaction functions.[5] They estimate individual-specific intercepts for 83 members of the FOMC who served during this period and document some degree of heterogeneity in policy preferences across members. In common with earlier researchers, they find that, as a group, members of the Board of Governors preferred a looser monetary stance than Reserve Bank

[5] By so doing, they interpret individual votes as the reflection of individual preferences only ("sincere voting") and implicitly assume that there is no divergence of beliefs about the state of the world across individuals. They also rule out any form of individual learning or strategic behavior by assumption.

presidents. They also find support for the hypotheses that FOMC members' reaction function shifts toward ease when the Democrats assume the Presidency[6] and when elections are approaching. They also show that partisan pressures work both through direct influence from the President and indirectly through the power of appointment—governors appointed by Democrat Presidents tend to favour easier policies than those appointed by Republicans. Overall their results confirm the presence of political pressures on individual policymakers consistent with models of partisan politics.

Meade and Sheets (2005) also look at FOMC monetary policy decisions between 1978 and 2000 and present some interesting descriptive statistics.[7] This period includes 214 votes. Dissenting votes represent about 8% of total votes cast, with Board members and Bank Presidents dissenting at rates of 7.7 and 8.9%, respectively. However, if votes by the Chairman are excluded, the dissent rate for Board members rises to 9.2%, above that for Bank presidents. Of the 198 dissenting votes registered in their sample, two-thirds were dissents for tighter monetary policy, while one-third were for easier monetary policy. Dissenting votes cast by Board members were split about evenly between easing and tightening, while Bank presidents dissented for tighter monetary policy six times more frequently than for easier policy, a finding consistent with previously discussed evidence.

Turning now to the UK, Gerlach-Kristen (2003) analyzes votes at the 72 MPC meetings at the Bank of England between June 1997 and April 2003. She finds that external policymakers have dissented more frequently, for longer periods of time and have tended to favour lower interest rates than the majority. However, looking directly at the original voting records available on the Bank of England's website, the degree of disagreement expressed through voting appears rather small overall.

More recently, Riboni and Ruge-Murcia (2008) estimate the individual reaction function of each member of the Bank of England's MPC between June 1997 and June 2006. They find evidence of systematic heterogeneity, which appears to be related to the nature of the membership. In particular, they find that external members react more strongly to unemployment than internal members, but that there is no clear pattern regarding their reaction to inflation.

Studies based solely on voting records are problematic because voting may not be sincere. In fact Blinder et al. (2001, p. 39) note that the "FOMC does vote in a formal sense, but it is widely known that individual members often do not vote their true preference. Instead, each committee member decided whether to support or oppose the chairman's policy recommendation, which is almost always made

[6] Note that they do not establish any causality in this respect.

[7] Meade (2002) compares dissent rates at the FOMC and at the Bank of England's MPC. She finds that the dissent rate at the Federal Reserve between February 1970 and August 2002 was 7.8%, compared to a dissent rate of 16.6% at the MPC of the Bank of England (BoE) between June 1997 and May 2002 (these numbers exclude votes by the committee chairman). During the same periods, dissents were registered at 48% of the FOMC meetings compared to 63% at the BoE's MPC.

first. And a Fed tradition dictates that a member should "dissent" only if they find the majority's—that is the Chairman's—opinion unacceptable." Given this reality, several authors have also analyzed transcripts of FOMC meetings to determine the true extent of dissent and of preference heterogeneity.

Examining transcripts of 72 face-to-face FOMC meetings between 1989 and 1997, Meade (2005) indeed finds that voiced dissent on the short-term interest rate happens in 28.2%, compared to 7.5% for official dissent. The rate of voiced dissent is even higher for non-voting FOMC members; in that case, it reaches 34%. Regarding the policy "bias,"[8] voiced dissent reaches a rate of 49% for voters and 44% for non-voters. Focusing on the period 1992–1996, Meade (2002) notes that the difference between the mean and the median preference—as inferred through the transcripts—does not help predict the change in interest rates, but is correlated with the policy bias. This finding suggests that the bias is instrumental in achieving consensus on the interest rate decision. The discussion in Meade (2005) also supports this conclusion.

Meade (2002) finds that voiced dissent rates are smaller during the period 1992–1996, which implies that voiced dissent must have been very high during the early Greenspan years. As suggested by Meade and Stasavage (2008), this may be because policymakers became more wary of voicing dissent after 1993, when the transcripts of FOMC meetings became public. This finding is interesting as several ECB officials, including Issing (1999), have strongly objected to the publication of GC meetings transcripts, arguing that it would be prejudicial to the quality and frankness of the internal debates.

What are the implications of these studies? They suggest that some degree of preference heterogeneity exists at the FOMC and the Bank of England MPC but it is likely to be small when expressed in voting data. For example, although statistically significant, the difference between Democrat and Republican appointed Governors appears slight. Chappell et al. (2005) find that a typical Democrat-appointed Governor prefers a funds rate that is about 19 basis points lower than a typical Republican-appointed colleague. In spite of the caveats attached to the methodology used to estimate individual preferences, this finding casts doubt on the economic relevance of preference heterogeneity for MPC design in the current context of U.S. monetary policy institutions. Riboni and Ruge-Murcia (2008) seem to find somewhat greater heterogeneity across BOE MPC members, but this does not seem to be a concern for Governor Mervyn King who once said "From the outset, commentators have been unable to resist labelling members of the Committee as either "hawks" or "doves." I have argued before that it makes no sense to use these descriptions because each member of the Committee has the same objective" (King 2002, p. 5).

---

[8] This "bias" is a post-meeting statement by the FOMC regarding the likely course of future monetary policy.

6.2.3.2 Differences Due to Home Bias in Individual Objective Function

In the context of an enlarged Eurozone, a concern is that the prime source of heterogeneity may not be the relative weight attached to inflation relative to output stabilization but the home bias of national governors' policy objectives as they remain accountable to their home country even if the ECB is independent and its objective of price stability in the euro area as a whole appears to be well anchored (Berger et al. 2004). Unfortunately, in the absence of any transcript of ECB policy meetings, it is hard to gauge the validity of these concerns.

Interestingly, Meade and Sheets (2005) find that US policy-makers take into account developments in regional unemployment when casting votes on monetary policy, and that these regional developments are more important for Board members than for Reserve Bank presidents. However, the magnitude of the effects they identify seems too small to have any actual impact on policy decisions. In fact, although various GC members may suffer from home biased preferences, the averaging of these preferences through the collective decision-making procedure may deliver an outcome that is not far from the optimum. The results presented by Bénassy-Quéré and Turkisch (2009) are reassuring in that respect. They first compute the interest rate preferred by each GC member in a 22-country Eurozone, assuming maximal home bias for all governors and then compare the interest rate chosen under various collective decision rules. They find that the rotation system chosen in the 2003 reform would deliver an interest rate outcome very close to that obtained under complete centralization, i.e., the best from the euro area perspective. Similar results are reported by Berger et al. (2004). In other words, the risk of monetary policy decisions being distorted owing to home biased preferences in an enlarged euro area appears quite limited. We therefore conclude this subsection by noting that preference heterogeneity should probably remain a second-order concern.

6.2.4 Belief and Judgment Aggregation

A second important dimension of heterogeneity across policymakers is their belief regarding the state of the economy and/or its structure, for example, the size of the output gap or the strength of the various transmission channels of monetary policy. In the context of the Governing Council, each national governor may also add to a common understanding of macroeconomic and financial data by sharing his interpretation of domestic developments and using his knowledge of domestic economic institutions. To the extent that individual private information is valuable and that it is not fully correlated across members, it would thus seem that a larger and more diverse committee would collectively possess strictly more information and therefore would have the potential to make better decisions. It would seem also that the decision rule would be largely irrelevant if all useful information were shared between committee members before any vote took place. However, the economics and social psychology literature provide reasons to be less assertive.

6.2.4.1 Theoretical Caveats from the Economics Literature

Four simple but important theoretical caveats should be kept in mind. First, as shown by Persico (2004), a larger committee size may decrease the motivation to gather (and/or interpret) information when information acquisition is costly. As a consequence, the interaction between the decision rule and the size of the committee needs to be carefully considered in order to preserve individual motivation. Second, if information is not fully shared between committee members before the decision is made, then it is sub-optimal to give the same voting weight to two individuals with different precisions of information. In other words, an increase in the committee size may be detrimental if the new members have lower information precision than older members. Third, communication in the form of cheap talk can become a concern when individual preferences are too dissimilar, although repeated interactions among policymakers and reputational concerns within the committee could significantly moderate the amount of untruthful information sharing. Fourth, if communication and/or coordination costs increase with committee size, then obviously the optimal size of a committee must be finite.

6.2.4.2 Caveats from the Social Psychology Literature

Interestingly, the social psychology literature also points to the danger of various sources of biased judgment, which arise during the process of group interaction. In the course of an MPC deliberation, members exchange arguments, ideas and information, which affect each other's position and belief. A common assumption in the MPC economics literature is that the deliberation phase would most likely enable the full disclosure of private information, rational updating, and convergence of individual beliefs. However, the social psychology literature presents instances where these channels of informational influence from one member to another may be obstructed or biased. In particular it suggests that individuals tend to treat other people's information as less precise than their own, omit to discuss information that is not initially collectively shared and may bias their collective information search and examination. It also emphasizes the importance of normative influence on top of informational influence, a distinction that is typically ignored by economists.

The Influence of Anonymous Advisors

From the perspective of an individual member firming his opinion about the appropriate course of future monetary policy, other MPC members are akin to a group of advisors providing potentially useful information. The literature on the influence of advice is therefore helpful to understand how individuals change opinions. In a series of experiments, Yaniv (2004) explores the effect of (anonymous) advice on individual accuracy in judgment. He presents evidence showing that (i) people tend to place a higher weight on their own opinion than on the advisor's opinion; (ii) more knowledgeable individuals discount the advice more; (iii) the weight of advice decreases as its distance from the prior opinion increases; and (iv) the use of advice improves accuracy significantly, though not optimally. Using a similar experimental context, Yaniv and Milyavsky (2007) analyze how individuals make use of multiple sources of advice. They find that individuals trim egocentrically the opinion sets such that opinions distant from their own are greatly discounted, and that—in the specific task they study—the marginal beneficial effects of increasing the number of advisors above two are small. These studies suggest that useful informational influence is likely to take place in the GC, but that the more autocratic the decision rule is, the less efficient is information aggregation, unless expertise is positively correlated with voting power.

Information Exchange Among Members of a Group

Not only do individuals fail to take full advantage of benevolent advisors' opinions, they also do not seem to share fully their own information with other group members. Stasser (1991) and Wittenbaum and Stasser (1996) find that groups often do not discuss all the information that their members possess, but concentrate instead on information that members initially share. When the group must consider information that is initially unshared to make a correct decision, the bias toward discussing shared information can lead to an incorrect decision. Larson et al. (1998) also find that group leaders are more likely than others to repeat unshared information. Active leadership may therefore increase its impact and improve the group decision-making's efficiency.

Gigone and Hastie (1997) propose that shared information affects group decision quality through its impact on individual members' judgment prior to the discussion ("common knowledge effect"). From this perspective, group discussion is mainly an occasion for normative influence, in which members negotiate the weighting of their pre-discussion opinions.

The "Groupthink" Phenomenon and Selective Information Seeking in Groups

Problems associated with failure to exchange views are highlighted in Janis's (1982) famous analysis of "groupthink" in a series of case studies. According to Janis, factors such as high cohesion, structural faults (e.g., directive leadership), homogeneity of members' social background, and a provocative situational context (e.g., external threats) produce a concurrence-seeking tendency, excessive confidence of the group, closed mindedness, and pressures toward uniformity, which in turn lead to defective decision making, including an incomplete survey of available options, a failure to assess the risks of the preferred option, and a selective bias in processing information. As a result, the group is less likely to make a good decision and more likely to become psychologically entrapped in a poor decision.

In spite of its popularity as a way of explaining poor group decisions, groupthink has received mixed empirical support, in particular in laboratory studies (Aldag & Fuller 1993). Nevertheless these studies highlight the importance of distinguishing the effect of each individual factor, which Janis included as a cause of groupthink. The factor that has received the most consistent support is directive leadership. But the other central variable of cohesiveness has not been found to play a negative role in group performance. In fact, this factor may even be positive by promoting morale and confidence (Choi & Kim 1999).

In a related study, Schulz-Hardt et al. (2000) provide evidence that groups, just like individuals, prefer supporting instead of conflicting information when making decisions.[9] They document that the strength of this bias depends on the distribution of the group members' initial favourite option: the more group members had chosen the same alternative prior to the group discussion, the more strongly the group preferred information supporting the alternative. This study, as well as Janis's (1982) book, suggests therefore that information acquisition and processing is likely to be less biased in MPCs where a variety of perspectives are represented.

The Effect of Discussion and the Group Polarization Phenomenon

Moscovici and Zavalloni (1969) provide evidence of a phenomenon called group polarization, which describes the tendency for individuals' opinions to become more extreme (in whatever direction they originally favoured collectively) after discussion than before. Both informational and normative explanations of group polarization have been proposed, but Kaplan (1987) argues that normative influences are relatively more likely with judgmental issues than with intellective issues. Since monetary policy decisions have both judgmental and intellective dimensions, it is likely that normative influences associated with group polarization have some relevance in a MPC context. In that case, deliberation could lead to too extreme beliefs and decisions, especially if a strong majority favours the same action initially.

6.2.5 *Experimental Evidence on the Effects of Size and Composition*

The previous discussion highlighted how information could be less than perfectly acquired and communicated in groups during the process of collective judgment

---

[9] A large literature in psychology has been devoted to documenting systematic biases in individual judgment. One could wonder which biases are magnified and which are attenuated when decisions are made by groups. In their review of the relative susceptibility of individuals and groups to fifteen systematic judgmental biases, Kerr et al. (1996) found no clear general pattern and we will therefore not explore this topic further.

formation. In this section, we shall focus on outcomes rather than processes and discuss how the three main aspects of MPC structure we are interested in (size, composition and decision rule) are empirically related to several performance measures in a variety of experimental contexts. In all of these experiments, the interests of all individuals in a group are perfectly aligned, and potential motives for strategic manipulation of information should be of no concern.

Available evidence does not provide fully convincing guidance about the optimal size of a MPC and suggests that some degree of heterogeneity of perspectives is likely to be beneficial. Exactly how much is a question that has not been directly addressed. The literature leaves us with a number of trade-offs relevant for MPC design rather than firm quantitative indications.

6.2.5.1 Effects of Group Size

Social psychologists have long been interested in comparing the quality of individual and group decisions. Michaelsen et al. (1989) and Watson et al. (1991) find that when groups solve problems repeatedly, average group performance over time can often exceed the average performance of the best member, although groups do not outperform the best individual at the level of the single test, as shown by Tindale and Larson (1992) or Stasson and Bradshaw (1995).

More recently, Blinder and Morgan (2005, 2008) and Lombardelli et al. (2002) conducted a series of experiments, which imitated real-life monetary policy decisions. They found that decisions made by groups of five members were on average better than individual decisions. Furthermore, groups of eight members outperformed groups of four members by a small margin. Interestingly, Blinder and Morgan (2008) found that groups without a leader performed as well as groups with a leader (selected on the basis of his/her prior individual performance in the monetary policy game). This result is therefore suggestive that the distribution of power within the group may not be that important, at least for the type of ordinary macroeconomic situations replicated in the game.

The experiments by Blinder and Morgan (2005, 2008) and Lombardelli et al. (2002) did not directly address the question of the optimal size of the committee. When addressing this type of question, social psychologists insist on the following trade-off. On the one hand, when a group grows larger, it has access to more resources, so its performance would be expected to improve. But in larger groups, coordination losses are also more likely, as are motivation losses due to social loafing and free riding (Levine & Moreland 1998). This trade-off may explain the empirical evidence presented by Berger and Nitsch (2008) who find a U-shaped relation between the membership size of MPCs and inflation in a panel data set of 30 countries between 1960 and 2000. Their result suggests that the lowest level of inflation would be reached by MPCs with about seven to ten members. However, their results are only suggestive as they are obtained in pooled regressions and do not hold when country fixed effects are added. In fact, the magnitude of the econometric estimates is so large that increasing the size of an MPC from 10 to 20 members would have an inflation cost of more than 10 percentage points, which looks very large, at least for the case of the ECB.

6.2.5.2 Effects of Group Composition

One source of evidence on the benefits of aggregating various viewpoints—even without any communication—comes from the economic forecasting literature, which has documented that forecasting is improved by combining individual forecasts using different models. Surveying the literature on forecast combination, Timmermann (2005) observes that empirical findings suggest in particular that simple combination schemes are difficult to beat and that forecasts based exclusively on the model with the best in-sample performance often lead to poor out-of-sample forecasting performance.

Research by social psychologists on diversity shows that it can affect both the dynamics and performance of groups. According to Levine and Moreland (1998), the effects of diversity on group dynamics are largely negative. For example, as the heterogeneity of a group increases, its members tend to communicate less often, and in more formal ways, with one another. In contrast, diversity can have positive effects on group performance since it endows a group with flexibility, which can be valuable if the group's tasks change or become more complex. Diversity also fosters innovation and can improve a group's relation with various outsiders, who are often diverse themselves.

In a famous experiment that highlights the value of opinion diversity within a group, Hall (1971) asked teams to rank by order of importance fifteen items that persons might use for returning to the mother ship if they were lost on the Moon. He found that "the best-performing groups (…) were those which were least consensual in the early stages of discussion, exploring all possible avenues and ideas. Groups which established a common consensus quickly were often ineffective, suggesting that at least some disagreement is beneficial for committee performance because it stimulates discussion and hard thinking." Thus cacophony in an enlarged GC could be beneficial, as long as it remains behind the closed doors of ECB Headquarters.

6.2.6 Experimental Evidence on the Effects of the Decision-Making Procedure

The practice in the GC has so far been to make decisions by consensus, whereas the ECB statute provides for simple majority voting. The existing experimental literature on the effects of the decision-making mechanism in groups typically compares these two rules and highlights several virtues of decision-making by consensus. It suggests in particular that consensus promotes the exploration of more alternatives and is conducive to a better atmosphere prevailing in the group, a factor that could be important for group morale. On the other hand, majority rule seems to enable the preservation over time of a diversity of viewpoints within the group, which could prove useful if the group has to acknowledge a bad decision made in the past or adapt to a new environment.

6.2.6.1 Effect on Group Decision Outcome and Performance

Social psychologists have generally found that unanimity rule results in more compromise decisions than versions of majority rule (Miller 1985, 1989; Kaplan & Miller 1987). Blinder and Morgan (2005) observe that groups of five perform better than the average individual under both decision rules, and that the two rules do not yield significantly different results. However, they also observe that in their experiment, "majority decisions quickly evolved into unanimous decisions. In almost all cases, once three or four subjects agreed on a course of action, the remaining one or two fell in line immediately." This suggests that the task in their experiment was much more intellective than judgmental and therefore was less likely to generate persistent dissent.

A study by Holloman and Hendrick (1972) found that consensus decisions were significantly more accurate than decisions made by majority rule. They argued that a stricter decision rule heightened pressures on group members to exchange information and search more intensively for better solutions.

The decision rule may also have an effect on performance through the convergence of beliefs within the group. Kameda and Sugimori (1993) analyze how an assigned decision-rule, majority or unanimity, affects the extent to which a group is subject to psychological entrapment. This phenomenon refers to a faulty-decision-making process whereby individuals escalate their commitment to a previously chosen, though failing, course of action. In a group context, the sunk investments at stake may not necessarily be limited to physical costs such as money, time or energy but are also likely to include social and interpersonal investments. Proposing a change may cause loss of face for some members and may violate group harmony. In a series of two experiments, they show that the use of majority rule is more likely to reduce the unity of a group and thus may hinder collective entrapment; in contrast, the use of unanimity may promote group cohesiveness and foster collective entrapment, as in the groupthink phenomenon described above. They suggest that a potentially entrapping situation may cause a greater tendency to rationalize the ongoing action in unanimity rule than in majority rule groups, and that members who initially belong to the minority are more likely to keep playing the role of the devil's advocate in majority rule groups.

6.2.6.2 Effect on Positions of Individual Members

As suggested by the Kameda and Sugimori (1993) experiment, not only do group decision rules affect the group decision differentially, they also affect changes in the opinions of individual members of the group differentially. In unanimous rule groups, as compared to groups using variants of majority rule, substantial convergence occurs during the decision-making process (Hastie et al. 1983; Kaplan & Miller 1987). This convergence effect occurs not only with respect to the publicly stated positions of the members, but also with respect to their privately held opinions as well in the case of judgmental issues (Kaplan & Miller 1987). Those members with less popular preferences are less likely to maintain their initial positions under unanimous rule than under majority rules. It is possible that the public expression of an opinion contrary to one's private position creates dissonance that leads to a change in the private position (Festinger & Carlsmith 1959). Thus it would seem that the de facto practice of consensus within the GC could generate greater convergence of views than majority voting, which may explain why it has been the practice in the GC where ex ante heterogeneity of views is likely to be greater than in other major central banks' MPC.

6.3 Different Governance Structures for Different Functions

A common assumption in economic policy modelling is that the institution making decisions has a unique governing structure. Indeed, this was our implicit assumption in most of the previous section. In circumstances where there is only one instrument whose setting is determined by the institution, this assumption is satisfactory. However, in most real life situations, institutions have multiple goals and multiple instruments to achieve those objectives. In the area of monetary policy, for example, there is the setting of interest rates, the management of liquidity conditions—which takes centre stage at the zero bound; decisions concerning acceptable collateral and overall risk management—which have made headlines in late 2009–early 2010 with the downgrading of some Eurozone countries' sovereign debt ratings; asset management (financial, physical and human capital); and communication strategy. One might also consider a second set of decisions comprising unconventional operations which may be of less unambiguous legitimacy.[10]

One common way of coping with the diversity of instruments and policies that need to be chosen within an organization is the creation of a hierarchy of governance bodies[11] whose power is received by delegation from the supreme authority. Those bodies receiving delegated authority may have a broader or narrower scope of membership compared to the supreme authority but usually

---

[10] The involvement of central banks in "unconventional operations", in some cases with quasi-fiscal aspects, has raised concerns about the legitimacy of those operations. See Crockett (2009).

[11] Governance bodies may differ in the composition of their members or in the voting rules applied in different situations. In other words we would consider a group making some decisions according to majority rule and others by unanimity, consensus or supermajority, as different governance bodies.

comprise specialist knowledge or expertise enabling gains from comparative advantage.[12] While there are gains to be obtained from delegation it may be the case that the political legitimacy of the delegated actor diminishes as the distance vis-à-vis the supreme authority increases. Thus one might conceive of a natural hierarchy within which the scope of operational power diminishes as distance from political legitimacy increases. For example, a three-tier structure would consist of those who agree on the fundamental design of the system who have direct political legitimacy; those who engineer the system who would be supervised by those with direct political power; and those who operate the system who would be supervised by those who engineered the system.

In as much as the supreme authority over an institution can always alter the legislation governing its design and policy execution it is important for lower bodies in the hierarchy to operate within the bounds set to them to ensure that their operational authority remains robust to future legislative changes. Viewed within this framework, opportunities arise to define *operational* activities which may be quite independent and *policy* activities of lesser or greater hierarchy that would have differently designed governance structures best attuned to ensure their robust legitimacy. What then becomes important is the careful design of the delegation mechanism—precision of the powers that have been granted independence—and how well the monetary authorities operate within the prescribed bounds and according to the defined decision mechanism. Ill-defined bounds and non-transparent decisions are unlikely to be robust to the ultimate legislative authority of the supreme political body and may drain credibility from the policy makers.

Before discussing divisions of responsibility within the central bank it will be useful to focus on the reasons for the primal division of monetary and fiscal policies, i.e., the distinction between the central bank and the Treasury.[13] Clearly, the essential benefit is to obtain a second governance structure—different from that of the Treasury. The motive behind central bank independence—the general rubric under which this movement to a second policy structure has been discussed—was to provide some independence from political considerations (see Berger et al. 2001). Political manipulation of monetary policy was widely understood in the 1980s to have been an important cause of poor monetary policy performance during the 1970s inflation episodes.

Independence from politics is primarily a negative criterion and immediately raises issues of democratic accountability and legitimacy. We will see below that the robustness of the legitimacy of central bank actions will always be an issue for this very reason. Legitimacy is here being understood as a quality that maintains an institution or individual in place over an extended time horizon. Institutions or individuals can always be replaced or deprived of their effective power by the

[12] See Lybek and Morris (2004), and BIS (2009) for surveys and discussions of central bank board structures. Berger et al. (2008) discuss determinants of board size.

[13] Don Kohn, Vice Chairman of the Federal Reserve Board, has argued that at the zero interest rate bound it becomes very difficult to distinguish between fiscal and monetary policies (see Kohn 2009).

constituencies they purport to represent. Illegitimate representation is unstable—subject to replacement. Legitimate representation is stable, unlikely to be fundamentally reformed within the relevant time frame.

In resolving this tension between independence and legitimacy the European and American methods differ. The European solution involved an extremely careful design of the institution and strong formal legal mechanisms to ensure independence, while the American solution had more the characteristics of a designed balance of political powers between institutions whose resolution would be accomplished through conflict, coordination and trial and error.

How should central bank governance structures differ from those of the Treasury? That is, how to provide positive attributes to the institution? There may be a knowledge specialization—the central bank might be better equipped to understand the long run neutrality of money, the subtle monetary policy transmission mechanism, the long run vertical Phillips curve, and—in general—be more inclined to "indirect" controls over financial markets.

A second way to conceive the central bank is that it simply is "tougher" than average in terms of willingness to sacrifice short term real economic conditions to the long run objective of price stability—Rogoff's (1985) modelling of the objective function. Alternatively, rather than simply seek intrinsic differences in preferences central bankers may be subject to contractual constraints on their behaviour such as in Walsh's (1995) model.

Designing the terms of office of central bankers may be sufficient to accomplish the appropriately socially desired policy. For example, the socially optimal monetary policy might be completely understood among all policymakers but election cycles could lead elected officials to adopt a second best "survival" strategy. Providing the central bank governing body a long term in office, hence a different subjective rate of time discount, might be sufficient to lead them to adopt the optimal policy. This conceptualization of the function of a central bank supports a particular type of governance structure—a committee. A committee structure permits a trade off between duration and renovation of the governance body. A three-person committee, each person having a six-year term, would—if properly spaced—allow for a new committee member every 2 years. A one-person governance structure with a six-year term would allow for no renovation during the six-year term.

As discussed earlier, the structure of the ECB presents an inherent tension between the ultimate raison d'être of the EU—a desire for unified European policies—and the fundamental logical fact that a single policy for a disparate group of states may impact some more favourably than others at given points in time. Nor can there be, over any finite time horizon, any guarantee that the benefits and costs of a unified policy will even out for each state. When considering central banking policies, however, it must be understood that they comprise a small subset of the gains from the EU and that the tension discussed above may be resolved in a "meta game" where each EU member is in fact better off within the Union than outside, summing across all the dimensions of the membership cost benefit matrix. Hence we assume there is some general level of stability within EU institutions that, provided that it has voice and representation within certain bounds, each member can accept consensus decisions even when they are not favourable to itself.

The EU Treaty already establishes a differential governance structure for decisions impacting the ECB profit and loss statement and those relating to monetary policy. That is, decisions pertaining to the ECB budget, distribution of seigniorage and loss sharing among member central banks, are taken in accord with the capital key.[14] In these decisions, members are represented in proportion to their financial interest in the ECB. One can understand that these decisions, which touch on the financial sustainability of the ECB, and the legitimacy of its financial independence, are taken with due regard to the views of the central banks that are financing the bulk of ECB operations and receive the largest proportional share of profit. Since the Treaty ensures the financial independence of the ECB, it should never be the case that financial conditions drive policy decisions, nor should this be the case for any NCB.[15] Interestingly, however, issues of risk management connected with monetary policy are ruled by a common policy—a common collateral list and equal treatment of sovereign debt. This may be thought necessary to ensure fairness among member states. Various commentators have suggested that different treatment for different assets, for example sovereign risk, would be more efficient in that it would reward countries with solid fiscal finances and penalize those without. Does this implicit subsidy to poor performing states make the coalition less stable? It is also the case that member NCBs share losses connected with monetary policy operations. The 2008 ECB financial statements make it clear that while the NCBs with direct exposure to Lehman Brothers, Indover Bank and two Icelandic banks should make provisions for possible losses, *any realized losses* will be shared according to the capital key.

Perhaps the most critical area where a different governing structure, i.e., broad representation, is necessary is unconventional operations. These operations by definition are not commonplace and may be introduced in an ad hoc way. Just as it is never possible to write a fully state-contingent contract among individual parties—all possible contingencies cannot be foreseen—it is not possible for legislation to define all possible measures that a central bank may find necessary to achieve its objectives. In such circumstances there clearly needs to be an option to innovate but also a mechanism to provide legitimacy to the operations in "real time". A broader governing structure—with greater political representation would serve this function. Of course this governing structure would be an intermediate one, ultimately the legislatures and/or courts would determine the ultimate legitimacy of the central bank actions and direct future legislative changes that would codified the ultimate ruling.

---

[14] It is also the case that emergency liquidity operations require the authorization of a supermajority within the European System of Central Banks.

[15] In the early decades of the Federal Reserve System, profit and loss considerations often influenced individual Federal Reserve Bank positions on proposed monetary operations.

The idea of assigning a different governance structure to different functional roles, particularly in unusual or emergency circumstances is not a new idea. In commenting on the ECB decision adopted by the European Council on March 12, 2003 concerning a new voting scheme, the French report "...recommended that operational decisions be delegated to an enlarged EB while keeping the one-member-one-vote principle for institutional/strategic decisions within the GC conditional on a demographic threshold (double majority requirement)."[16] That is, execution or implementation of policy can be delegated—distanced from political authority—but strategic decisions must be taken within a governing structure more in conformity with that of the supreme authority.

In the US, the powers exercised under the Gold Reserve Act of 1934 to manage the U.S. foreign reserves are shared by the U.S. Treasury and the Federal Reserve.[17] Monetary policy authority is also shared between two governance structures. The FOMC determines the policy rate and directs open market operations[18] while the Board of Governors has the authority to set required reserves and authorize changes in the discount rate. Authority granted the Fed under the Federal Reserve Act (FRA) under section 13.3 is further refined: "in unusual and exigent circumstances" to provide discounts to individuals, partnerships and corporations, requires "...the affirmative vote of not less than five [out of seven] Board members...."[19] Similarly, the central banks of Argentina, Chile, Costa Rica, Korea and the Philippines require a super majority vote to authorize extraordinary or emergency central bank operations.

In Japan, emergency lending by the Bank of Japan must be approved by the Prime Minister and the Minister of Finance. In Thailand, both the Bank of Thailand Financial Institutions Policy Board and the Cabinet must approve emergency lending. Such operations must be approved in Jordan by both the central bank board and the Council of Ministers. In both Korea and the Philippines, the Monetary Policy Board, not the general board, holds power in an emergency.[20]

In the specific case of the ECB one would have to ask the question whether a super-majority of Board members is enough to provide legitimacy to "unconventional operations" or whether extra-central bank parties ought to be involved in the process, for instance, Ministries of Finance. While this might be seen as an infringement of ECB autonomy, it is precisely in cases where the ECB may be exceeding its known authority to act, that extra-institutional support would be requested. That is, an infringement on authority can only be definitely claimed in cases where the ECB clearly has the legal authority to engage in an action. In some cases, such as the Bank of Japan, the Federal Reserve, and the Bank of England

---

[16] Bénassy-Quéré and Turkisch (2009, p. 34).

[17] See Broaddus and Goodfriend (1996).

[18] As will be discussed below, this was not the case pre-1935.

[19] The FOMC consists of all seven Board members, the President of the FRBNY and four Reserve Bank presidents alternating among the remaining 11 FRBs.

[20] See Stella (2010).

certain assurances of financial support are sought from the Treasury to backstop operations whose fiscal risk is seen as placing them at the fringe of allowable operations.

During the recent crisis, the Norges Bank requested that the Ministry of Finance provide support to the mortgage-backed bond market through a swap with Treasury securities. These operations had no impact on the Norges Bank balance sheet. This solution was quite clean and could provide an alternative model for the ECB going forward. However, the issue of whether this would somehow cede ECB powers to Ministries of Finance would have to be debated and decided. In either case, delimiting clearly the scope for fiscal and monetary policies—combined with whatever new responsibilities the ECB might obtain in the field of financial market supervision and stability (see Chap. 7 for further details) will be essential to preserve legitimacy.

6.4 Moving Towards Greater Centralization: The Federal Reserve Experience 1913–1935[21]

This section concerns the evolution of the governance structure of the Federal Reserve System from 1913 through the Banking Act of 1935. During that period the Fed moved toward more centralized control and more unified policymaking. This change was driven both by economic and political forces and a brief review may prove illustrative of how similar pressures may be resolved in the Eurozone. The economic forces were primarily the increased integration of U.S. financial markets and the political forces were Congressional and governmental concerns that the Fed was not responsive enough to the perceived need to undertake a more simulative policy during the Great Depression.

It is important to understand that some elements of the fundamental legal structure of the Federal Reserve have not changed since 1913 when the FRA was approved. The System consists of 12 legally separate Federal Reserve Banks with separate balance sheets and boards of directors who select the president, or CEO, of their Reserve Bank. At the outset of the Fed, it was not clear how policy decisions would be governed although it appears as though individual Reserve Banks were to be given broad powers to act independently with the central "national" perspective of the Board given a supervisory role.[22]

As to the distribution of power among the 12 Reserve Banks, New York—owing to its proximity to the nation's most important financial market and the latter's ties with the London and continental European markets—had a natural advantage. It was also significantly larger than the other Reserve Banks owing to

---

[21] This section draws heavily on Meltzer (2003).

[22] At the outset, the Secretary of the Treasury and Comptroller of the Currency were "ex officio" members of the Board, with the Secretary as Chairman.

the way in which the capital structure of the Banks was determined. The capital of the Reserve Banks is essentially a uniform fraction of the member commercial banks in its district. Thus New York, particularly in the early years, had a dominant economic weight. Its Board of Directors could also count on participation of the elite banking, commercial, and industrial titans of the time.

In the early years of the Federal Reserve System, the influence of New York was largely an informal one. Concerns about the possibility of New York dominance galvanized opposition, both from the other regional Banks, the Board in Washington, and among certain members of Congress. The distribution of power was finally decided formally with the establishment of the FOMC which provided New York with a permanent vote (in 1942) in contrast with the other 11 Federal Reserve Banks obtaining the right to vote during a given year through a rotation system approximately every third year. However, between the 1935 Banking Act and 1942, New York lost its special power owing to the radical shift in the locus of power to the Board in Washington.[23]

The original distribution of power outlined by the FRA appeared to have been set according to the American principle of "checks and balances". "The final structure included Wilson's compromise—a politically appointed Federal Reserve Board in Washington and regional banks in principal centers, run by bankers, with no clear division of authority between the two" (Meltzer 2003, p. 67). At the beginning, tensions existed between the center and the periphery and within the periphery itself. Not only between New York and the other Banks but between individual Banks and the informal committee formed by the Banks.

The Committee on Centralized Purchases and Sales "…role was limited to recommendations and executions of orders sent by the reserve banks. Responsibilities for decisions remained with the individual banks and their directors, who retained the right to purchase and sell at their discretion and to purchase directly from member banks in their districts." "The committee [of FRB governors (later they would be called "presidents")[24]] was an informal extralegal arrangement. The Board, acting in its supervisory role, had to approve purchases and sales. The line between supervision and decision-making was never clear, so the procedures irritated some Board members and became a source of friction. Friction increased as open market operations became the principal policy instrument" (Meltzer 2003, p. 146).

The Banking Act of 1935 resolved this conflict. "Board members became members of the Federal Open Market Committee for the first time and held seven of the 12 seats and chairmanship of the committee. New York lost its leadership role. The New York bank did not regain a permanent seat on the committee until 1942… The 1935 act permanently shifted the locus of power to the Board. The Federal Reserve became a central bank. The 12 regional reserve banks lost their semiautonomous status and much of their original independence" (Meltzer 2003, pp. 4–5).

[23] The extent of the Board dominance can be seen in the fact that it also obtained the right to dismiss Reserve Bank officers.

[24] Authors' parenthetical insert.

Elements of the conflict between the Reserve Banks and Washington continue to exist today, for example, in the operation of the discount window. The Board cannot change "the" discount rate but can only approve requests to change rates from individual Reserve Banks. In practice, in the first two decades of Fed operation, different Banks had different discount depending on conditions in their geographical market sector. At that time, the U.S. financial markets were not fully unified and restrictions on commercial bank branching limited interbank arbitrage among FRB districts. The gradual unification of U.S. financial markets was a constant underlying factor driving the System toward the logic of centralization.

The Banking Act of 1935 not only dramatically altered the locus of power within the Federal Reserve System but it was passed in a climate conducive to a drastic curtailment of monetary policy independence. During this period, Congress passed legislation threatening to directly issue currency (for example, to veterans of the First World War) if the Federal Reserve did not ease monetary policy. This effectively forced the Fed to respond directly to political pressures.[25]

The economic and political consequences of the Great Depression, combined with the weak and faulty Federal Reserve policy response, provided Congress the impetus to resolve the ambiguity of powers both within the System and between the Federal Reserve and the legislature.

6.5 Conclusion: Summary Assessment and Way Forward

The findings and discussion in this chapter clearly suggest that the design of ECB governance structures matters. It is critical both for the efficiency and legitimacy of the institution that all relevant factors and considerations are taken into account in the light of enlargement.

The precise design of the optimal governance structure is less clear. A rotation system may be awkward but the best compromise. Such a system has been durable in the United States where there has been a similar legacy of "independent regional central banks" morphing into a unified structure. That said, the literature is far from conclusive regarding optimal MPC design.

As to robust frameworks, a long-term steady state governance structure could be dual: monetary policy decisions could be taken by a "denationalized" committee of 7–9 ECB bureaucrats while the council of governors would meet regularly to perform oversight. However, this alternative may be at least one generation away as the legitimacy of the ECB and other EU institutions needs to be strengthened and political integration will likely need to make further progress. Meanwhile, a careful examination and delineation of ECB functions—perhaps to change as a consequence of reforms to be adopted after the current crisis has been

[25] In 1933 President Roosevelt invoked the War Powers Act and declared it illegal for private persons to hold gold. This, combined with the devaluation of the dollar against gold was effectively monetary policy.

resolved—may provide the opportunity to articulate more refined and specialized governance structures most, or more, functionally appropriate to them. There is no reason to impose on those disparate functions a governance structure identical to that for conventional monetary policy operations.

References

Aldag, R., & Fuller, S. (1993). Beyond fiasco: A reappraisal of the groupthink phenomenon and a new model of group decision processes. *Psychological Bulletin, 113*, 533–552.

Baldwin, R., Berglof, E., Giavazzi, F., & Widgren, M. (2001). Preparing the ECB for enlargement. CEPR Policy Paper No. 6.

Bank for International Settlements (2009). Issues in the governance of Central Banks. A report from the Central Bank Governance Group. Basle: BIS.

Bénassy-Quéré, A., & Turkisch, E. (2009). The ECB Governing Council in an enlarged euro area. *Journal of Common Market Studies, 47*, 25–53.

Berger, H. (2002). The ECB and Euro-area enlargement. IMF Working Paper No. 02/175.

Berger, H. (2006). Optimal central bank design: Benchmarks for the ECB. CESifo Working Paper No. 1697.

Berger, H., De Haan, J., & Eijffinger, S. C. W. (2001). Central Bank independence: An update of theory and evidence. *Journal of Economic Surveys, 15*, 3–40.

Berger, H., De Haan, J., & Inklaar, R. (2004). Restructuring the ECB. In H. Berger & T. Moutos (Eds.), *Managing European Union enlargement* (pp. 29–66). Cambridge, MA: MIT Press.

Berger, H., & Nitsch, V. (2008). Too many cooks? Committees in monetary policy. CESifo Working Paper No. 2274.

Berger, H., Nitsch, V., & Lybek, T. (2008). Central Bank boards around the world: Why does membership size differ? *European Journal of Political Economy, 24*(4), 817–832.

Blinder, A. S. (2007). Monetary policy by committee: Why and how? *European Journal of Political Economy, 23*(1), 106–123.

Blinder, A., Goodhart, C., Hildebrand, P., Lipton, D., & Wyplosz, C. (2001). How do central banks talk? *Geneva Reports on the World Economy* (Vol. 3). London: CEPR.

Blinder, A., & Morgan, J. (2005). Are two heads better than one? Monetary policy by committee. *Journal of Money, Credit, and Banking, 37*(5), 789–811.

Blinder, A., & Morgan, J. (2008). Leadership in groups: A monetary policy experiment. *International Journal of Central Banking, 4*, 117–150.

Broaddus, J. A., & Goodfriend, M. (1996). Foreign exchange operations and the Federal Reserve. *FRB Richmond Economic Quarterly, 82*(Winter), 7–22.

Buiter, W. H. (1999). Alice in Euroland. *Journal of Common Market Studies, 37*(2), 181–209.

Chappell, H., McGregor, R. R., & Vermilyea, T. (2005). *Committee decisions on monetary policy, evidence from historical records of the Federal Open Market Committee*. Cambridge, MA: MIT Press.

Choi, J. N., & Kim, M. U. (1999). The organizational application of groupthink and its limitations in organizations. *Journal of Applied Psychology, 84*(2), 297–306.

Crockett, A. (2009). Should the Federal Reserve be a systemic stability regulator? In J. D. Ciorciari & J. B. Taylor (Eds.), *The road ahead for the Fed* (pp. 137–150). Stanford, CA: Hoover Institution Press.

De Larosière, J., Balcerowicz, L., Issing, O., Masera, R., Mc Carthy, C., Nyberg, L., Pérez, J., & Ruding, O. (2009). *Report of the high level group on financial supervision in the EU*. Brussels: European Commission.

Erhart, S., & Vasquez-Paz, J.L. (2008). Determinants of the size of a monetary policy committee: Theory and cross-country evidence, Banco Central de Reserva del Peru, Working Paper No. 2008-001.

Festinger, L., & Carlsmith, J. M. (1959). Cognitive consequences of forced compliance. *Journal of Abnormal and Social Psychology, 58*, 203–210.

Fujiki, H. (2005). The monetary policy committee and the incentive problem: A selective survey. Bank of Japan, Institute for Monetary and Economic Studies Discussion Paper No. 2005-E-4.

Gerlach-Kristen, P. (2003). Insiders and outsiders at the Bank of England. *Central Banking, 14*(1), 96–102.

Gerling, K., Gruner, H. P., Kiel, A., & Schulte, E. (2003). Information acquisition and decision making in committees: A survey. ECB Working Paper No. 256.

Gigone, D., & Hastie, R. (1997). Proper analysis of the accuracy of group judgments. *Psychological Bulletin, 121*(1), 149–167.

Gildea, J. (1990). Explaining FOMC members' votes. In T. Mayer (Ed.), *The political economy of American Monetary Policy* (pp. 211–228). Cambridge, UK: Cambridge University Press.

Gros, D. (2003). Reforming the composition of the ECB Governing Council in view of enlargement: How not to do it! Briefing paper for the Monetary Committee of the European Parliament, February 2003.

Hall, J. (1971). Decisions, decisions, decisions. *Psychology Today*, November, pp. 51–54 and 86–88.

Hastie, R., Penrod, S., & Pennington, N. (1983). *Inside the Jury*. Cambridge, MA: Harvard University Press.

Havrilesky, T., & Schweitzer, R. (1990). A theory of FOMC dissent voting with evidence from the time series. In T. Mayer (Ed.), *The political economy of American Monetary Policy* (pp. 197–210). Cambridge, UK: Cambridge University Press.

Heisenberg, D. (2003). Cutting the bank down to size: Efficient and legitimate decision-making in the European Central Bank after enlargement. *Journal of Common Market Studies, 41*(3), 397–420.

Holloman, C., & Hendrick, H. (1972). Adequacy of group decisions as a function of the decision-making process. *Academy of Management Journal, 15*, 175–184.

Issing, O. (1999). The Eurosystem: Transparent and accountable, or "Willem in Euroland", *Journal of Common Market Studies, 37*(3), 503–519.

Issing, O., Gaspar, V., Angeloni, I., & Tristani, O. (2001). *Monetary policy in the Euro area. Strategy and decision-making at the European Central Bank*. Cambridge: Cambridge University Press.

Janis, I. (1982). *Groupthink: Psychological studies of policy decisions and fiascoes* (2nd ed.). Boston, MA: Houghton Mifflin.

Kameda, T., & Sugimori, S. (1993). Psychological entrapment in group decision-making: An assigned decision rule and a groupthink phenomenon. *Journal of Personality and Social Psychology, 65*(2), 282–292.

Kaplan, M. (1987). The influencing process in group decision-making. *Review of Personality and Social Psychology, 8*, 189–212.

Kaplan, M., & Miller, C. (1987). Group decision making and normative vs. informational influence: Effects of type of issue and assigned decision rule. *Journal of Personality and Social Psychology, 53*, 306–313.

Kerr, N., MacCoun, R., & Kramer, G. (1996). Bias in judgment: Comparing individuals and groups. *Psychological Review, 103*(4), 687–719.

King, M. (2002). The monetary policy Committee: Five years on, speech delivered to the society of business economists at the Royal College of Pathologists, May 22, 2002 (London).

Kohn, D. L. (2009). *Interactions between monetary and fiscal policy in the current situation, speech given at the Conference on monetary–fiscal policy interactions, expectations, and dynamics in the current economic crisis*. Princeton, NJ: Princeton University.

Krause, G. (1996). Agent heterogeneity and consensual decision-making on the Federal Open Market committee. *Public Choice, 88*, 83–101.

Larson, J. R., Jr., Christensen, C., Abbott, A. S., & Franz, T. M. (1998). Diagnosing groups: The pooling, management, and impact of shared and unshared case information in team-based medical decision making. *Journal of Personality and Social Psychology, 75*, 93–108.

Levine, J., & Moreland, R. (1998). Small groups. In D. Gilbert, S. Fiske, & G. Lindzey (Eds.), *Handbook of social psychology* (Vol. 3, pp. 415–469). New York: McGraw-Hill.
Lombardelli, C., Proudman, J., & Talbot, J. (2002). Committees versus individuals: An experimental analysis of monetary policy decision-making. Bank of England Working Paper No. 165.
Lybek, T., & Morris, J. (2004). Central Bank governance: A survey of boards and management. IMF Working Paper No. 04/226.
Meade, E. (2002). Central Bank decision: How does one good head compare with a rule? Center for Economic Performance, London School of Economics. Unpublished.
Meade, E. (2005). The FOMC: Preferences, voting and consensus. *Federal Reserve Bank ofSaint Louis Review, 87*(March/April, Part 1), 93–102.
Meade, E., & Sheets, N. (2005). Regional influences on FOMC voting patterns. *Journal of Money, Credit, and Banking, 37*(4), 661–677.
Meade, E., & Stasavage, D. (2008). Publicity of debate and the incentive to dissent: Evidence from the US Federal Reserve. *The Economic Journal, 118*, 695–717.
Meltzer, A. H. (2003). *A history of the Federal Reserve, Vol. 1: 1913–1951*. Chicago: University of Chicago Press.
Michaelsen, L., Watson, W., & Black, R. (1989). A realistic test of individual vs. group consensus decision making. *Journal of Applied Psychology, 74*, 834–839.
Mihov, I., & Sibert, A. (2006). Credibility and flexibility with independent monetary policy committees. *Journal of Money, Credit, and Banking, 38*, 23–46.
Miller, C. (1985). Group decision-making under majority and unanimity decision rules. *Social Psychology Quarterly, 48*, 51–61.
Miller, C. (1989). The social psychological effects of group decision rules. In P. B. Paulus (Ed.), *Psychology of group influence* (pp. 327–355). Hillsdale, NJ: Erlbaum.
Moscovici, S., & Zavalloni, M. (1969). The group as a polarizer of attitudes. *Journal of Personality and Social Psychology, 12*, 125–135.
Persico, N. (2004). Committee design with endogenous information. *Review of Economic Studies, 71*(1), 165–194.
Riboni, A., & Ruge-Murcia, F. (2008). Preference heterogeneity in monetary policy committees. *International Journal of Central Banking, 4*(1), 213–233.
Rogoff, K. (1985). The optimal degree of commitment to an intermediate monetary target. *Quarterly Journal of Economics, 100*(4), 1169–1190.
Schulz-Hardt, S., Frey, D., Luthgens, C., & Moscovici, S. (2000). Biased information search in group decision making. *Journal of Personality and Social Psychology, 78*(4), 655–669.
Sibert, A. (2006). Central Banking by committee. *International Finance, 9*(2), 145–168.
Stasser, G. (1991). Pooling of unshared information during group discussion. In S. Worchel, W. Wood, & J. Simpson (Eds.), *Group process and productivity* (pp. 48–67). Newbury Park, CA: Sage.
Stasson, M., & Bradshaw, S. (1995). Explanations of individual-group performance differences: What sort of 'bonus' can be gained through group interaction? *Small Group Research, 26*, 296–308.
Stella, P. (2010). "Minimizing Monetary Policy", forthcoming BIS Working Paper.
Tabellini, G. (1987). Reputational constraints on monetary policy: A comment. *Carnegie Rochester Conference Series on Public Policy, 26*, 183–190.
Timmermann, A. (2005). Forecast combinations. CEPR Discussion Paper No. 5361.
Tindale, R., & Larson, J. (1992). Assembly bonus effect or typical group performance? A comment on Michaelsen, Watson, and Black. *Journal of Applied Psychology, 77*, 102–105.
Vandenbussche, J. (2006). Elements of optimal monetary policy committee design. IMF Working Paper No. 06/277.
Waller, C. E. (2000). Policy boards and policy smoothing. *Quarterly Journal of Economics, 115*(1), 305–339.
Walsh, C. E. (1995). Optimal contracts for central bankers. *American Economic Review, 85*(1), 150–167.

Watson, W., Michaelsen, L., & Sharp, W. (1991). Member competence, group interaction, and group decision making: A longitudinal study. *Journal of Applied Psychology, 76*, 803–809.
Wittenbaum, G., & Stasser, G. (1996). Management of information in small groups. In J. Nye & A. Brower (Eds.), *What's social about social cognition? Social cognition research in small groups* (pp. 3–28). Newbury Park, CA: Sage.
Yaniv, I. (2004). Receiving other people's advice: Influence and benefit. *Organizational Behavior and Human Decision Processes, 93*, 1–13.
Yaniv, I., & Milyavsky, M. (2007). Using advice from multiple sources to revise and improve judgments. *Organizational Behavior and Human Decision Processes, 103*(1), 104–120.
Yellen, J. (2005). Policymaking on the Federal Open Market Committee (FOMC): Transparency and continuity, presentation to the bank of Japan's 12th International Conference of the Institute for Monetary and Economic Studies.

Chapter 7
The ECB, Financial Supervision, and Financial Stability Management

Dirk Schoenmaker

7.1 Introduction

After more than 10 years of monetary stability, it is time for the European Central Bank (ECB) to develop its financial stability role as well. The recent financial crisis has highlighted the need for the ECB to take a role in maintaining financial stability. In this chapter, I first make the case that financial stability needs to be managed at the European level. Next, I indicate that the ECB has set a first step towards maintaining financial stability with the publication of a Financial Stability Review since 2004. In addition, during several bouts of financial instability over the last ten years, such as the financial turmoil in the aftermath of terrorist attack in 2001 and the current financial crisis, the ECB has proven to be an effective general lender of last resort (LOLR), providing adequate liquidity when needed.

Following the De Larosière Report (2009), the ECB is about to expand its role in macro prudential supervision. This report proposes to set up a European Systemic Risk Board consisting of the members of the ECB General Council, plus the Chairs of the three European Supervisory Authorities (CEBS, CEIOPS and CESR) and a member of the European Commission. The ECB will play a key role in this new European Systemic Risk Board. In this new capacity, the ECB will face two challenges. First, the ECB will need tools to manage financial stability. For instance, what can the ECB do when an asset price bubble is building up or credit growth is excessive? Second, the ECB will depend on the European Supervisory Authorities and the national central banks and supervisors for the provision of information. Timely information is crucial to make an up-to-date assessment of the stability of the European financial system and to act pro-actively when needed.

D. Schoenmaker (✉)
Banking and Insurance, VU University Amsterdam, Amsterdam, The Netherlands
e-mail: dschoenmaker@feweb.vu.nl

D. Schoenmaker
Duisenberg School of Finance, Amsterdam, The Netherlands

J. de Haan and H. Berger (eds.), *The European Central Bank at Ten*,
DOI: 10.1007/978-3-642-14237-6_7,

There is, as yet, no role envisaged for the ECB in the field of micro prudential supervision of individual institutions. A tight link between macro and micro prudential supervision is important for a full and timely flow of supervisory information. But there are two hurdles for a micro supervisory role for the ECB. The Maastricht Treaty requires a unanimous vote of all EU Member States for transferring financial supervision to the ECB. Even if this hurdle would be taken, the Maastricht Treaty only allows the transfer of banking/securities supervision and not supervision of insurance companies and pension funds. A sectoral supervisory approach makes it difficult to take the cross-sectoral nature of the financial landscape fully into account.

7.2 Monetary and Financial Stability

The Maastricht Treaty provides the ECB with a clear mandate for maintaining price stability. The ECB has established a strong track record on price stability, containing inflation throughout the start of the currency union. Moreover, the ECB has effectively managed to restrain inflation expectations. The ECB has gained a reputation as a capable and independent central bank.

Traditionally, central banks have two major objectives: monetary stability and financial stability. In a sense, these objectives are two sides of the same coin. Failures or disruptions in the financial system have an impact on the real economy, with related effects on output and inflation. Likewise, monetary imbalances may lead to financial instability. The current financial crisis has inter alia been fed by a prolonged period of overly expansionary monetary policy. Following the era of monetary targeting and subsequently of inflation targeting, we will need to think about a new framework for monetary policy taking adequate heed of financial stability (Mishkin 2008; Kremers & Schoenmaker 2009). Looking at the history of central banking, the nineteenth century central banks played a major role in averting financial panics (Goodhart 1988). At that time, the central bank's concern for financial stability was arguably more important than monetary stability. After World War II, the Bretton Woods arrangements led to a prolonged period of stable financial markets. But prices were less stable, with bouts of high inflation (e.g., the oil price shock in the 1970s). Consequently, in modern history the central bank's monetary role has come to the forefront.

At the time when EMU was designed in the 1990s, Folkerts-Landau and Garber (1992) published a paper titled: "The European Central Bank: A Bank or a Monetary Policy Rule?" in which they introduce two concepts of central banking. The narrow concept only includes monetary stability (monetary policy rule), while the broad concept includes monetary as well as financial stability (like the lender of last resort (LOLR) function and supervision of financial institutions). The ECB is largely modelled after the Bundesbank (which has only a limited, indirect role in supervision)[1] and follows the narrow central banking concept focussing on monetary stability. The Maastricht Treaty defines maintaining price stability as the primary objective (art 105.1) of the European System of Central Banks (ESCB), and specifies that the ESCB should only contribute to the supervision and financial stability policies of the national authorities (art 105.5). Folkerts-Landau and Garber (1992) argue that the narrow mandate for the ECB may hamper the development of the EU financial system.

Still, the ECB is slowly moving to become a full-fledged central bank by developing its 'banking' functions. It has started publishing a Financial Stability Review (see Sect. 7.4). Moreover, the ECB acted as LOLR throughout the recent financial crisis during which there were severe problems in the wholesale interbank market. Surplus banks became unwilling to lend to deficit banks because of concerns about their solvency due to losses on and exposure to sub-prime mortgages. The ECB was pro-active and provided short-term funds to deficit banks and absorbed funds from surplus banks. The ECB provided liquidity through its instrument of open market operations (OMO) and standing facilities (marginal lending facility and deposit facility). This is the so-called general LOLR function, under which liquidity is available for all banks against collateral in a standardised way. The ECB's policy was successful in stabilising the euro-area interbank market.[2] By its generous provision of liquidity to all banks (and a broader range of eligible collateral), the ECB has come close to becoming a LOLR for ailing individual banks. However, individual LOLR operations and possible recapitalisation of banks are in the realm of national authorities (Padoa-Schioppa 1999).

So, what do we learn from the financial crisis? The ECB has established itself as an effective European crisis manager. But the ECB has no powers to prevent and manage crises in the financial system, including problems with cross-border banks. Before we examine the appropriate role of the ECB in that field, we need to establish whether financial stability should be managed at the national or European level.[3]

---

[1] Formal banking supervision rested with the Bundesaufsichtsamt für das Kreditwesen (which was subsequently merged into BaFin). The Bundesbank was always involved in providing the data necessary and monitoring the banks, and managed the emergency fund through which banks could obtain financing if they face acute liquidity problems.

[2] However, at the EU-wide level the ECB and the Bank of England (BoE) followed different policies and did not coordinate. Fearful of overreliance on central bank funds by banks (moral hazard), initially the BoE did not provide extra liquidity. Liquidity shortages in the UK interbank market caused severe funding problems for Northern Rock culminating in a bank run on retail deposits in September 2007. The BoE provided a massive lender of last resort loan to keep Northern Rock afloat and the UK government subsequently nationalised Northern Rock.

[3] Section 7.3 heavily draws on De Haan, Oosterloo, and Schoenmaker (2009).

7.3 Financial Stability: A National or European Concern?

Financial stability is a public good, as the producer cannot exclude anybody from consuming the good (non-excludable) and consumption by one person does not affect consumption by others (non-rivalness). An important question is whether governments can produce this pubic good at the national level in today's globalised financial markets. Especially in Europe, an important challenge for maintaining financial stability arises from cross-border banking. Pan-European banks may create cross-border externalities in case of (potential) failure (Schoenmaker & Oosterloo 2005). There are at least 46 EU banking groups with significant cross-border activities, accounting for 68% of overall consolidated EU banking assets (Trichet 2007).[4] This indicates that EU banks with significant cross-border activity hold a sizable share of total EU banking assets. Cross-border banking occurs across the EU and is not confined to the euro area. Especially financial intermediaries from the UK are central players. Moreover, banks from other European countries (EU-15) own most banking assets in the new EU Member States (EU-12).

The interaction of highly penetrated banking systems and national financial stability management might be a dangerously weak institutional feature. The reason is that national authorities have a mandate for maintaining financial stability in their own system and they may therefore be reluctant to help solving problems in other EU Member States. To formalise this issue, two different models of recapitalising banks are examined: a single country and a multi-country model.

7.3.1 Single Country Model of Bailout

Freixas (2003) presents a model of the costs and benefits of a bailout. The model considers the ex post decision whether to recapitalise or to liquidate a bank in financial distress. The choice to continue or to close the bank is a variable x with values in the space $\{0, 1\}$. Moreover, θ denotes the social benefits of a recapitalisation and C its cost. The benefits of a recapitalisation include those derived from avoiding contagion and maintaining financial stability. The direct cost of continuing the bank activity is denoted by C_c and the cost of stopping its activities by C_s and the difference is $C = C_c - C_s$. The case $C < 0$ is obviously possible, but is a case where continuing the bank's operations are cheaper than closing it, so that continuation is preferred and the recapitalisation decision is simplified. In this situation, private sector solutions are possible and the central bank can play the role of 'honest broker'.

[4] It should be noted that these figures have changed during this crisis. Nevertheless, cross-border banking is still an important element of the European banking system.

The optimal decision for the authorities will be to maximise: $x^*(\theta - C)$ so that

$$\begin{cases} x^* = 1 \text{ if } \theta - C > 0 \\ x^* = 0 \text{ if } \theta - C < 0 \end{cases} \tag{7.1}$$

This simple model shows that a bank will be recapitalised whenever the total benefits of an intervention are larger than the net cost. In the case of a bailout, the authorities will contribute C.

7.3.2 Multi-Country Model of Bailout

In the multi-country model, Freixas (2003) considers the case where the mechanism is set in such a way that the bank is recapitalised only if a sufficient contribution from the different countries can be collected. This is an interpretation of improvised co-operation: the countries concerned meet to find out how much they are ready to contribute to the recapitalisation, denoted by t.[5] If the total amount they are willing to contribute is larger than the cost, the bank is recapitalised. The decision is:

$$\begin{cases} x^* = 1 \text{ if } \sum_j (t_j - C_j) > 0 \\ x^* = 0 \text{ if } \sum_j (t_j - C_j) < 0 \end{cases} \tag{7.2}$$

and the j-country objective will be to maximise:

$$x^*(\theta_j - t_j) \tag{7.3}$$

This game may have a multiplicity of equilibria, and, in particular, the closure equilibrium $t_j = 0$, $x^* = 0$ will occur provided that for no j we have:

$$\theta_j - \sum_j C_j > 0 \tag{7.4}$$

that is, no individual country is ready to finance the recapitalisation itself. Obviously, if this equilibrium is selected, the recapitalisation policy is inefficient, as banks will almost never be recapitalised.

That in most cases the closure equilibrium will occur can be explained by the fact that part of the externalities fall outside the home country (although it is safe to assume that in the current setting the country with the highest social benefits of a

---

[5] The term 'improvised co-operation' has been coined to convey the view of an efficient, although adaptive exchange of information and decision taking. It relies on the idea that maintaining financial stability is a goal that every individual country is interested in achieving, so there are good grounds for co-operation (Freixas 2003). It can be argued that improvised co-operation corresponds to the current situation in the EU.

recapitalisation is the home country).[6] The countries are grouped as follows: the home country denoted by *H*, all other European countries denoted by *E*, and all other countries in the world denoted by *W*. The social benefits can then be decomposed into the social benefits in the home country ($h \cdot \theta = \theta_h$), the rest of Europe ($e \cdot \theta = \theta_e$) and the rest of the world ($w \cdot \theta = \theta_w$):

$$\sum_{j=1}^{W} \theta_j = \theta_h + \sum_{j \notin H}^{E} \theta_{e,j} + \sum_{j \notin E}^{W} \theta_{w,j} \tag{7.5}$$

In this equation *h*, *e* and *w* are indexes for the social benefits (i.e., externalities caused by the possible failure of a financial institution) in the home country, the rest of Europe, and the rest of the world. The sum of *h*, *e* and *w* is 1. When the total social benefits are close (or equal) to the social benefits of the home country (θ is close to $\theta_{h,}$ so *h* is close to 1), the home country will be willing to bailout the financial institution. In all other cases ($h < 1$), the home country will only deal with the social benefits within its territory, while host countries expect the home country to pay for (a part of) the costs in the host country. Current national based arrangements undervalue externalities related to the cross-border business of financial institutions. As a result, insufficient capital will be contributed and the financial institution will not be bailed out. This model pinpoints the public good dimension of collective bailouts and shows why improvised co-operation will lead to under-provision of public goods, that is, to an insufficient level of recapitalisations. Countries have an incentive to understate their share of the problem so as to incur a smaller share of the costs. This leaves the largest country, almost always the home country, with the decision whether to shoulder the costs on its own or let the bank close, and possibly be liquidated. The outcome of this model is consistent with the findings of Schinasi (2007). Applying the theory on 'economics of alliances', he examines decision-making in a group of countries. Schinasi (2007) concludes that the provision of shared financial stability public goods results in an equilibrium that is sub-optimal from a European perspective, even though each country views its own decision as optimal and has no incentive to change its resource allocation decision if other countries maintain theirs.

A case in point is the rescue operation of Fortis in October 2008. The institutional setting with national authorities was not capable to reach a collective approach for Fortis, a cross-border bank with its main operations in the Benelux countries (Schoenmaker 2008). National authorities were responsible for crisis management. When Fortis was first recapitalised, the Belgian, Dutch and Luxembourg governments provided capital injections to the national banking parts (Fortis Bank, Fortis Bank Netherlands, and Fortis Bank Luxembourg, respectively) and not to the Fortis Group as a whole. When the first recapitalisation of EUR 11 billion proved to be insufficient, Fortis was torn apart along national lines: the

[6] This assumption is consistent with the post-BCCI Directive that stipulates that banks have to be headquartered in the country where most of their business is conducted.

Dutch parts were nationalised by the Dutch government and the solvent Belgian/Luxembourg parts were sold to the French banking group BNP Paribas.

In sum, national financial stability management leads to an under-provision of recapitalisation, and therefore more European based mechanisms for the management and resolution of cross-border financial crises need to be developed. This is because national authorities (central banks and ministries of Finance) only have a mandate for maintaining national financial stability and may therefore be reluctant to provide liquidity or solvency support to banks in other EU countries. They do not take cross-border externalities caused by financial institutions under their jurisdiction into account. When moving to a European mandate for financial stability (as for monetary stability), these externalities will be internalized leading to an efficient outcome. The next question is the appropriate role for the ECB in the management of European financial stability.

7.4 Financial Stability Framework

In order to maintain financial stability, central banks should have a structure in place that enables them to: (i) identify potential vulnerabilities at an early stage, (ii) take precautionary measures, which make it less likely that costly financial disturbances occur, and (iii) undertake actions to reduce the costs of disturbances and restore financial stability after a period of distress. Figure 7.1 shows such a framework.

7.4.1 Assessment

Central banks need to monitor and analyse all potential sources of risks and vulnerabilities, which requires systematic monitoring of individual parts of the financial system (financial markets, intermediaries, and infrastructure), the interplay between these individual elements, as well as macroeconomic conditions. To come up with a comprehensive view of the stability of the financial system, different steps have to be taken. First, central banks assess the individual and collective robustness of the intermediaries, markets, and infrastructure that make up the financial system. There is no standard framework to analyse financial stability. In an effort to improve the quality and comparability of basic data, the International Monetary Fund (IMF) has developed a set of Financial Soundness Indicators (FSIs) as a key tool for macro-prudential surveillance (see IMF 2004).

Central banks need to identify the main sources of risk and vulnerability that could pose challenges for financial system stability in the future and assess the ability of the financial system to cope with a crisis, should these risks materialise. The overall assessment will make clear whether any (remedial) action is needed.

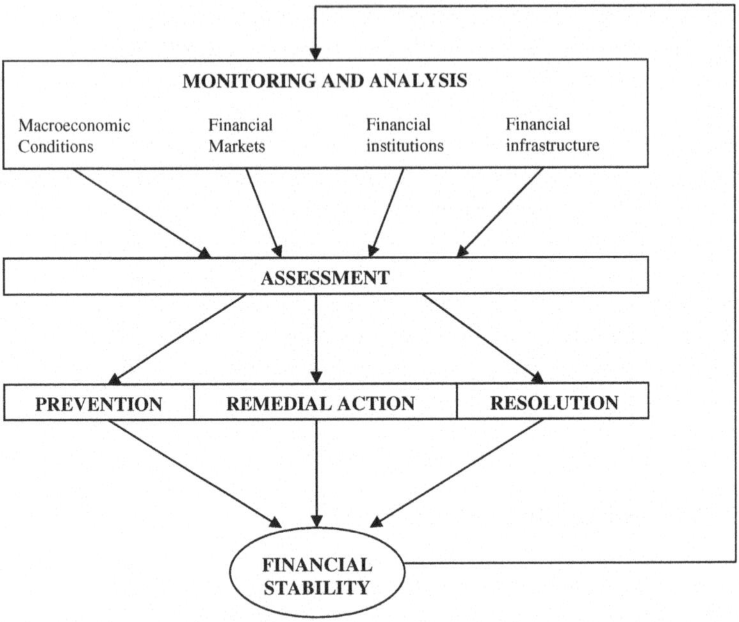

Fig. 7.1 Framework for maintaining financial stability. *Source*: Houben, Kakes, and Schinasi (2004)

If the assessment does not suggest any immediate dangers, continued supervision, surveillance, and macroeconomic policies, are key to preserve the stability of the financial system. In addition, communicating on these issues is important. There are various ways of communicating to the public on financial stability policies. One such method is the publication of a Financial Stability Review (FSR). The purpose of publishing a FSR is to promote awareness in the financial industry and among the public of issues that are relevant for safeguarding the stability of the financial system. By providing an overview of the possible risks to and vulnerabilities of the financial system, the FSR can also play a role in preventing financial crises. In this respect, Svensson (2003, pp. 26–27) argues that publication of a FSR serves "to assure the general public and economic agents that everything is well in the financial sector when this is the case. They also serve as early warnings for the agents concerned and for the financial-regulation authorities when problems show up at the horizon. Early action can then prevent any financial instability to materialize, keeping the probability of future financial stability very low." The growing interest of central banks in monitoring and analysing risks and threats to the stability of the financial system has spurred the publication of FSRs. During the last decade, the number of central banks that publish a FSR has increased rapidly from 1 in 1996 to over 40 in 2005 (see Fig. 7.2).

Tools for measuring system-wide risks and calibrating policy tools are far from straightforward (Borio & Drehmann 2009) and the analyses and recommendations put forward in the FSRs can be improved upon. As for the latter,

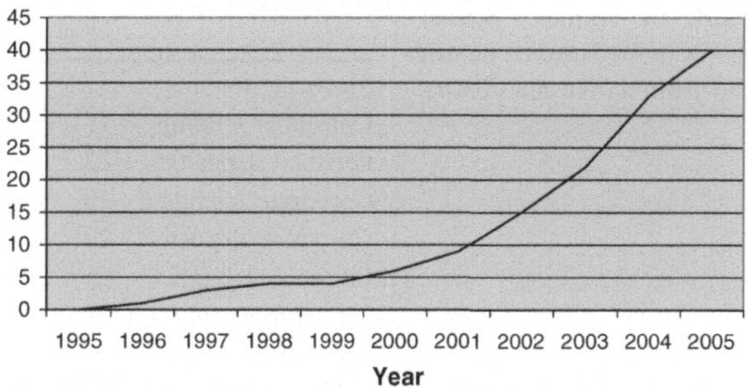

Fig. 7.2 Number of central banks that publish a Financial Stability Review, 1996–2005. *Source*: Oosterloo, De Haan, and Jong-A-Pin (2007)

Cihák (2006) argues that this includes clarifying the aims of the FSRs, providing an operational definition of financial sector soundness, clarifying the core analysis that is presented in FSRs consistently across time, making available the underlying data, discussing more openly risks and exposures in the financial system, making greater use of disaggregated data, focusing more on forward-looking measures rather than backward-looking description of indicators, and presenting stress tests that are comparable across time, and among other things include scenarios, liquidity risks, and contagion.

The ECB published its first Financial Stability Review in December 2004. At the outset, there was discussion within the ECB about the appropriate level: the EU level (because of the EU Internal Market for financial services) or the euro-area level (because of the monetary responsibility for the euro currency). The ECB decided to examine the stability of the financial system at the euro-area level. Most authors agree that financial stability should be managed at the European level, but there is no agreement on the precise scope. Some argue that financial stability is primarily a concern for the euro area (Pisani-Ferry, Aghion, Belka, von Hagen, Heikensten, & Sapir, 2008), while others consider financial stability as an issue for the EU as a whole (Goodhart & Schoenmaker 2006; Nieto & Schinasi 2007).

There are three arguments for focusing on the euro area (Pisani-Ferry et al. 2008). First, financial integration is deeper in the euro area. Banks in the euro area are more closely linked. Second, central banks' emergency provision of liquidity to banks affects the Eurosystem (ECB and the national central banks in the euro area) as a whole. Ring-fencing turmoil in national money markets is not possible in an integrated euro area. Third, the political support for European coordination of financial stability arrangements is larger in the euro area than in the non-euro area countries.

The choice for the EU is based on different arguments. First, it is difficult to manage financial stability in Europe without incorporating its financial centre, London (Goodhart & Schoenmaker 2006). Large banks conduct a significant part of their business in the London wholesale market (e.g., Deutsche Bank has 30% of its assets in London). Second, financial stability is a particular concern for the new Member States, as a large part of their banking system is owned by banks from other EU countries. Third, financial stability is related to the wider regulatory and supervisory framework of the EU Single Market, which allows banks to expand throughout the EU without additional supervision by the host countries.

Table 7.1 Nordea's market shares in the Nordic countries (%). *Source*: Vesala (2006)

	Denmark	Finland	Norway	Sweden
Mortgage lending	17	32	12	16
Consumer lending	15	31	11	9
Personal deposits	22	33	8	18
Corporate lending	19	35	16	14
Corporate deposits	22	37	16	21
Investment funds	20	26	8	14
Life and pension	15	28	7	3
Brokerage	17	5	3	3

Reviewing the arguments, it is not clear from the data that banks are more linked in the euro area. There are a few Scandinavian banks (e.g., Nordea (see Table 7.1) and Danske Bank) that operate throughout the region, both in the ins (Finland) as in the outs (Denmark and Sweden). The merger of Santander (Spain) and Abbey National (UK) and the takeover of ABN Amro (Netherlands) by a consortium of banks consisting of Fortis (Belgium), Santander (Spain), and Royal Bank of Scotland (UK) indicate that cross-border consolidation is not confined to the euro area. Finally, the financial stability function is closer related to the regulatory and supervisory function than to the monetary function.

7.4.2 Preventive and Remedial Action

The next step in the framework of Fig. 7.2 is taking action on the basis of the assessment (something that has clearly been lacking in the build-up of the 2007–2009 financial crisis). If there are any indications of possible financial distress, it is up to the competent authorities (central banks and supervisors) to react properly. The public authorities can take informal action through correspondence and discussion with the affected institutions(s) to solve these problems. They can also use informal pressure to influence the behaviour of financial players. Generally, the public authorities might exert moral suasion in two different situations. First, when they want to influence expectations of the general public through external statements or speeches, and second, when they attempt to persuade financial intermediaries to modify their behaviour in the interest of the sound development of markets. If moral suasion fails, other policy instruments, such as surveillance and supervision, need to be intensified in order to correct the situation at hand. In the next two sections, we discuss the ECB's role in surveillance and supervision. We make a distinction between the macro level (Sect. 7.5) and the micro level (Sect. 7.6).

If financial conditions nevertheless worsen and a financial crisis occurs, one cannot pinpoint a single set of instruments that should be used. Generally, crises are never exactly alike and options differ as to which particular approach is 'best' for resolving them.

The ECB is the key player for liquidity support measures. Emergency assistance to the market as a whole (general LOLR) has been provided to relieve market pressure following an adverse exogenous shock (for example, the 9/11 terrorist attacks and the financial crisis of 2007–2009). But what would happen if a pan-European banking group would suddenly experience a liquidity shock? Decisions to provide emergency liquidity assistance to banks (individual LOLR) are up to the national central banks in the respective countries where banking groups are licensed and operate. However, this national responsibility can lead to multiple coordination problems (see Sect. 7.3). Section 7.6 offers a discussion on the present ambiguity regarding the allocation of individual LOLR responsibilities in the EU, but first I will turn to the ECB's role in maintaining financial stability.

7.5 Macro Prudential Supervision

A typical distinction made in prudential supervision is between macro and micro prudential supervision. Micro prudential focuses on the risks within individual institutions and does not address any effects on the wider financial system (externalities). By contrast, macro prudential supervision focuses on the stability of the financial system as a whole. The case for macro prudential supervision has been reinforced by the current financial crisis. Financial imbalances may be building up in the system, while individual players are looking fine. This point was already known before the crisis, both in academic circles (Hartmann, Straetmans, & de Vries, 2004) and policy circles (Borio 2003). Hartmann et al. (2004), for example, investigated whether financial markets crash jointly. The more markets crash simultaneously the more banks will be in danger, even large banks that hold widely diversified trading portfolios. The number of markets affected by a crisis situation may also determine the severity of any real effects that might follow. Hartmann et al. (2004) find evidence that stock market returns are statistically dependent during crises. Nevertheless, the present EU supervisory arrangements mainly focus on supervision of individual firms, and hardly on the macro-prudential environment in which these firms operate.

What are the key channels for system risk in the financial system? Linkages among financial institutions may cause shocks propagating from one financial institution (or market) to another. In the case of the failure of Lehman Brothers in September 2008, many financial (and non-financial) institutions were exposed to Lehman Brothers. Worries about the vulnerability of Lehman's counterparties caused a general loss of confidence in the financial system. A second propagation channel is common exposures. Joint failures may arise from common exposures to shocks that come from outside the financial system (e.g., exposures to sub-prime mortgages). Next, to these systemic risk channels, pro-cyclicality amplifies the negative or positive effects throughout the cycle. The dynamics of the financial system and the real economy reinforce each other. In good times, banks have ample capital (through retained earnings) causing or contributing to asset bubbles and credit booms. Conversely, in bad times, banks face reduced capital (through losses) and tighten lending standards leading to credit crunches.

The task of macro prudential supervision is to identify these channels and to mitigate these sources of instability. This is typically a central bank task for two reasons. First, monetary and financial stability are interrelated, as explained in Sect. 7.2. Second, Brunnermeier, Crockett, Goodhart, Persaud, and Shin (2009) identify the need for macroeconomists to be involved in macro prudential supervision. Goodhart, Schoenmaker, and Dasgupta (2002) have conducted a cross-country survey of the skill profile of central bankers and supervisors. Using a dataset of 91 supervisory agencies, they find that central banks employ more economists and fewer lawyers in their supervisory/financial stability wing than non-central bank supervisory agencies. Economists have the capacity to analyse the impact of macro-economic trends on the financial system as a whole. The empirical findings of Goodhart et al. (2002) suggest that a setting with central bank involvement in macro prudential supervision is more likely to produce a macro-approach than a setting without such central bank involvement.

7.5.1 De Larosière Proposals on Macro-Prudential Supervision

In October 2008 the European Commission mandated a High Level Group chaired by former managing director of the IMF Jacques De Larosière to give advice on the future of European financial regulation and supervision. The Group presented its final report on 25 February 2009 and their recommendation provided the basis for legislative proposals by the Commission later that year.

According to De Larosière Report, a key lesson to be drawn from the crisis is the urgent need to upgrade macro-prudential supervision in the EU for all financial activities. In the report of the High Level Group, it is stressed that central banks have a key role to play in a sound macro-prudential system. However, in order to be able to fully play their role in preserving financial stability, they should receive an explicit formal mandate to assess high-level macro-financial risks to the system and to issue warnings where required.

The High Level Group suggests establishing a new independent body, the European Systemic Risk Board (ESRB), responsible for safeguarding financial stability by conducting macro-prudential supervision at the European level. The ESRB would include the members of the ECB General Council plus the Chairs of the three European Supervisory Authorities (CEBS, CEIOPS and CESR) and a member of the European Commission. To ensure appropriate geographical coverage and a well-balanced composition, the De Larosière Report proposes ECB involvement via the ECB General Council, which includes the President of the ECB, the Vice-President of the ECB, and the governors of the national central banks (NCBs) of all 27 EU Member States, rather than that of the Governing Council.

The main task of the ESRB would be assessments of stability across the EU financial system in the context of macro-economic developments and general trends in financial markets. In case of significant stability risks, the ESRB would provide early warnings and, where appropriate, issue recommendations for remedial action. The addressees of warnings and recommendations would subsequently be expected to act on them unless inaction can be adequately justified.

7.5.2 Financial Stability Tools Needed

De Larosière Report is silent on the tools for macro prudential supervision. However, the ECB needs tools to actively manage financial stability. Tinbergen, one of the first winners of the Nobel Prize for economics, already showed that one instrument is needed for each policy goal. The ECB has two goals: monetary and financial stability. The ECB has a clear instrument, setting the interest rate, to serve monetary policy. It also needs a clear instrument for financial stability. The ECB can then pro-actively decide about applying the tool.

Two different tools have been proposed. The first proposal is to revisit Basel's system of capital requirements and make it more cycle-neutral (e.g. Brunnermeier et al. 2009; Kremers & Schoenmaker 2009). The Basel system is geared towards the stability of individual financial institutions, and does little to take account of their interaction with their environment and its stability. Capital requirements that "breathe with the cycle" may help avoid banks overly expanding credit when capital is ample in boom-time and, conversely, help avoid them tightening credit in the aftermath precisely when this is least conducive to financial stability. A simple way to introduce countercyclical capital buffers is to scale the minimum capital requirement multiplicatively. When credit or GDP growth is at its neutral level, the multiple is set to 1. If credit/GDP growth is above trend, the multiple is proportionally set above 1. Vice versa, the multiple is set below 1, if credit/GDP falls below trend. The challenge is to get a proper indicator for credit and GDP growth and to establish the required adjustment to the minimum capital requirement.

A second proposal is to impose liquidity charges. Perotti and Suarez (2009) argue that in all crises that spread beyond the original shock, liquidity runs forcing fire sales are a main cause of propagation. If systemic crises involve liquidity runs, which only liquidity insurance by central banks can absorb, then it is appropriate for the central bank to be responsible to monitor the buildup of risks and to manage the liquidity insurance provision with effective tools. Perotti and Suarez (2009) propose to establish a mandatory liquidity charge, to be paid continuously during good times to the central bank, which in exchange will provide emergency liquidity during systemic crises. The charge would be set according to the principle that future regulation should work like Pigouvian taxes on pollution, discouraging bank strategies that create systemic risk for everyone. Hence, it should be increasing in the maturity mismatch between assets and liabilities, and should be levied on all financial institutions with access to the LOLR. So, if the ECB observes an increase in short term funding of a bank (while asset maturities remain constant), it will increase its liquidity charge for that bank.

Moving to crisis management, the ECB needs a tool to resolve a general financial crisis affecting the whole financial system. For that purpose, the ECB can act as general LOLR flooding the interbank market with liquidity when needed. The Statute of the ESCB provides the basis for this classical central banking tool (art 18.1) "In order to achieve the objectives of the ESCB and to carry out its tasks, the ECB and the national central banks may … conduct credit operations with credit institutions and other market participants, with lending based on adequate collateral". So, the ECB needs to take adequate collateral. During the 2007–2009 financial crisis, the ECB has expanded the range of eligible collateral. As the range of collateral expands beyond safe assets, such as Treasuries, credit risk increases. The ECB has made a provision of EUR 5.7 billion for the increased credit risk of its general LOLR operations. The NCBs have underwritten this provision according to their capital key in the share capital of the ECB (De Nederlandsche Bank, 2009, p. 174). As each NCB is backed up by its own government, the ECB's expansion of collateral rules is implicitly underwritten by the national governments of the euro area. By expanding its role as general LOLR, the ECB is coming close to becoming an individual LOLR to (ailing) banks. But individual LOLR operations are in the realm of the NCBs as will be discussed in Sect. 7.6.

7.5.3 Information Challenge

Timely information on the condition of financial institutions and markets in the EU is crucial to make an up-to-date assessment of the stability of the EU financial system and to act swiftly when needed. A main challenge for the ESRB, is a full flow of information from NCBs and national supervisors to the ECB (see Sect. 7.6 for a discussion about the information flow between national central banks and supervisors). Game theory suggests that the envisaged arrangements are not incentive compatible. The ECB has a mandate for the stability of the EU-wide financial system (European mandate), while the remit of NCBs is limited to the stability of their respective national financial system (national mandate). If the interests of the ECB and the NCBs are aligned, NCBs may provide the necessary information to the ECB. But if there is a conflict of interests between a NCB and the ECB, there is no incentive for this NCB to provide timely information (Cihák & Decressin 2007). A case in point are emerging problems with a national bank in one of the EU Member States. While a NCB may have an incentive to help a major player of their national banking system and to wait (and hope) for better times (forbearance), the ECB may want to act swiftly to prevent the problems spreading to the wider EU financial system (prompt corrective action). However, without the information from the NCB that is closer to the ailing bank, the ECB cannot act timely.

The solution to this incentive problem is to align mandates. I propose removing the national mandate of NCBs and replace it with a European mandate. This has been done for monetary policy from the start of EMU. The Maastricht Treaty provides the Eurosystem with a clear mandate to maintain price stability in the euro area.

7.6 Micro Prudential Supervision

This section examines micro prudential supervision aimed at the risks of individual institutions. Different proposals to establish a European structure of financial supervision have been put forward, as documented by Schoenmaker and Oosterloo (2008). The three main policy options are:

1. Appoint a lead supervisor for the supervision of cross-border financial groups. In practice, this will mean that the home country authority of a pan-European financial group is given full responsibility for EU-wide operations, both branches and subsidiaries.
2. Establish a single EU supervisor either for all EU banks or merely for the large cross-border banking groups (i.e., a so-called two-tier system), and
3. Establish a European System of Financial Supervisors, in which a central agency works in tandem with national supervisors. The role of the central agency is to foster cooperation and consistency among members of the System, but could leave the day-to-day supervision of cross-border financial groups with the consolidating supervisor.

7.6.1 Lead Supervisor

According to the European Financial Services Round Table (EFR 2005), a clearly defined lead supervisor (usually the home supervisor) for prudential supervision of large cross-border financial institutions would be an important step towards a more coherent and efficient supervisory framework in the EU. The lead supervisor should in particular be the single point of contact for all reporting schemes, validate and authorise internal models, approve capital and liquidity allocation, approve cross-border set-up of specific functions, and decide about on-site inspections. Furthermore, the lead supervisor should not only be responsible for supervision on a consolidated level, but also on the level of individual subsidiaries.

The EFR agrees that host countries should be involved in the supervisory process, as local supervisors have generally a better understanding of the local market conditions. The EFR suggests forming colleges of supervisors (one for each specific group) in which all supervisors involved share relevant group-wide and local information regarding the financial group in question. The lead supervisor, i.e., the home supervisor of the parent company, would chair the college of supervisors that would comprise, at a minimum, all supervisory agencies in whose jurisdictions the financial institution has sizeable operations. The lead supervisor would make intelligent use of the expertise and knowledge of the local supervisors in the college and entrust tasks to them by means of the delegation of tasks and, where appropriate, responsibilities. A mediation mechanism would be available if disagreements were to arise between the lead supervisor and other members of the college.

In comparison with the current situation, the efficiency of supervision is enhanced under this option as duplication is eliminated. Nevertheless, the concept of a lead supervisor does poorly with respect to financial stability, as its national mandate does not induce the lead supervisor to incorporate the cross-border externalities of a failure of a financial institution in its decision-making.

7.6.2 Single Supervisor

Some have argued that developments in the EU banking sector call for establishing a single pan-European supervisor assuming full responsibility for the supervision of both branches and subsidiaries of all EU banks (e.g., Schüler 2002). There may indeed be merit in centralising day-to-day supervision and pooling of information, allowing for effective market surveillance of European-wide systemic risks. However, a major drawback of a central European supervisory authority could be that the distance between the central authority and the supervised institutions may be too large—both physically as well as in terms of familiarity with local circumstances. Bank supervision may therefore be better executed at the local level, because of the availability of specific expertise of the local market.

Another option would be to set up a two-tier system, i.e., a system in which large cross-border banking groups are supervised by a central pan-European supervisory authority, while local banks are supervised by the existing national supervisory authorities. However, this option may risk creating an un-level playing field in supervision between pan-European banks and banks operating at the national level, while both are competing on the same market. The potential problems with respect to the distance to the activities of the large cross-border banking groups may also be applicable to this option.

7.6.3 European System of Financial Supervisors

Vives (2001) and Schoenmaker and Oosterloo (2008) propose a European System of Financial Supervisors (ESFS) with a European Financial Authority (EFA) at the centre of the system and national supervisory authorities (NSAs) in the different countries. Such a system could be set up along the lines of the European System of Central Banks (ESCB). A key issue is the appropriate level of (de)centralisation of the central authority. Supervision is primarily a micro-policy as day-to-day supervision should be conducted close to supervised institutions. Nevertheless,

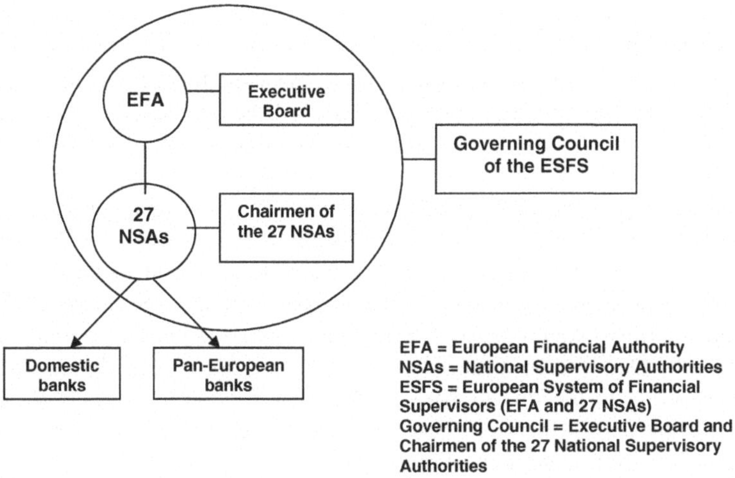

Fig. 7.3 A decentralised European System of Financial Supervisors (ESFS). *Source*: Schoenmaker and Oosterloo (2008)

there may be some merit in centralising policy-making and pooling information, allowing effective market surveillance of European-wide systemic risks. The drawback of a central European supervisor could be that the distance between the central authority and the supervised institutions may be too large, both physically and in terms of familiarity with local circumstances.

A decentralised ESFS could combine the advantages of a European framework with the expertise of local supervisory bodies. Figure 7.3 illustrates such a framework with an EFA at the centre working in tandem with the 27 decentralised national supervisory branches. A crucial element of the proposal is that the ESFS operates under a European mandate. In this proposed system, small and medium-sized banks (as well as insurers), which are primarily nationally oriented, are supervised by one of the 27 national supervisors. Pan-European banks are supervised by the consolidating or lead supervisor (usually the supervisory team of the home country). This national supervisor will be the single point of contact for all reporting schemes (no reporting to the host authorities), validate and authorise internal models, approve capital and liquidity allocation, approve cross-border set-up of specific functions and decide about on-site inspections. With respect to the latter, the lead supervisor can ask host authorities to perform on-site inspections on its behalf. The lead supervisor is compelled to inform host authorities concerning its activities and host authorities should have access to all reporting schemes (i.e., a common database of the ESFS). If a host authority feels the lead supervisor does not take account of its interests and no agreement can be reached, it can present its concerns to the EFA. If necessary, the EFA can overrule the lead supervisor and enforce the European mandate.

In this approach, crisis management is also done on a European basis. While the national supervisor in the home country takes the lead during a crisis at an individual institution (gathering information, making an assessment of the situation), the ESFS is involved to ensure an adequate EU-wide solution. When a crisis hits more (large) financial institutions at the same time, the involvement of the EFA (in close co-operation with the ECB) will be intensified.

Key supervisory decisions (for example, the assessment of potential cross-border mergers and acquisitions or crisis management decisions) as well as the design of policy are done at the centre by the Governing Council consisting of the Executive Board of the EFA and the Chairmen of the 27 National Supervisory Authorities (in the same way as the ESCB takes decisions on monetary policy). In this way, host country authorities are fully involved and the interests of their depositors are fully taken into account (i.e., potential cross-border externalities are incorporated). Day-to-day supervision is conducted by one of the 27 national supervisors close to the financial firms. The EFA will be responsible for information pooling and is therefore best equipped to perform EU-wide peer group analysis of large European financial groups.

The EFA is responsible for the correct and uniform application of supervisory rules (level playing field) and it can also act as a mediator in case of problems between home and host country authorities. In doing so, it may give instructions to the 27 national supervisors. A drawback of a system with a central authority and 27 national supervisors is that the decision-making structure can become rather complicated.

7.6.4 De Larosière Proposals on Micro-Prudential Supervision

After having examined the present arrangements, the De Larosière Report (2009) considers that the structure and the role bestowed on the existing European supervisory committees are not sufficient to ensure financial stability in the EU. It is argued that although the level 3 supervisory committees have contributed significantly to the process of European financial integration, there are a number of inefficiencies that can no longer be dealt with within their present legal structure (i.e., as advisory bodies to the European Commission). To address these inefficiencies, the Report makes a clear choice for the third model, i.e., the European System of Financial Supervision (ESFS).

The ESFS is supposed to become an integrated network of European financial supervisors. The level 3 committees will be transformed into European Supervisory Authorities. According to the De Larosière Report (2009), this largely decentralised structure will fully respect the proportionality and subsidiarity principles of the EU Treaty. Existing national supervisors, who are closest to the markets and institutions they supervise, will continue to be responsible for day-to-day supervision and preserve the majority of their present competences. However, in order to be in a position to effectively supervise an increasingly integrated and consolidated EU financial market, the European Authorities will perform a defined number of tasks that are better performed at the EU level.

The Report therefore argues that, in addition to the competences currently exercised by the level 3 committees, the Authorities should have the following key-competences: (i) legally binding mediation between national supervisors; (ii) adoption of binding supervisory standards; (iii) adoption of binding technical decisions applicable to individual financial institutions; (iv) oversight and coordination of colleges of supervisors; (v) designation, where needed, of group supervisors; (vi) licensing and supervision of specific EU-wide institutions (e.g., credit rating agencies), and binding cooperation with the ESRB to ensure adequate macro-prudential supervision.

7.6.5 No Supervisory Role for the ECB

In the second and third model, the ECB could have been designated to become the European financial supervisor. The Treaty offers the possibility to give prudential tasks to the ECB. According to article 105.6 "the Council may, acting unanimously on a proposal from the Commission and after consulting the ECB and after receiving the assent of the European Parliament, confer upon the ECB specific tasks concerning policies relating to the prudential supervision of credit institutions and other financial institutions with the exception of insurance undertakings".

But there are two hurdles for a supervisory role for the ECB. Although several EU countries (like France, Italy, Spain, Portugal, Greece and the Netherlands) support the central bank model for supervision (Padoa-Schioppa 2003), the Treaty requires a unanimous vote of all EU Member States for transferring financial supervision to the ECB. In particular, Germany and the United Kingdom (UK) are against direct central bank involvement in financial supervision. Germany believes that monetary policy should be fully independent. The monetary reputation should not be tarnished by supervisory failures. In Germany, the Bundesbank model had a strong monetary reputation and no direct involvement in banking supervision (Goodhart & Schoenmaker 1995). In the UK, the incoming Labour government gave the Bank of England full monetary powers in 1997, while hiving off its supervisory powers. The different UK supervisory agencies were put together in a single supervisor, the Financial Services Authority (FSA). So, the UK also wants to separate monetary and supervisory powers. [7] More importantly, the UK does not want to give the ECB supervisory powers, as it is outside the euro area and thus has (almost) no leverage over the ECB.

Next, the Maastricht Treaty only allows the transfer of banking and securities supervision and not the supervision of insurance firms. However, a sectoral

[7] The Conservative Party wants to abolish the FSA and make the Bank of England responsible for prudential supervision. It also wants to establish some sort of conduct of business supervisor. The Conservatives would thus move to a twin peaks model, with a prudential and a conduct of business supervisor.

supervisory approach ignores the cross-sector nature of the financial landscape (see also De Haan et al. 2009).

7.6.6 But An Expanded LOLR Role

In the current setting for financial supervision and stability, national authorities are responsible for individual LOLR operations and possible recapitalisations of banks (Padoa-Schioppa 1999). So, the NCBs are performing the individual LOLR operations. If and when the financial supervision and stability arrangements are moved to the European level, the ECB is well placed to play the individual LOLR role (Boot & Marinč 2009). The ECB would incorporate the cross-border externalities of possible bank failures in its decision-making. A centralized LOLR function would thus optimise the LOLR decision, as argued in Sect. 7.3. The Statute of the ECB allows this LOLR role (art 18.1). Another advantage of a centralized LOLR is that it could lead to a more prudent use of the LOLR facility (Vives 2001; Boot & Marinč 2009). The ECB has less of an incentive to 'protect' national banks (other than for systemic risk reasons) than national central banks.

A key issue is how to deal with the credit risk on LOLR operations. Although officially LOLR support is meant to deal with liquidity problems of banks, liquidity problems often turn into solvency problems (Goodhart & Schoenmaker 1995). So LOLR operations are risky. Central banks can create unlimited amounts of liquidity, but their capacity to bear losses is constrained to their capital base. Governments are typically the owner of central banks and thus the provider of capital. There is a national government behind each national central bank. But who will assume the credit risk on the LOLR operations of the ECB?[8] European politicians still have to answer that question. Goodhart and Schoenmaker (2009) argue for burden sharing rules among national governments to deal with the credit risk on LOLR and possible recapitalisations of ailing banks. Such burden sharing will only work if the rules are agreed upon ex ante and are legally binding. The argument for burden sharing is that systemic risk in an integrated EU financial system can only be managed at the EU level (see Sect. 7.3). However, so far politicians seem not willing to give up part of their sovereignty to spend taxpayers' money.

7.6.7 Information Challenge

As LOLR to individual banks, the ECB needs full access to supervisory information on these banks. This information is crucial to make an informed judgment

[8] Art. 32 of the Statute specifies that income from monetary operations (as well as any losses) will be shared among the participating NCBs according to their capital key in the share capital of the ECB. However, a decision to take up the individual LOLR role at the ECB would need political endorsement.

about the solvency and liquidity position of a bank facing financial problems (Goodhart & Schoenmaker 1995). This is a major challenge in a supervisory structure where central banking and supervision are separated. The bank run on Northern Rock in 2007 is a clear illustration of this challenge. Up to the very last moment, the Bank of England was unaware of the funding problems (caused by the underlying maturity mismatch between long-term assets and short-term funding) at Northern Rock. An effective LOLR therefore needs to be closely linked to the prudential supervisor. That is why Padoa-Schioppa (2003) argues for implementing the so-called twin peaks model in Europe. In this model, there is a prudential supervisor monitoring the solvency of financial institutions (internal dimension) and a conduct of business supervisor monitoring the treatment of customers (external dimension). Padoa-Schioppa favours that the central bank performs the prudential supervisory task. The ECB would then combine monetary policy and prudential supervision and consequently have direct access to supervisory information on banks.

However, the ECB is not likely to get a direct role in micro prudential supervision, as explained above. The functioning of the ESRB in which the ECB, NCBs and European Supervisory Authorities operate, is crucial to foster financial stability in Europe. In the set-up of the ESRB, attention should be paid to a proper incentive structure so that both the central banks and the supervisors will inform each other timely within the newly envisaged structure.[9] Otherwise, the ESRB runs the risk to become just another talking shop.

7.7 Conclusions

I have argued that financial supervision and stability arrangements should be moved to the European level in response to the emerging European financial system. In that European setting, the ECB has to take up its appropriate role as full central bank with two equally important objectives of monetary and financial stability. On the latter, the ECB has already proven to be an effective general lender of last resort (LOLR) in the recent financial crisis providing the market with sufficient liquidity.

The micro (prudential) supervisory role is designated to a new European System of Financial Supervisors (ESFS), consisting of a network of national financial supervisors who work in tandem with the new European Supervisory Authorities, as proposed by De Larosière Report. The ECB will not have a direct role in micro prudential supervision, and the ESFS will operate separately from the

[9] Boot and Marinč (2009) argue that national authorities could be more willing to share information with the ECB, since only then support can be expected. But on the negative side, there is the bureaucracy effect (Kremers & Schoenmaker 2009). Bureaucratic agencies are notoriously bad in exchanging information. In the Northern Rock case, the second effect has dominated.

ECB. However, the De Larosière Report proposes that the ECB will play a key role in macro prudential supervision (i.e., monitoring and assessing risks to the stability of the financial system as a whole). The European Institutions (i.e., the European Commission, the European Council and the European Parliament) are currently working to put these proposals into legislation.

I fully support this approach. To be an effective player on the financial stability front, the ECB needs to go further than publishing a Financial Stability Review (FSR) and acting as general LOLR. The work of the new European Systemic Risk Board (ESRB), consisting of the ECB and the new European Supervisory Authorities, will involve analysing developments within the financial system, provide early warning of systemic risks that may be building up and, where necessary, provide recommendations to address these risks. The warnings and recommendations of the ESRB will, however, not be binding and there is a risk that addressees will not act upon them. I therefore argue that the ECB also needs appropriate tools to take preventive action (e.g., increasing capital requirements during booms) and remedial action (e.g., acting as individual LOLR in addition to general LOLR). This final step has not yet been taken. Before the ECB can assume LOLR operations to individual banks, governments should agree on a burden sharing arrangement to deal with the credit risk of such operations.

References

Boot, A., & Marinč, M. (2009). Crisis management and lender of last resort in the European banking market. In P. Alessandrini, M. Fratianni, & A. Zazzaro (Eds.), *The changing geography of banking and finance* (pp. 233–250). Heidelberg: Springer.

Borio, C. (2003). Towards a macroprudential framework for financial supervision and regulation. *CESifo Economic Studies, 49*, 181–216.

Borio, C., & Drehmann, M. (2009). *Towards an operational framework for financial stability: 'Fuzzy' measurement and its consequences*. BIS Working Paper No. 284.

Brunnermeier, M., Crockett, A., Goodhart, C., Persaud, A., & Shin, H. (2009). *The fundamental principles of financial regulation*. Geneva report on the World Economy, No 11.

Cihák, M. (2006). *How do central banks write on financial stability*? IMF Working Paper No. 06/163.

Cihák, M., & Decressin, J. (2007). *The case for a European banking charter*. IMF Working Paper No. 07/173.

De Haan, J., Oosterloo, S., & Schoenmaker, D. (2009). *European financial markets and institutions*. Cambridge (UK): Cambridge University Press.

De Larosière, J., Balcerowicz, L., Issing, O., Masera, R., Mc Carthy, C., Nyberg, L., et al. (2009). Report of the high level group on financial supervision in the EU, Brussels.

De Nederlandsche Bank. (2009). *Annual Report 2008*. Amsterdam: De Nederlandsche Bank.

European Financial Services Round Table. (2005). *On the lead supervisor model and the future of financial supervision in the EU*. Brussels: EFR.

Folkerts-Landau, D., & Garber, P. (1992). The ECB: A bank or a monetary policy rule? In M. Canzoneri, V. Grilli, & P. Masson (Eds.), *Establishing a central bank: Issues in Europe and lessons from the US* (pp. 86–110). Cambridge: Cambridge University Press.

Freixas, X. (2003). Crisis management in Europe. In J. Kremers, D. Schoenmaker, & P. Wierts (Eds.), *Financial supervision in Europe* (pp. 102–119). Cheltenham: Edward Elgar.

Goodhart, C. (1988). *The evolution of central banks*. Cambridge, MA: MIT Press.
Goodhart, C., & Schoenmaker, D. (1995). Should the functions of monetary policy and banking supervision be separated? *Oxford Economic Papers, 47*, 539–560.
Goodhart, C., & Schoenmaker, D. (2006). Burden sharing in a banking crisis in Europe. *Economic Review, 2*, 34–57. (Sveriges Riksbank, Stockholm).
Goodhart, C., & Schoenmaker, D. (2009). Fiscal burden sharing in cross-border banking crises. *International Journal of Central Banking, 5*, 141–165.
Goodhart, C., Schoenmaker, D., & Dasgupta, P. (2002). The skill profile of central bankers and supervisors. *European Finance Review, 6*, 397–427.
Hartmann, P., Straetmans, S., & de Vries, C. G. (2004). Asset market linkages in crisis periods. *Review of Economics and Statistics, 86*, 313–326.
Houben, A., Kakes, J., & Schinasi, G. (2004). *Towards a framework for financial stability*. De Nederlandsche Bank Occasional Study No. 2(1).
International Monetary Fund. (2004). *Compilation guide on financial soundness indicators*. Washington, DC: IMF.
Kremers, J., & Schoenmaker, D. (2009). The US proposals for regulatory reform. In D. Mayes, R. Pringle, & M. Taylor (Eds.), *Towards a new framework for financial stability* (pp. 489–497). London: Central Banking Publications.
Mishkin, F. (2008). *How should we respond to asset price bubbles*? Speech at Wharton, Philadelphia, May 15.
Nieto, M., & Schinasi, G. (2007). *EU framework for safeguarding financial stability: Towards an analytical benchmark for assessing its effectiveness*. IMF Working Paper No. 07/260.
Oosterloo, S., De Haan, J., & Jong-A-Pin, R. M. (2007). Financial stability reviews: A first empirical analysis. *Journal of Financial Stability, 2*, 337–355.
Padoa-Schioppa, T. (1999). EMU and banking supervision. *International Finance, 2*, 295–308.
Padoa-Schioppa, T. (2003). Financial supervision: Inside or outside central banks? In J. Kremers, D. Schoenmaker, & P. Wierts (Eds.), *Financial supervision in Europe* (pp. 160–175). Cheltenham: Edward Elgar.
Perotti, E., & Suarez, J. (2009). *Liquidity insurance for systemic crises*. Policy Insight No. 31, London: CEPR.
Pisani-Ferry, J., Aghion, P., Belka, M., von Hagen, J., Heikensten, L., & Sapir, A. (2008). *Coming of age: Report on the Euro area*. Bruegel Blueprint No. 4, Brussels.
Schinasi, G. (2007). Resolving EU financial-stability challenges: Is a decentralized decision-making approach efficient? mimeograph.
Schoenmaker, D. (2008). Resolving the stability trilemma. *Financial Regulator, 13*(3), 45–53.
Schoenmaker, D., & Oosterloo, S. (2005). Financial supervision in an integrating Europe: Measuring cross-border externalities. *International Finance, 8*, 1–27.
Schoenmaker, D., & Oosterloo, S. (2008). Financial supervision in Europe: A proposal for a new architecture. In L. Jonung, C. Walkner, & M. Watson (Eds.), *Building the financial foundations of the Euro—experiences and challenges* (pp. 337–354). London: Routledge.
Schüler, M. (2002). *The threat of systemic risk in banking—evidence for Europe*. Deutsche Bank Research Notes, No. 3, Frankfurt.
Svensson, L. E. O. (2003). *Monetary policy and real stabilization*. NBER Working Paper No. 9486.
Trichet, J.-C. (2007). *Towards the review of the Lamfalussy approach: Market developments, supervisory challenges and institutional arrangements*. Speech at the First CEBS Conference, London, 9 May.
Vesala, J. (2006). *Remarks at a workshop organized by National Bank of Belgium on Financial Stability Monitoring and Assessment in a Multilateral Environment*. Available at: http://www.rahoitustarkastus.fi/NR/rdonlyres/9F7E459B-F462-4EE6-A029-CFD2586650FC/0/Vesala_Brussels_notes_140606.pdf.
Vives, X. (2001). Restructuring financial regulation in the European Monetary Union. *Journal of Financial Services Research, 19*, 57–82.

The manufacturer's authorised representative in the EU is Springer Nature Customer Service Centre GmbH, Europaplatz 3, 69115 Heidelberg, Germany. If you have any concerns regarding our products, please contact ProductSafety@springernature.com

Printed and bound by CPI Group (UK) Ltd, Croydon, CR0 4YY
01/10/2026
02225968-0001